IMAGINING THE GLOBAL

Joseph Turow

SERIES EDITOR

THE NEW MEDIA WORLD

DIGITALCULTUREBOOKS, an imprint of the University of Michigan Press,
is dedicated to publishing work in new media studies and the emerging
field of digital humanities.

Imagining the Global

TRANSNATIONAL MEDIA AND POPULAR CULTURE BEYOND EAST AND WEST

Fabienne Darling-Wolf

University of Michigan Press

ANN ARBOR

Published in the United States of America by the
University of Michigan Press
Manufactured in the United States of America
♾ Printed on acid-free paper

2018   2017   2016   2015   4   3   2   1

A CIP catalog record for this book is available from the British Library.

DOI: http://dx.doi.org/10.3998/nmw.12748915.0001.001

Library of Congress Cataloging-in-Publication Data

Darling-Wolf, Fabienne.
    Imagining the global : transnational media and popular culture beyond East and West /
Fabienne Darling-Wolf.
        pages cm. — (New media world)
    Includes bibliographical references and index.
    ISBN 978-0-472-07243-9 (hardcover : alk. paper) — ISBN 978-0-472-05243-1 (pbk. : alk.
paper) — ISBN 978-0-472-12079-6 (e-book)
    1. Mass media and culture.   2. Mass media and globalization.   3. Mass media—Social
aspects—United States.   4. Mass media—Social aspects—France.   5. Mass media—Social
aspects—Japan.   I. Title.
P94.6.D365 2014
302.23—dc23

                                                                          2014020615

Artist Statement: The art I designed for the cover of this book is part of a series of works titled
Signs of Our Times. This series of original paintings draws from visual elements—graffiti and
other street art, signs, posters—collected in my travels in North America, Europe, and Japan to
create phenomenological collages of contemporary urban life. Rather than focusing on my own
engagement with landscapes in different parts of the world, this particular collage, however, references key elements of the book's journey through reality television, news coverage of disaster,
global magazines, French rap, and Japanese animation. Taken as a whole, the image illustrates
the hybrid and polysemic nature of global culture.
    John Darling-Wolf

Acknowledgments

Many people supported me in various ways in the process of researching and writing this book. At Temple University, I am grateful to all of my colleagues who provided the intellectual and moral support that made this project possible. In particular, I thank Carolyn Kitch for her continuing encouragement over the years, for her assistance in developing a book proposal, and, more generally, for serving as the most amazing (albeit frustratingly unattainable) role model. I am deeply indebted to Andrew Mendelson for his willingness to give me the flexibility to conduct research abroad in his capacity as chair of the Journalism Department and for his help and support as a friend. I thank Nancy Morris and Patrick Murphy for their willingness to read the manuscript, for their insightful comments, and for cheering me on when I faltered. Also crucial was Temple University's financial support for my fieldwork provided through two summer research grants and a sabbatical leave.

At the University of Pennsylvania, I thank Marwan Kraidy for being a constant inspiration, for our numerous productive chats, for sharing his knowledge of academic publishing, and for his feedback on various drafts of the manuscript. I thank the Annenberg School for Communication for inviting me to present at the "Real Worlds: Global Perspectives on the Politics of Reality Television" conference. I also thank series editor Joseph Turow for helping me write a stronger and clearer book that people might actually want to read.

My graduate students in the Media and Communication doctoral program were the source of many provocative conversations and revisions to the text. The reviewers' comments and suggestions provided another invaluable guide to the numerous rounds of revisions. I am deeply thankful that they were willing to find the time in their busy schedule to read the manuscript and provide a fresh perspective on the text. Some of the materials included in chapter 1 appeared in Marwan Kraidy and Katherine Senders' edited collection *The Politics of Reality Television: Global Perspectives* (Routledge, 2011). The inspiration for chapter 2 came from an article I published in *Journalism Studies* 9, no.3 (2008) titled "Holier-than-Thou: News of Racial Tensions in a Trans-national Context." Chapter 4 builds on reflections I started to develop in "Getting over Our

'Illusion d'optique': From Globalization to Mondialisation (through French rap)" (*Communication Theory* 18, no.2 [2008]).

Perhaps most importantly, this research would not have been possible without the help of my informants in France, Japan, and the United States, who generously gave their time and opened their homes to me. I am particularly grateful to those informants in Japan who have kept me in touch with the rapid developments in Japanese popular culture throughout the years and who often helped me secure the basic material support and information necessary to do my work when I first entered their lives as a graduate student. Words cannot describe their generosity or how grateful I am for their continuing involvement. I have chosen to refer to them throughout the book as "informants" rather than "participants" or "co-researchers" not to minimize their incredible contribution to my work but, on the contrary, to highlight how I am disproportionately benefiting from their willingness to share their knowledge. I am particularly indebted to my interpreter and research assistant Yasumi Okame who has been with me since the beginning even when I had very little to offer as compensation for her incredibly hard work. I also want to thank all the friends and neighbors on the "400 block" who have supported my research in Philadelphia.

The fact that my mentor Hanno Hardt will not get to read this book simply breaks my heart, but I am glad I had a chance to discuss the project with him the last time we were together in Slovenia. He will always be present in my writing even though he is no longer with us. I thank his wife Vida for her continuing support and hospitality in the summers.

Finally, my husband John and daughters Hana and Mei were instrumental in bringing this project to completion. I am grateful for their willingness to accompany me in the field and to put up with my writing-induced absent-mindedness. I thank Hana and Mei for the role they have played in keeping me connected with Japanese animation and French television programming and for helping me keep things in perspective by bringing daily joy to my life. I thank John for serving as a patient sounding board for my ideas, for his unwavering moral support, and for designing the book's magnificent cover image. I dedicate this work to them with all my love.

Contents

Introduction: A Translocal Approach to Imagining the Global

Winnie the Pooh, Snow White, Batman, Pikachu, Zorro, Spiderman, two flamenco dancers, and a kimono-clad Japanese girl shading herself with a waxed umbrella walked along with a collection of cowboys, Indian girls in saris, Venetian beauties, knights, Native Americans, ninjas, and musketeers (all d'Artagnans), toward the small center square. The beat of the Brazilian percussion band that had followed the procession's journey through the hills from the neighboring village suddenly stopped as a man advanced toward the straw figure set atop a woodpile. The Carmentran (a friendly looking scarecrow dressed in old jeans and a lumberjack shirt) was to be set on fire to symbolize the end of winter—a local Southern French tradition on this carnival day.

The short vignette above, drawn from my experience in a small French community, illustrates the extent to which elements of "the global" have come to permeate individuals' daily lives. As space- and time-defying communication technologies facilitate virtual mixing on an increasingly global scale, this kind of hybrid engagement with a wide array of globalized cultural forms has become commonplace. The fact that the culture we experience as "local" (or even, in this case, "traditional") is inescapably embedded in broader global processes is increasingly difficult to ignore. Globalization theorists identify this "collective *awareness* of growing global interconnectedness" (Pieterse, 2009, p. 16, emphasis in original) as a defining element of our contemporary condition. They point to the fact that globalization is marked by a new role for the imagination in social life as individuals simultaneously envision "the global" and negotiate their own locality through their engagement with flows of cultural products, images, and information increasingly disconnected from their place of origin (Castells, 2000; Giddens, 1990; Tomlinson, 1999). "The global," in other words, is a space that is envisioned and imagined rather than directly experienced (Appadurai, 1990, 1996, 2001). It is a space built upon the spread of increasingly culturally mixed, or hybridized, mediated texts embedded in increasingly complex processes of transcultural exchange that result in the development of a "plurality of imagined worlds" (Appadurai, 1996, p. 5).

Recognizing, however, that the hybrid products of global interconnectedness are inescapable and that the imagination they foster is a key component of our contemporary global order is merely a necessary first step in understanding our historical moment. A more important—and significantly more difficult—task lies in exploring hybridity's "finer points and meanings" (Pieterse, 2003/2009, p. viii). The most critical question to ask, in other words, is not whether hybridity exists or even matters (we know it does), but *how* it matters. How do individuals "imagine the global" as cultural products and social relations are lifted out from local contexts to be restructured "across indefinite spans of time space" (Giddens, 1990, p. 21)? What kinds of "imagined worlds" do they construct? How is this imagination built and negotiated through processes of production, distribution, and consumption of globalized cultural forms? How does it intersect with "local" and/or "national" conditions? How does it relate to other elements of individuals' identities? How, as scholars, can we better conceptualize its complex dynamics as a space of both potential domination and resistance, neither "purely emancipatory" nor "entirely disciplined" (Appadurai, 1996, p. 4)? How can *we* better "imagine the global"?

This book explores these questions through an examination of the transnational forces at work in the relationship between three sites (listed in alphabetical order throughout the book): France, Japan, and the United States. These sites were chosen in response to global media scholars Marwan Kraidy and Patrick Murphy's call for a "multisited, translocal approach" to global communication studies "working comparatively *between and within* various locals" (2008, pp. 346, 351, emphasis in orginal; see also Shohat, 2002, p. 78). A number of other scholars have pointed to the need to move beyond the recognition that "globalization means radically different things to different people in different places" (Sorge, 2005, p. 8) to explore what we can learn from these differences. A translocal approach focuses on the concrete conditions under which various local/national environments *relate to each other* in a globalized world.

While working comparatively, a translocal perspective moves beyond a traditional comparative approach by putting the emphasis on the multifaceted relations, connections, and dynamics between the sites rather than on each site individually. It focuses, as media scholar Terhi Rantanen puts it, "on *places* rather than *place*" (2005, p. 12, emphasis in original). It draws from the works of scholars, particularly within the British Cultural Studies tradition, who have proposed to trace the trajectories of modern cultural practice through a theoretical and methodological model "based on the articulation of a number of distinct processes whose interaction can and does lead to variable and contingent outcomes" (Du Gay, 2013, p. xxx).

Starting from the assumption that "theory is always a response to a particular context" (Grossberg, 1993, p. 5) the concept of articulation allows us to study cultural practice "without falling into the twin traps of reductionism and essentialism" (Slack, 1996, p. 113). From a methodological point of view, articulation offers an empirically driven framework through which to approach different dimensions of cultural analysis in relationship to each other as mutually constituted elements. It "provides a mechanism for shaping intervention within a particular formation, conjecture or context" (Slack, 1996, p. 113) while keeping a critical eye on broader power dynamics (see also Grossberg, 1996). A translocal perspective builds on articulation's "radical contextualism" (Grossberg, 1993, p. 5) as both a theoretical agenda and a methodological strategy. It proposes to challenge the binarism of global vs. local—where the local typically acts as "the global's presumptive victim, its cultural nemesis, or its coerced subordinate" (Kraidy and Murphy, 2008, p. 339)—to consider the local/national/global as *mutually constitutive* elements. It helps us embed "large-scale realities in concrete life-worlds" (Appadurai, 1996, p. 55).

This book illustrates what a translocal approach looks like, and what it can theoretically teach us, by exploring multiple dimensions of the transnational relationship between the "power triad" (Warnier, 2004) identified above. This three-way comparative focus offers opportunities to reflect on dimensions of the global rarely considered—such as, for instance, the implications of the French consumption of nostalgic representations of America in globally distributed Japanese animation. Making such connections between local social spaces encourages us to address thus far neglected local-to-local links and productively rethink local-global dynamics. To put it differently, a translocal approach allows us to explore not only how "the global" is negotiated and imagined in different contexts (what hybridity) but also what we can learn from both the differences and the similarities between these contexts about the nature of larger processes of globalization (how hybridity matters). Thus, developing a translocal perspective is both an empirical task and a theoretical one. Taking as a starting point the notion that the global/national/local are mutually constituted, this book empirically explores, through the study of globally distributed hybrid cultural forms and their "local" negotiation, the ways in which these three central sites define their imagined national/cultural/local identities in relationship to each other. The three sites are considered in different configurations throughout the book, each one adding to our understanding of the relationships between them—and, ultimately, to our theoretical understanding of broader processes of transnational influence and identity formation.

The Japan/France/U.S. Triad

Relatively recent historical developments, including the rise of China and East Asian economies, seem to suggest that economic globalization can no longer be characterized solely as a process of "'Triadization,' confined to the 'interlinked economies' of Europe, North America, and Japan" (Pieterse, 2003/2009, p. 13). The consequences of this common history of global hegemonic power—in particular as it relates to transnational cultural influence—are, however, yet to be fully explored. The "power triad" of France, Japan, and the United States thus remains a productive focus. It allows us to consider how powerful global cultural producers negotiate the global/national/local nexus in relationship to each other—just as "the global" contains an imagined dimension, the nation/national is a contested site, "an evolving, imaginary construct rather than an originary essence" (Shohat and Stam, 2003, p. 11). Because it involves sites that have historically, and at times contentiously, been positioned as "Western" (France and the United States) and "Eastern" (Japan), it also offers opportunities to complicate, and possibly deconstruct, "East/West" and well as "West/West" dynamics.

There is no denying that the United States has historically been an influential force in the development of global popular cultural forms. This book will demonstrate that this historical legacy remains a significant, even if contested, element of individuals' imagination of the global. Furthermore, while there is evidence that the global influence of the U.S. media is declining, exactly what this decline might mean for both U.S. and "global" media audiences is yet to be fully articulated. Studies of global media "flows" such as, for instance, Jeremy Tunstall's (2008) *The Media Were American* (written as a revision to his 1979 classic *Media Are American*) usefully point to a number of new actors entering the scene of transnational popular cultural influence (Bollywood movies, telenovelas, animation). A number of scholars have critically analyzed various aspects of these texts. Fewer works, however, have empirically and comparatively examined how these relative newcomers' entry onto the global popular cultural scene might intersect with transnational audiences' negotiation of the global—or how they might, concretely, shift the balance of power of transnational cultural influence beyond the most obvious economic level.

Global media scholar and feminist critic Radhika Parameswaran suggests that "the 'American dream' and the 'American ways of life'" remain "persuasive ideological constructs that circulate in varied transnational contexts to produce shifting global allegiances that in turn revive the idea of America as a mythical national space of unbridled freedom and democracy" (2009, p. 201). What this means for different audiences *including those in the United States* needs to be carefully considered. Cultural historian Francis Shor suggests, for instance, that this mythical vision of the United States "as the repository of good in the world" (2010, p. 32) is preventing U.S. citizens from coming to terms with the reality of its declining global power. He concludes that our ability to develop a more egalitarian global order rests in part on our ability to raise U.S. media consumers' consciousness about the nature of their nation's relationship to the rest of the world. Or, as cultural critics Ella Shohat and Robert Stam argue, "In the current situation, U.S. power is global, yet the knowledge of too many of its citizens is local and monoperspectival. At this point in history, as a consequence, transnationalizing media studies has become a political and pedagogical responsibility" (2009, p. 5).

The relationship between France and the United States—described by *New York Times* reporter William Grimes as "a folie à deux that's lasted nearly three centuries" (Grimes, 2006, p. 33E)—provides a terrain on which to explore West-to-West relationships characterized by significant cultural and linguistic differences. Defining France as a "'paradigmatic' European nation-state . . . historically linked to foundational theorizations of nations and nationalism," Stam and Shohat remind us that "the France-United States relationship began as a passionate romance" characterized by a reciprocal movement of ideas (at the time of the French and American revolutions), even if the two countries have since then been engaged in "a perennial love-hate relationship . . . accompanied by the emotions associated with sibling rivalry" (2012, pp. 26, 44, 482). While the United States surpassed France in its economic hegemony in the 20th century, the largest western European nation remains an influential global media producer—thanks to a combination of heavily subsidized cultural industries and the legacy of colonialism, which helped secure a global francophone market. Perhaps more importantly, France's official positions on a number of political, economic, and philosophical issues significantly differ today from those of the United States—the boycotting of French wine and renaming of "freedom fries" in some U.S. locales following France's opposition to the U.S. intervention in Iraq is a relatively recent reminder of how contentious these differences of opinion can become. In other words, and to borrow from Bourdieu, the United States and France represent "two imperialisms of the universal" (cited in Stam and Shohat, 2012, p. 482).

Most significantly for the purpose of this book, France's view on cultural policies powerfully contrasts with that of the United States (and, incidentally, the United Kingdom). While the United States has historically actively resisted trade restrictions to global media flows—as its withdrawal from UNESCO following the New World Information and Communication Order debate in the mid-1980s illustrates (it rejoined in 2003; McPhail, 2010)—France has long asserted that the unique nature of cultural products means that they cannot simply be treated like any other goods on the market. Its strongly culturally protectionist policies (the much defamed "quotas") aim at protecting French culture and the French language from (mostly U.S.) "cultural imperialism" but also serve to secure the country's position as a global media exporter.[1]

Japan's relationship to the United States is equally (if not more) tortured and complex. The formation of the Japanese nation itself is entangled in the country's relationship with "the West" and is a thoroughly *modern* endeavor. Cultural anthropologist Marilyn Ivy points to the lack of "a discursively unified notion of the 'Japanese' before the eighteenth century" and to the need to recognize "the coincident modernity of Japan and the West" (1995, p. 8). Japan as a *nation-state* was born from the territory's sudden forced engagement in transnational relationships sparked by Commodore Perry's 1853 arrival on its shores—in response to the threat of domination by Europe and the United States.

The process of "self-westernization" that characterized Japan's Meiji restoration starting in 1868 (Duus, 1998) is frequently equated to colonization. It significantly differed, however, from the forms of U.S. or European colonial violence found in other parts of the world. Japanese leaders' decision to "Westernize" stemmed from the desire to avoid a much more direct form of colonial influence. Fueled by anti-foreign rhetoric, the borrowing was selective, rational, and intentional, and while the importation of technology from Europe and the United States was (self-)consciously recognized, the form industrialization took was argued to be specifically Japanese (Boyle, 1993). Furthermore, if Japan started embracing "Western" ideas after Perry's arrival, the process was not unilateral. The Meiji era also marks a period of strong Japanese transnational influence, particularly in France where the *Japonisme* movement started. Indeed, some of the most celebrated elements of French culture—from impressionism to cubism—drew heavily from artists' and intellectuals' active engagement with Japanese culture. As we will see in chapter 5, this historical exchange would set the stage for a continuing process of transnational cultural engagement between the two nations.

Finally, Japan's colonial aggression in other parts of Asia further complicates the picture of its relationship to the rest of the world. While the postwar occupation resulted in more direct—even if contested—U.S. intervention, it is also the period during which Japanese leaders worked to strategically frame Japan as a war victim and erase its aggression in China from official memory (Dower, 1993; Duus, 1998). In a move that historian Carol Gluck (1993) characterizes as public amnesia, Japanese leaders advocated a total break from the past and promoted the notion of a new Japan entirely reformed, and focused on economic prosperity. Because of its spectacular rise as one of the most influential global economies in the second half of the 20th century, globalization scholars often simply do not know where to "fit" Japan in their maps of global geopolitics. In other words, Japan's history and geopolitical position as a quasi-colonized colonizer, as "Westernized" yet assertively "non-Western," as a nation positioning itself "in and above Asia" (Iwabuchi, 2004), powerfully blur the boundaries between colonizer and colonized, East and West, aggressor and victim, and points to the political and problematic nature of all of these categories.

Moving beyond East and West

Indeed, as globalization theorist Jan Nederveen Pieterse reminds us, the division of the world along East/West lines was always "an artificial and polemical" one that "played a much larger role in rhetoric and representation than in reality" (2003/2009, p. 126). The hybrid and multidirectional nature of 21st-century transnational cultural exchange makes this fact particularly difficult to ignore today. As "new frameworks of hybridity are being produced where the linear logic of East-West, or for that matter even West-East, simply does not hold" (Shome, 2006a, p. 120), scholars have struggled to develop new conceptual maps that more adequately take into account the complex and often contradictory subject positions that mark our contemporary condition (Grewal and Kaplan, 2003). This, however, has not been an easy task.[2]

One problem with conceptualizing global dynamics along an East/West axis is that it erases differences and tensions within regions/nations/local sites, and consequently makes it difficult to address (or easier to deny) power relations that do not follow the traditional lines of "the West" vs. "the Rest." In the case of Japan, for instance, strategically locating the Japanese nation in binary opposition to "the West" has historically served to direct attention "away from the doubleness of Japanese (post)colonial experience as a non-Western colonizer" (Iwabuchi, 2002, p. 61).

The division further results in a tendency to associate "the global" with "the West," with global-local interactions "predominantly studied in terms of how the Rest resists, imitates, or appropriates the West" (Iwabuchi, 2002, p. 50). In a related rhetorical twist, "the West" is also frequently merged with the United States—as if the latter were the inherent designated representative of the former. This failure to recognize differences within "the West" translates into an easy dismissal of other "Western" nations' concerns with perceived U.S. cultural imperialism and consequent attempts to protect themselves (see, for example, Hachten, 2005, p. 71). More disturbingly, it obscures the presence of other modes of organization, knowledge production, and distribution as valid *Western* alternatives. It contributes, for instance, to the neoliberal-era positioning of U.S.-style consumerism as "the norm of capitalism" (Pieterse, 2003/2009, p. 20) by denying the existence of different interpretations of capitalism in other parts of "the West."

Recognizing these quandaries, scholars have attempted to move beyond essentializing characterizations of both East and West. The lack of adequate vocabulary available to more sensitively speak of different areas of the world while at the same time recognizing the historical legacy of their engagement with each other has, however, made this task particularly challenging. Even scholars clearly attuned to these dynamics tend, for instance, to merge Anglo-American experiences with those of the rest of "the West." In an essay powerfully critiquing the West/Rest divide, cultural critics Raka Shome and Radha Hegde conclude that "global mass culture is firmly entrenched in the *West*. It absorbs differences within the larger, overarching framework of what is essentially an *American* conception of the world" (2002, p. 185, emphasis mine).[3] Likewise, in his influential critique of pessimistic interpretations of globalization as a homogenizing process of "Westernization," John Tomlinson recognizes that various elements of "Western" culture "do not constitute an indivisible package" (1999, p. 168), but the elements *he* describes are nevertheless all drawn from Anglo-American culture—McDonald's, Coca-Cola, Levi Jeans, Sesame Street.

Scholarly work originated in non-U.S. Western locales is also frequently positioned in an awkward liminal position "in and outside the West." For instance, Hamid Mowlana describes early postmodernist writing as "mostly an intellectual exercise in the French social science tradition" whose "appeal to and acceptance by *Western* social scientists was to come much later, in the 1980s" (1986/1997, p. 213, emphasis mine). Shome similarly distinguishes French intellectual work from the "Western" tradition when addressing the politics of translation of scholarship into English: "a French intellectual— given the 'high culture' connotations of French intellectual thought—is far more likely than, let's say a Bangladeshi intellectual—to find a publisher to translate her/his work through which it can enter high brow arenas of *western* intellectual space" (2009, p. 708, emphasis mine). This may be true, but are French scholars not "Western" unless translated into English?[4]

Generally, while scholars have effectively confronted essentializing constructions of "the East," the notion that "the West" is not a homogenous totalizing whole has been less successfully addressed. This is due in part to the fact that, as Pieterse reminds us, the polarities of North/South, East/West, colonizer/colonized were, historically, "such overriding fields of tension that differences within the West/North, among imperialist countries and within capitalism faded into the background" (2003/2009, p. 50). The resulting tendency in much academic work to "pit a rotating chain of marginalized communities against an unstated white or Western norm" (Shohat, 2002, p. 69) has dire consequences, however. On the most basic level, it simply does not do justice to the complexity of contemporary processes of transnational cultural influence—to globalization's "jagged contours" (Hegde, 2011a, p. 2). It problematically tends to locate issues of marginalization, poverty, or even nationalism outside of "the West"—as if "Western" nations were comfortably installed in postmodernity and free from the process of (re)defining their own cultural, racial, gender, class, and/or national identities (Dov, 1996). It obscures the fact that powerful "Western" nations negotiate their hegemonic global position in relationship to each other as well as to "the Rest" (Stam and Shohat, 2012). Finally, by putting the focus on East/West power dynamics, this conceptual binarism marginalizes the experiences of individuals experiencing prejudice and discrimination *within the West*.

A more critical engagement with what it means to be "Western" (particularly in the "non-U.S. West") is clearly needed, both in considerations of global dynamics and in the often heated debates about the politics of representation in academic work surrounding issues of who can speak for whom and in what context(s). The politics of translation of non-English language "Western" intellectual work in academic production are yet to be fully explored. How might the experience of a Greek scholar, for instance, be different from that of a French intellectual attempting to enter the canon of "Western" academic texts? How might the marginalization of the non-English-language intellectual work of "Western" scholars (a large number of whom are, after all, non-native English speakers) help secure the United States's/Britain's position as the sole/most significant representative of "the West"? In what ways does it serve to conceal the presence of a "Western" intellectual conversation taking place outside of the United States and Britain—an alternative to Anglo "Westernism"?

This is not to suggest that the critique of U.S. and/or European imperialism has become irrelevant, or that "the West" is an entirely empty concept—many European nations and the United States do share some cultural/racial/ideological biases as well as the historical culpability of imperialism. To put it differently, like Eurocentricism, "the West" is best understood as a historically significant discursive-ideological concept, an "implicit positioning" (Stam and Shohat, 2012, p. 62) taking its roots in colonialism rather than as an actual geographic space. In contemporary times, however, "the shifting fault lines of economic and cultural power" also result in "new forms of articulations and disarticulations, new configurations of power, and new planes of dis/empowerment" (Shome and Hegde, 2002, p. 175). This is particularly true when considering cultural dynamics that are considerably more difficult to trace than flows of capital. Under such conditions, terms such as "Western," "non-Western," "postcolonial," or even "subaltern" must be used (self-)consciously.

A critical deconstruction of "the West" requires a parallel engagement with the common association of globalization with "Western" modes of cultural, political, and economic organization—with, in other words, "Western-style" modernity. Noting that Westernization is not the only path to modernity, scholars have suggested that we theorize globalization "as a set of regionally differentiated patterns of modernization" (Straubhaar, 2007, p. 28). Rather than conceptualize modernization as a linear chronological process—from "developing" to "modern" to, potentially, "postmodern"—drawing from the historical experiences of an essentialized "West," they propose that we think, instead, of modernities (plural). This "specter of *different modernities*" (Pieterse, 2003/2009, p. 46, emphasis in original), of "modernization without westernization" helps complicate our understanding of globalization—or, more precisely, of globalizations (plural).

Scholars have started to explore these multiple modernities and have examined the trails cultural globalization takes in their wake (see, for example, Kraidy, 2009a). By drawing comparisons between two (very different) "Western" nations and a "non-Western" (yet highly economically powerful) one, this book continues on this intellectual path. Its translocal approach aims to illustrate the ways in which the East/West divide may be used as an essentializing tool on both sides of the axis. It proposes, in turn, to develop a more nuanced understanding of how this process of strategic positioning intersects with other dimensions of transnational and transcultural dynamics and of individuals' identities under conditions of globalization. These more theoretical considerations will be taken up toward the end of the book as a way to reflect on what scholars can learn from applying a translocal approach to global media studies. Like the observations made in other chapters, however, these theoretical reflections will be based on empirical evidence drawn from the comparison between the three sites' engagement with global media.

Gendered Hybridities and the Politics of Representation

One particularly problematic characteristic of the essentialized division of the world along East/West lines is its intersection with issues of gender, race, and class. Scholars have noted how opposing "Western" nations to "the Rest" frequently serves to strategically locate class, racial, or gender oppression outside "the West" and, conversely, to position the latter as the champion of equality, justice, progressive sexual politics, cosmopolitanism, and progress (see, for example, Dov, 1996; Hegde, 2001; Niezen, 2004). They point to the fact that the United States and Europe have often historically justified their imperialist aggression by defining themselves as liberators of "non-Western" women from the particularly severe oppression of "their" men. For instance, when the United States opposed itself to Japan at the turn of the 20th century, it linked Japan's ability to "Westernize" to a successful shift in Japanese women's status (Iriye, 1967). In a more contemporary context, Hegde (2011) discusses how the foregrounding of Afghan women as victims in media coverage of the war on terror helped provide a moral justification for the United States' actions.

But if "sexuality has historically played a central role in the ways in which dominant *Western* views on cultural differences are coded" (Hegde, 2011, p. 2, emphasis mine), discourses about "Eastern" racial purity, homogeneity, and appropriate gender roles have similarly drawn from the opposition between an allegedly racially homogeneous and Confucian-influenced "East" and a "West" imagined as racially mixed and "gender liberated" (Iwabuchi, 2002). In other words, issues of gender, race, class, and/or ethnicity remain contentious both in "the West" and elsewhere, and powerfully intersect with local/ national/cultural identity formation and processes of globalization—"gender is, and always has been, global—whether recognized or not" (Shome, 2006b, p. 255; see also Durham, 2001; Enloe, 2004; Hegde, 2011b; Parameswaran, 2009). Ethnicity is similarly produced in part through the process of imagining the global/national—as Appadurai notes, minorities under conditions of globalization provide "a constant reminder of the incompleteness of national purity" (2006, p. 84).

Women's frequent positioning as representatives of the nation and/or keepers of cultural tradition has also rendered their negotiation of transnational influence (and globalized media forms) particularly complex. Scholars have analyzed how mediated representations of femininity intersect with constructions of national/global/racial identities in a variety of cultural contexts (for recent examples see Kraidy, 2009a; Parameswaran, 2011; Parameswaran and Cordoza, 2009; Valdivia, 2011; Volčič and Erjavec, 2011). For instance, locating beauty pageants against the backdrop of the spread of "Western-style" consumerism in India, Parameswaran concludes in an examination of their media representation:

> Newspaper and magazine stories celebrate global beauty queens' material accomplishments, but also strive to ensure that readers are aware of these women's loyalty to their own cultural traditions and family values. . . . Using the language of nationalism, some media reports idolize the Indian beauty queen for setting innovative global standards for ideal femininity. (2005, pp. 424–25)

Gender constructions may thus be negotiated simultaneously as acts of resistance against foreign influence (*nationalism*), means to safeguard "indigenous" elements of culture (*own cultural tradition*), and as claims of membership in global geopolitics (*innovative global standards*).

The trope of hybridity is a significant subtext of this negotiation. Offered as alternatives to globally dominant ideals of "Western/White" femininity and to "pre-modern" "local" gender dynamics, the constructions of ideal Indian beauty Parameswaran describes deploy hybridity as "a mutually interactive combination of global and national cultural images, values, and symbols" (2005, p. 424). As we will see in chapter 3, scholars have observed a similar process in Japan where hybridized representations of ideal Japanese beauty are offered as acts of resistance against "Western" global hegemony while simultaneously feeding a self-Orientalizing discourse (Creighton, 1995; Darling-Wolf, 2006; Yegenoglu, 1998). These examples illustrate the need to continue to explore the intersection of gender, race, class, and nation with the construction of hybridized cultural forms under conditions of globalization.

Because of the tendency, identified above, to focus on how "the Rest" resists, imitates, or appropriates "the West," this intersection has been most assertively addressed in "non-Western" contexts. As feminist scholar Chandra Talpade Mohanty reminds us, however, "the interwoven processes of sexism, racism, misogyny, and heterosexism are an integral part of our social fabric *wherever in the world we might be*" (2003, p. 3, emphasis mine). This book consequently pays particular critical attention to these matters in the development of its translocal approach. It responds to the call for "situated and empirically driven research on globalization" with a critical eye on "how *globalized media practices articulate gender*" (Shome, 2006b, p. 181, emphasis mine). The empirical examples provided here will indeed demonstrate that gender, race, and class are constant—and at times eerily similar—elements of the imagination of the global regardless of the context and of the angle of analysis used to approach it.

"The Global" and the Media

As Shome's quote above suggests, the notion of the global would not exist, at least not in its current form, without the media. Because relatively few people are able to acquire the extensive first-hand knowledge of different cultural environments needed to develop "a primarily global identity" (Strauhbaar, 2007, p. 6) the media become a crucial site on which impressions of "the global" are formed and negotiated (Rantanen, 2005). As Argentinian-Mexican cultural critic Néstor García Canclini puts it, "we construct what is ours with greater intensity against the backdrop of what we imagine about others" (2001, p. 62).

By blurring "the lines between the 'realistic' and fictional landscape" the "mediascapes" formed by flows of information and images provide the scripts through which individuals create "imagined worlds" and "constitute narratives of the 'other'" (Appadurai, 1990, p. 299). The media are, in other words, a central component of the imagination of the global that, according to Appadurai (1996, p. 31), "is now central to all forms of agency." As cultural critic Radha Hegde explains:

> In the global context, questions of culture, subjectivity, and everyday life have to be situated against the ubiquitous presence and proliferation of communication technologies and their ability to transcend time and space. Increasingly embedded in the circuits of social life, media forms collide with established cultural practices, forcing reconfigurations of categories such as private/public, tradition/modernity, and global/local. (2011a, pp. 5–6)

Thus, examining globally distributed media "provides a point of departure for elaborating the production of the transnational imaginary" (Shome and Hegde, 2002, p. 182).

The empirical materials used in this book to explore this process are cultural products that are noteworthy for the extent to which they intersect on the global, national, and local levels with the three sites that are its central focus. These are globally distributed texts, genres, and formats that are (and have long been) adapted to (and negotiated in) a wide variety of cultural environments, forming a useful basis for comparison. As noted, they allow us to look at dynamics rarely considered and thus help us address new dimensions of the global/national/local intersection. They also allow us to draw connections between contexts rarely considered in relationship to each other. In a sense, they are examples of what Condry (2006, p. 90) terms "*genba* globalization."[5] *Genba* (literally, "scene" or "actual place" in Japanese, as in "the scene of a crime") are sites of cultural production where global, local, and national identities and representations intersect and that "actualize . . . the global and the local simultaneously" (Condry, 2006, p. 90). These are texts that allow us to explore, in other words, the multiple "tonalities" (Geertz, 1983) of global culture.

The rise of digital communication, the Internet, and/or social media has recently received much scholarly attention. The texts discussed in this book, however, further demonstrate that the time-space compression (Castells, 2003; Giddens, 1999; Harvey, 1989) that results from individuals' engagement with global media predates these recent developments. A number of scholars have warned against the tendency to dismiss "old" theories in the face of rapid technological change as if new technologies did not share a historical link with earlier media forms and automatically rendered previous insights obsolete (see, for example, Livingstone, 2004; Morley, 2006; Sterne, 2007). Digital media scholar Kelly Gates suggests that rather than uncritically "celebrating recent innovations as radically different and inherently better" we must strive "to recognize the deeply embedded ways that the past is still with us in the present" (2013, p. 7). Back in 1996, Appadurai already noted that the new forces at work in the development of the global imagination were built on technological changes taking place *over the past century or so* (1996, p. 5, emphasis mine). The texts included in this book represent this relatively longer view. While, as we will see, the rise of digital communication may have accelerated and expanded their global spread (allowing, in particular, non-English-language texts to reach U.S. audiences in greater numbers), these were highly globally influential cultural products long before the Internet or YouTube.

Some of the specific programs or artists mentioned in the following chapters may not be familiar to U.S. readers. Additional information (in English) about each of these texts and/or genres is readily available through a quick Internet search. The texts themselves (episodes of animated series, songs and their lyrics, magazines) are also easily accessible online—illustrating the point above about the role of digital media—if the reader wants to get a sense of their texture.

This book, however, goes beyond the study of texts. While examining media can help us develop a sense of how the local/national/global are rhetorically negotiated, local identities cannot be fully accessed through textual analysis (García Canclini, 2001). As Murphy and Kraidy note, "While globalization may be discursively situated in terms of broad economic, political and cultural trends, media consumption is . . . perhaps the most immediate, consistent and pervasive way in which 'globality' is experienced" (2003, p. 7). Appadurai proposes that scholars find new ways to explore the increasingly global and deterritorialized link between the imagination and social life through an ethnography "that is not so resolutely localizing" (1996, p. 55). In response to these suggestions, the insights provided here are also based on countless informal discussions, extensive participant observation, and more than 80 formal interviews with some 160 media consumers (and, occasionally, producers) in Japan, France, and the United States conducted over the course of several years of fieldwork. These informants' enthusiastic responses to the various texts discussed and their insightful comments on the nature of globalization provide a rich terrain through which to explore the imagination of the global. They provide us with the thick descriptions necessary to start answering the question of how hybridity matters.

In addition to their importance as global cultural producers and to the multidimensional nature of their historical relationships, the three sites that constitute the focus of this book were chosen because they are sites that have shaped my identity as a scholar and on which I can claim some level of expertise. Born and raised in France, I have spent most of my adult life in the United States where I currently teach. I am also engaged in an ongoing relationship with Japan where I moved for the first time as an English teacher more than 18 years ago, and which became the main focus of my research (and my ethnographic field-site) shortly thereafter. In addition to spending several years on the island of Shikoku and returning to my field-site on a regular basis, I frequently spend my summers teaching in Tokyo. French is my native language and I can function in Japanese (even though I typically conduct formal interviews in Japan with the help of my wonderful interpreter, Yasumi Okame, who also more generally serves as my research assistant). The interviews with Japanese informants cited throughout this book were conducted in 1998–99, 2009, and 2011. Some of the media consumers cited were interviewed in each of these time periods, allowing me to develop a "longer view" on their engagement with global media—several were still in high school when I started my research in the community.

The bulk of this book was, however, written from a small village in Southern France not far from where I grew up, and where I own a home. My interactions with the local community there over the course of several years starting in 2006—including a one-year stay (from August 2009 to August 2010) specifically focused on gathering data for this work—provided a useful backdrop to many of the insights developed here. The majority of the formal interviews with French informants cited in this work were conducted in 2010, but I also returned to the village in the summers of 2011, 2012, and 2013 and conducted further participant observation and informal interviews.

Interviews with U.S. consumers were conducted in 2011 and 2012 in the Philadelphia area. While attempts were made to include individuals of all ages and of different socio-economic backgrounds in all three cultural contexts, it is important to note that the U.S. media consumers who participated in my research tended to be more urban (even though they were not all originally from Philadelphia) and somewhat more highly educated than their French and Japanese counterparts. The U.S. sample also tended to be relatively more racially and ethnically diverse. I believe the data will demonstrate that this discrepancy does not invalidate the comparison, but it is something the reader should keep in mind when considering the comments included in this book.

Finally, it is also important to note that the "chosen transnationality" that affords me the luxury to compare these three cultural contexts is significantly different from the forced translocality of migrant workers, of immigration as a result of political strife or intense economic hardship, or of postcolonial experience. For most people, transnationality or hybridity is not a choice, but "results from having to satisfy basic needs by participating in a system of production and consumption not of one's choosing" (Yúdice, 2001, p. xv). Keeping these caveats in mind, this book is intended as one voice in a larger conversation on global media between scholars in different disciplines and representing different areas of the world—a conversation hopefully based on "mutual engagement rather than theoretical chauvinism" (Kraidy, 2009b, p. 90).

Mapping the Book

As noted, this book builds an empirically informed theory of translocalism by considering how the process of imagining the global takes place through the negotiation of globally distributed hybrid cultural forms on three sites: France, Japan, and the United States. Because of the complexity of transnational dynamics, it is necessarily partial. Far from proposing to "represent" the entire world—at best an exercise in futility, at worst one in stereotyping—it concentrates on these three central sites as a means to explore interrelations and links within a broader global context. Drawing from specific examples, it considers how the process of imagining the global intersects with constructions of local, national, racial, and gendered identities in each of these sites as they engage with global culture, including each other's media. Each empirical example serves as a starting point for a reflection on what we can learn, both empirically and theoretically, from the similarities and differences within and between these economically powerful global cultural producers. This means that some relationships and dynamics will not be fully explored here. I realize, for instance, that the various cultural references mentioned in the vignette opening this chapter do not all have the same connotations in terms of the politics of transcultural borrowing. Sporting an Indian sari or Native American dress is not the same as dressing up like a Disney princess—even if French media consumers' awareness of these different sartorial choices may come from the same global sources (such as, for instance, Hollywood). A thorough engagement with the remaining legacy of colonialism/orientalism that permeates French consumers' relationship to India or with the ways in which less privileged individuals in cultural contexts marked by a history of colonial violence might negotiate global cultural references differently would fall, however, beyond the scope of this book.

The reasons behind the choice of specific texts will be briefly addressed at the beginning of each chapter. Each site will be considered in different configurations throughout the chapters—as producer, receptor, or mediator of cultural flows. Because of the complexity of contemporary transnational cultural exchange, however, we will soon see that these roles frequently overlap and/

or merge. Finally, the term "transnational" will be used throughout the book to refer to relations between the sites in which the national level is ostensibly (and, often, discursively) emphasized—as in the case, for instance, of global news. I chose the term "transnational" rather than "international" because it suggests a more fluid movement through spaces and borders beyond official state relations. The term "transcultural" will be used to reflect the more complex mix of cultural influences taking place on multiple levels characteristic of our hybrid contemporary condition.

Chapter 1, "Un-American Idols: How the Global/National/Local Intersect," empirically explores the most basic argument of this book: the idea that the global, national, and local are mutually constituted in contemporary popular culture. The genre of reality television, predicated on the "local" adaptation of highly "global" formats, provides a useful starting point for this exploration. Scholars have demonstrated how format adaptation creates a cultural space where local, national, and gendered identities are actively debated, contested, and negotiated (Kraidy, 2009a; Kraidy and Murphy, 2008). Reality TV's active engagement with communication technologies in its construction of "the real" also serves to heighten viewers' awareness of our worldwide connectedness. The chapter more specifically explores this global/national/local nexus through an examination of the adaptation of one global format to the French national television market. In keeping with the book's intent, it also considers how the show's construction of local, national, and global identities intersected with its narratives about race and culture to demonstrate how these different dynamics are all mutually constitutive, and often contentious, elements of contemporary cultural forms.

Having illustrated how the global/national/local are mutually constituted in contemporary media, the book goes on to apply a broader translocal lens to this process and to its intersection with racial and cultural dynamics. Chapter 2, "Holier-than-Thou: Representing the "Other" and Vindicating Ourselves in International News," explores how all three sites negotiated the global/national/local nexus in relationship to each other in their coverage of dramatic news events. Focusing on events that generated debates about racial and/or cultural dynamics in each of these sites (Hurricane Katrina, the race riots that shook France in 2005, and the March 2011 Japanese earthquake and tsunami), it draws parallels between the ways in which the French, Japanese, and U.S. press negotiated these issues both "at home" and in "international" news. The choice of news provides opportunities to reflect on the ideological nature of a medium whose claims to "represent" reality, if not always unquestionably accepted, are generally taken more seriously than those of more "popular" cultural forms, such as reality television. The chapter shows that the three sites all engaged in a very similar process of employing translocal comparisons to downplay the implications of crises "at home," particularly as they related to racial tensions. It also illustrates, however, how the French and U.S. discourse about the Japanese disaster further engaged in a process of "othering" Japan by interpreting Japanese reactions to the event as illustrative of distinctive cultural/racial traits contrasted to those of "Western" nations.

Building on this last conclusion, chapter 3, "Talking about *non-no*: (Re) fashioning Race and Gender in Global Magazines," turns to Japan as a site of reception to investigate how its status as a "non-Western/non-majority white" social context might shape its relationship to "the global" and to the other sites considered in the book. This chapter also adds a more careful consideration of gender and class into the mix, by examining how the Japanese negotiation of race interlocks with that of gender and class in globalized cultural forms. Finally, it considers how these dynamics take shape not only discursively, but also in individuals' experiences. Employing global fashion magazines as its empirical starting point, the chapter first examines the multiple ways in which culture, race, gender, and the global are invoked in Japanese texts. It then moves beyond textual representations to explore how Japanese women negotiate these constructions through their media consumption. The chapter demonstrates how individuals' imagination of "the global" and their negotiation of both transnational influence and national/cultural identity cannot be separated from their experience of gender, race, and class. It also illustrates how the local/national/global are mutually constituted not only in globalized media but also in individuals' daily lives.

Having demonstrated the often-political nature of processes of representation and positioning against the backdrop of an imagined global community in popular cultural forms, the book turns to the examination of a similarly myopic process of positioning in academic work *about* globalized media. The next two chapters build connections between empirical examinations of the local/national/global intersection to address the problematic consequences of biases commonly found in academic discourse. They employ translocal examinations of two globalized genres—hip-hop and Japanese animation—to illustrate the need to develop new theoretical models that move beyond essentialized characterizations of large areas of the world.

Chapter 4, "Disjuncture and Difference from the *Banlieue* to the *Ganba*: Embracing Hip-hop as a Global Genre," considers what applying a translocal lens to hip-hop as a *global* phenomenon can teach us about the politics of representation of race, class, and gender not only in hip-hop itself but also in academic discussions surrounding its contested definitions of cultural, racial, ethnic, and gender identities. Considering hip-hop through a translocal lens, it demonstrates how the positioning of hip-hop as an African/Latino/a American genre and the focus on limiting definitions of authenticity in academic discourse lead to problematic characterizations of hip-hop's global dynamics. It also considers how discussions of hip-hop's global dimensions are yet to fully address the genre's misogynist subtext. The chapter illustrates the productive potential of developing a more translocal approach to these questions, and the need to decentralize the United States in our examinations of global processes.

In response to this last argument, chapter 5, "What West Is It? Anime and Manga according to *Candy* and *Goldorak*," turns to Japan as a site of production and to a genre (Japanese animation) frequently identified as challenging U.S. cultural hegemony. The chapter demonstrates, however, that while intending to point to Japan's growing influence and to a concomitant decline in U.S. power, the academic and popular discourse in the United States about Japanese animation's "global" popularity has paradoxically resulted in the re-centralizing of the United States as both a global cultural producer and a consumer of globalized cultural forms. The chapter points to the ways in which this discourse is problematic by contrasting the genre's trajectory into the French cultural context to its influence in the United States. Drawing from interviews with French consumers as well as historical evidence, it illustrates the cultural significance of the Japanese genre in France. It also demonstrates how analyses too narrowly focused on a U.S./Japan axis result in dangerously essentializing characterizations of both "the West" and "Japan." The chapter concludes that this "global" genre was negotiated quite differently in the United States than it was in other areas of the world, due, in large part, to the United States' historical dominance of global cultural markets.

The consequences of the United States' history of (and possibly continuing) transnational cultural influence are further taken up in chapter 6, "Imagining the Global: Transnational Media and Global Audiences." Building on what we have learned so far in the book about the nature of globalized cultural forms and on additional conversation with media consumers in France, Japan, and the United States, the chapter provides a broader final reflection on individuals' experiences of "the global." Drawing parallels between the three sites, it considers how French and Japanese media consumers' imagination of the global was similarly shaped by the historical omnipresence of U.S. cultural products on their respective cultural landscapes. The chapter points to the need to keep in mind the imagined nature of individuals' engagement with different cultural contexts through the media, and, in particular, the imagined nature of their relationship with "America." It also demonstrates how the different histories of transnational influence in the three sites that constitute the focus of this book have resulted in U.S. media consumers having a different relationship to "global" texts than their Japanese and French counterparts. It concludes that this, again, points to the need to decentralize the U.S. cultural experience in our analyses of global processes and deconstruct "the West" as well as "the Rest."

The final chapter of the book, "Lessons from a Translocal Approach—or, Reflections on Contemporary Glocamalgamation," reflects on what we can draw theoretically from the translocal mosaic charted in its different chapters. Reflecting on the recurring dynamics found throughout the book, it returns to the central question of how hybridity matters—both empirically and theoretically. It emphasizes how hybridity results in a normalization of the global in individuals' daily lives, in an increased awareness of our inescapable engagement in it. It further reflects on the often-contentious nature of globalized hybridity, particularly as it intersects with racial and gender dynamics and explores its productive potential. Noting the dearth of adequate vocabulary available to describe the mutual transformations of cultural forms that characterize the imagination of the global, it proposes that we think about the messiness of global culture's intersection with local subjectivities as a form of "glocamalgamation." It concludes that glocamalgamation, as explored through the translocal approach of this book, forces us to move beyond narrow conceptualizations of the world and to decentralize the United States' cultural experience in our considerations of global processes while keeping an eye on its continuing economic power.

The book closes with a brief discussion of the productive potential of a critical theory of translocalism for future research and of the challenges involved in developing such an approach. It concludes that an empirically driven translocal perspective can help overcome the "fateful optical illusion" (Warnier, 2004, p. 91) created by the socio-cultural context surrounding us (including that of academia), and that French anthropologist Jean-Pierre Warnier argues is characteristic of contemporary discourses about globalization.

Noting that "an ill-formulated injunction suggests that we should not compare apples and oranges," Stam and Shohat argue that "in fact one can pursue comparison in many directions and for different ends" (2009, p. 481). Taking this suggestion seriously, the following chapters will draw connections between and within different "locals." Each will employ empirical evidence to reflect on different yet interlinked dimensions of the imagination of the global and how it intersects with constructions of local, national, racial, and gendered identities. Each will add a piece of the puzzle to our understanding of broader processes of transnational cultural exchange. Taken together, the chapters propose to sketch a theory of translocalism that might "serve as a trampoline for epistemological leaps" (Stam and Shohat, 2009, p. 489) allowing us to identify the blind spots in our own academic work and, ultimately, to develop a more multidimensional understanding of contemporary processes of cultural globalization.

The next chapter begins this translocal journey by empirically illustrating one of the theoretical starting points of the book: the idea that the global, national, and local are mutually constituted in contemporary popular culture. The chapter explores this process through the genre of reality television, with a specific focus on the adaptation of a widely globally distributed reality television format, *Star Academy*, to the French national television market.

ONE

Un-American Idols: How the Global/ National/Local Intersect

Reality TV has come to permeate the popular zeitgeist, occupying lucrative time slots across the globe and a prominent place in the cultural imaginary.
 —Ouellette and Murray, 2004, p. 2

The product of a combination of deregulation policies, the growing globalization and simultaneous fragmentation of television audiences spurred by cable's constant search for niche markets, efforts on the part of traditional networks to reclaim their audience, and across-the-board increased commercial pressures, reality TV emerges as a perfect exemplar of 21st-century transnational capitalism. With its success predicated on its ability to combine "a local cast and local viewer participation with a customizable transnational format" (Andrejevic, 2004, p. 12) the genre stands at the intersection of the "global" and the "local." Scholars have demonstrated that the process of adapting globally owned and distributed formats to an array of "local" contexts creates a privileged cultural space where local, national, and gendered identities are actively debated, contested, and negotiated in relationship to the global (Kraidy, 2009a; Kraidy and Murphy, 2008). The genre consequently offers a fertile terrain on which to explore one of the basic premises of this book: the notion that the local/national/global are mutually constituted in globalized cultural forms.

While reality TV is not the only cultural space where this process takes place, the genre's obvious entanglement in the global/national/local nexus provides a good empirical starting point to the development of a translocal perspective. This chapter starts with a brief description of the ways in which reality television has transformed global/local dynamics. It then turns to the case of the adaptation of one highly global format, *Star Academy*, into the French national market to illustrate how the process of localization generated specific constructions of French national identity in the show's narrative.

Moving beyond localization, it demonstrates how these constructions were developed in a symbiotic relationship with the show's engagement with an imagined global community. It closes with a short examination of the specific power dynamics permeating this relationship.

Reality TV's Entanglement with the Global/Local Nexus

The rise of format adaptation as a preferred form of transnational exchange—what global media scholar Joseph Straubhaar calls "genre imperialism" (2007, p. 68)—has inserted important new dynamics into global processes of transnational influence and their local negotiation.

On the broadest economic level, the extreme success of reality television starting in the first decade of the 21st century has engendered a subtle shift in global power relations. The move from selling "finished" and, consequently, significantly culturally marked media products—think of the global impact of *Happy Days*, *Dallas*, or *Sex and the City*—to selling more "culturally neutral" formats has eroded the relative economic advantage of powerful countries with the capital to develop extensive production facilities supported by a vast national market. As former head of Israeli television Yair Stern put it when describing the audiovisual landscape in his country in a personal conversation, "it used to be all American TV series, like *Dallas* or the hospital show . . . ER. Now it's all reality TV formats" (October 21, 2008). The rise of the small Dutch company Endemol to the status of reality TV giant is illustrative of this shift. It indicates that the low production cost of reality TV formats has allowed smaller players to start competing on the global market at a level previously unattainable to them (Kilborn, 2003). Today, Endemol has become a truly global company with subsidiaries and joint ventures in 23 countries, and has "forced Hollywood producers to take an increasing interest in imported programming formats" (Andrejevic, 2004, pp. 11–12).

The relationship of large format exporters to the various cultural environments in which they conduct business is different, however, than that of earlier global production giants, such as Hollywood, with stronger ties to an easily identifiable national culture. While yielding significant economic returns, the relatively culturally neutral nature of formats diminishes their cultural influence and allows for greater negotiation at the national level—which, as Straubhaar reminds us, is the level at which formats are typically adapted. Thus, format adaptation results in a "hybrid production in which imported elements, genres, and formats are adapted into national media systems and given national spins or interpretations. The outcome is neither national autonomy, nor cultural imperialism" (Straubhaar, 2007, pp. 167–68). The fact that formats may be exported to a wide array of national environments further complicates this picture by creating translocal relationships that may become more culturally significant than the "local" text's connection to its original format (Kraidy and Murphy, 2008). In other words, format adaptation powerfully illustrates the increased complexity of globalization in the 21st century.

The cultural discourse surrounding reality television is often couched, however, in quasi-anthropological language that, ironically, serves to position the genre as a microcosm of the "local" societies into which its global formats are adapted. French television scholar François Jost notes, for instance, that the intense debates generated by the first season of *Loft Story* (France's equivalent of *Big Brother*) centered on what could be learned from its teenaged participants about the character of younger generations, as if the program provided an "*in vivo* observation of French youth" (2002/2007, p. 63). Such claims are interesting in light of the fact that the owner of the format retains a high level of control over the various incarnations of the text. Elements interpreted as "local" may in fact be part of the format's global communication strategy. Thus, reality TV's engagement with the local is never fully divorced from the global context of production and distribution surrounding the genre. If "the global" is not always ostensibly represented in its local narratives, these narratives are nevertheless constructed against the backdrop of this broader framework.

Scholars further locate the rise of reality television as a popular genre in relationship to a historical and cultural moment in which our discomfort with surveillance technologies has been dulled by the age of interactive media and its incursion on individuals' personal privacies (Androjevic, 2004; Le Guay, 2005). An age, in other words, epitomized by the increased dual awareness of watching and being watched (Jost, 2002/2007). Indeed, as Chinese boys in a dorm room, cranky old ladies crossing the street, or talking kitties become instant transcultural YouTube phenomena, the presence of a global watching audience is more and more difficult to ignore. Reality television's active engagement with our contemporary hypermediated environment—24-hour web presence, ability for audiences to use their phone or the Internet to influence the outcome of a show—and its link to processes of global surveillance ultimately contribute to the *awareness of the global* symptomatic of our contemporary condition. They powerfully intersect with the construction of what globalization scholar Manfred Steger describes as "a rising global imaginary" (2009, p. 10).

This complex nexus of local/national/global linkages is an important broader context to keep in mind when examining the adaptation of reality television formats to various cultural environments. It helps us recognize that the local and the global do not exist "in suspended opposition" (Kraidy and Murphy, 2008, p. 339) but are constitutive parts of the same process of negotiation of socio-cultural and national identities under conditions of globalization. The rest of this chapter empirically explores how this negotiation took place in the adaptation of one reality TV format to the French national television market. It also considers how the show's construction of local, national, and global identities intersected with its narratives about race and culture to illustrate how these different dynamics are all mutually constitutive, and often contentious, elements of contemporary cultural forms.

Star Academy in Context

Owned by the Spanish branch of Endemol—to whom we also owe such successes as *Big Brother, Deal or No Deal,* and *Fear Factor*—*Star Academy*'s status as one of the most globally successful reality television formats to date makes it a logical choice for this investigation. Started in France in October 2001, the show's format has since been exported to some 50 different cultural environments ranging from Africa to Quebec through Lebanon and Russia. The show, however, was never successfully brought to the United States—even though it was initially inspired by the 1980 film *Fame,* featuring students at the New York City High School for the Performing Arts. While *Star Academy* experienced its popularity peak in France in the mid-2000s—it stopped broadcasting because of a decline in ratings after its 2008 season and the rights to the format were sold to a different channel in 2011—its influence on the reality TV genre is still strongly felt, and many of its other global incarnations, most notably its Arab World version (Kraidy, 2009a), are still running today.

Star *Academy*'s huge success rests in part on its ingenious merging of two extremely popular reality television formats. The show combines *Big Brother*–like 45-minute daily broadcasts from the "academy," the school for music and dance where candidates live, with weekly two and a half hour "primes"—in the vein of *Pop-Idol* in Britain or *American Idol* in the United States—broadcast, as their name suggests, during prime time. During the primes, students perform live in front of judges and an international audience. In the case of the French adaptation of the format, the official website for the program and a pay channel further provided live footage of life at the academy for 22 hours out of every 24-hour period. The French version of the show was originally broadcast on TF1, France's oldest television channel and one of its only two free private non-digital channels.[1]

An important backdrop to understanding the popularity of *Star Academy*—or *Star Ac'* as it is generally referred to in France—is the country's long history of game and variety shows. The early "radio crochets," the singing radio competitions that led to the discovery of some of France's most celebrated popular singers, can be considered one of *Star Academy*'s earliest precursors.

The fact that France has a long history of highly popular variety shows, often broadcast in prime time, is also relevant. In other words, while the current popularity of reality television might, at first sight, be interpreted as a relatively recent development, the reality TV phenomenon is not without historical precedent. Incidentally, *Star Ac'* itself has now spurred the development of other similar shows, such as *Nouvelle Star* initially broadcast on M6 (France's other analog private channel), which consists of a weekly prime (also lasting two and a half hours) that mixes the candidates' live performances with short humorous "behind the scenes" edited segments.

Particularly significant to the issues at hand is the fact that many of these game and variety shows have historically provided a space for national and cultural identity construction and representation. For instance, the *Eurovision* song contest, famously won by ABBA in 1974 and broadcast throughout Europe without interruption since 1956, pits European countries against each other in its annual one-day competition. Similarly, the game show *Jeux Sans Frontières* (Games Without Borders), broadcast for nine weeks every summer from 1965 to 1999, featured teams from different countries competing in outlandish costumes and crowned one nation its ultimate winner. The articulation of the global, national, and local in more recent reality television may be more subtle than in these earlier shows born out of a upbeat postwar effort to promote European unity through friendly competition,[2] but reality TV continues to serve as a terrain on which national and cultural identities are negotiated and constructed in relationship to the global. A closer look at *Star Academy* indicates that this complex negotiation takes place on several levels.

World Citizens "à la française": Localizing *Star Ac'* and Reconciling the French Nation

Most obviously, the French version of *Star Academy* beautifully illustrates the process of localization that global reality formats undergo when adapted to local cultural environments. Participants' daily life at the academy was steeped in references to what the audience was encouraged to interpret as "traditional" aspects of French culture. This was particularly apparent in the shows' daily broadcasts that followed the candidates' every move as they studied, ate, and slept together (pun intended).

The organization of the school itself was modeled after the French educational system. The complex process of selection of candidates for possible elimination on the Friday night prime orchestrated by professors throughout the week closely resembled, with its system of averages and "repêchage" (retest), the process of evaluation for the baccalauréat—the national exam French students have to take when exiting high school. The way classes were organized around a set schedule that all students were to abide by, the grading system on a 20-point scale, the emphasis on strong discipline, all referred to elements of life in a French lycée—elements the young audience and their parents were likely to be intimately (and at times painfully) familiar with. *Star Academy*'s version of French education was, however, clearly idealized. As Jost explains,

> To parents who deplore the abdication of educational responsibility on the part of professors and to children who condemn the school system for teaching boring subjects, Star Academy offers the image of a reconciled school, where adults and adolescents work together to reach a common goal. (2007, p. 107)

Star Academy similarly offered the image of a reconciled French cultural context constructed across regional and generational barriers. The world of *Star Academy* was one in which adult professors and the diverse casts of adolescents they taught were portrayed as sharing a common "French" cultural heritage celebrated throughout the daily broadcasts. This was accomplished by the physical presence on the show of French cultural icons ranging from older artists (Renaud, Michel Sardou, Johnny Hallyday) to relatively newer arrivals (Florent Pagny, Benabar), who served as the "patrons" of different seasons or came to perform with candidates during the weekly primes. This shared cultural heritage was further emphasized in the selection of songs to be interpreted by candidates, often drawn from the repertoire of celebrated French singer/songwriters such as Gilbert Bécaud, Hughes Aufray, and Yves Montand.

References to various French customs used to invigorate the otherwise rather dull reality of daily life at the academy served a similar purpose. When, in the show's seventh season, the mother of one of the candidates was invited to visit in February to make the traditional crèpes in celebration of the Catholic Candlemas, her exceptional intrusion into the otherwise autarkic life of the candidates not only helped break the monotony of schoolwork but also reminded viewers of this tradition.[3] Because each season of *Star Academy* ran for several months,[4] such allusions to "traditional" aspects of French culture could be made repeatedly.

The show's careful selection of candidates from various areas of France, despite the fact that media production in France is typically highly concentrated in the capital and rarely otherwise includes "the province" (the totality of France's other regions), extended the reach of this French imagined community to the country's entire map. As the candidates' regional diversity was made obvious in their online biographies, through allusions on the show to their hometowns or regions, and through regionally accented speech, audiences were reminded of the richness of France's diverse local cultures. Claims of geographic specificity quickly receded, however, once the candidates entered the academy, against the show's assertions of commonalities across regional differences and of shared national culture.

While an emphasis on "traditional" aspects of French culture suggests a nostalgic lens, the show also acknowledged—and reconciled the audience with—more contemporary cultural developments. French rap and French rock were mixed in with the famous folk songs of singer-songwriters. New fads were alluded to and discussed. Younger singers and newer genres were recognized as symbols of France's continuing engagement in popular cultural production—as the new generation of significant contributors to France's cultural identity. The show itself became such a symbol, as the winners from previous seasons, several of whom have gone on to successful singing careers, were invited to come back as instructors or guests. Their CD releases were heavily advertised during the show's commercial breaks. This bridging between young candidates and older professors, celebrated icons and newest fads served to reassure viewers that a new cohort of cultural producers aware of the debt they owe earlier generations were being groomed to assure their masters' succession—that "French" culture is alive and well.

Perhaps more significantly, Star Ac' reconciled its audience with the changing nature of the French socio-cultural and ethnic landscape. Candidates and professors on the show were clearly selected to represent the diverse racial, ethnic, and cultural makeup of the French population. In other words, the dynamics of race and ethnicity were a significant subtext of the show's construction of "French identity." Each season's cast of characters included several "minority" aspiring artists, most frequently black and/or North African, whose favored musical style was typically hip-hop, jazz, or R&B.[5] The show's host, Nikos Aliagas, was of Greek origin; Kamel Ouali, the show's artistic director, of Algerian descent. This mixing of races and ethnicities is typical of reality programs intent on creating drama by bringing together individuals of very different backgrounds.

The way Star Academy dealt with race, however, differed significantly from the strategies used to address the issue in similar U.S. texts. Scholars have demonstrated that instances of racial tension in the U.S. versions of Big Brother or The Real World become occasions to suggest that friendship and discussion can alleviate racism. This serves to conceal racism's structural nature by suggesting that "as long as some 'bad whites' can be fixed and brought to task, everything will be all right" (Shome, 2000, p. 369). In contrast, race was simply not addressed in Star Academy's narrative beyond the obvious visual clues provided by the candidates' physical selves. If, in the United States, The Real

World "constructs a reality that frees the audience of any implications in racism by blaming rural conservatives for the problem" (Kraszewski, 2004, p. 182) *Star Academy* constructed a reality in which racism simply did not exist.

This narrative intersects with France's official position of "color blindness" where "any recognition of ethnic particularity is presumed to dilute the force of the transcendental principle of 'equality before the law'" (Stam and Shohat, 2012, p. 145). Indeed, article 1 of the current French constitution essentially eliminates discussions of racial discrimination from official discourse (Sabbagh, 2003).[6] In keeping with this position, the show's narrative simply defined all candidates as (non-hyphenated) "French." One had to search beyond the confines of the show's official texts, including the official website that provided the 22-hour feed to the academy's daily life, to find more detailed elaborations on the candidates' racial or ethnic identities. So, for instance, while Yvane—a rapper known as Irie Kane in the French underground hip-hop scene who participated in the show's eighth season—moved to metropolitan France from his native Martinique[7] in 1998, his online profile on the show's website only stated that he was from Bourg-la-Reine in the department of Hauts-de-Seine. The website also failed to identify his work as a rapper.

Similarly, it is difficult to assess whether racial tensions emerged among candidates in their daily life at the academy. If they did, the show typically failed (or refused) to capitalize on them as dramatic elements of its narrative structure. Instead, everyone on the show, regardless of ethnic, cultural, or racial identity, was portrayed as equally sharing and enjoying the "French" cultural heritage described above, even if candidates were generally allowed to bring their own creative twist to these common cultural markers. Individuals whose "non-French" cultural origin was known due to their involvement in the broader French popular cultural scene, including Aliagas and Ouali, were portrayed as safely "integrated."

This reality TV–style reality stands in sharp contrast to the intense racial tensions that permeate the French socio-cultural landscape, as evidenced by the brutal riots that spread through the suburbs of France's major cities in the fall of 2005 following the death of two youths of African descent fleeing the police (to be further discussed in chapter 2). As we will see in chapter 4, it also stands in sharp contrast to the works of French rappers who, while asserting their French identity, also work to question, deconstruct, and possibly redefine what such an identity might mean in an increasingly hybridized cultural context marked by the legacy of postcolonial immigration.

Star Academy's construction of a space in which urban and rural youths of varied ethnicities and races can not only adequately function as a group, but can do so while embracing the values of tradition, hard work, and transgenerational respect, served, however, to safely reconcile white audiences with the increased diversity of French society. It also served to reassure members of ethnic and/or racial minority groups that they, too, could become celebrated contributors to the French popular cultural scene—if they were willing enough to comply with the rules of French cultural integration.

Beyond Localization: The Local/National/Global as Mutually Constitutive Elements

The above discussion illustrates how a global format can be localized to resonate with local audiences and even reconcile viewers with contested aspects of the socio-cultural landscape into which it is adapted. Focusing solely on this process of "localization of the global," as most studies of transnational media tend to do, only provides, however, a limited outlook on the negotiation of the local/global nexus in globalized cultural texts such as the one examined here. Identifying the defining lines along which a global format was turned into a "French" text (as I endeavored to do in the section above) is a necessary first step in recognizing the political nature of processes of localization. The next step, if we are to better understand the mutually constitutive nature of the local/national/global nexus, requires us to further locate this process within the larger context of the awareness of the global that characterizes our contemporary condition.

First of all, one must understand that the process of "localization" described above was actually one of "nationalization." While the show's narrative nodded at regional differences, these were brought together under the broader umbrella of a hegemonically defined national French identity constructed through the celebration of a "shared" cultural heritage—French songs, cultural icons, Catholicism, and so forth. Like any hegemonic definition, it had to be negotiated to integrate potentially contentious elements into its naturalization of the status quo. Thus, the French version of *Star Academy* sketched an idealized version of France as a nation in touch with its traditions yet open to new forms of cultural production (even ones arising as expressions of racial or ethnic difference), as long as these were safely integrated within an acceptable vision of French national unity. The "fiction réelle" [real fiction] (Jost, 2002/2007, p. 9) constructed in the show was one where France's policies of color blindness actually worked.

Perhaps more significantly, at least in terms of this chapter's main argument, this idealized vision of French *national* identity was constructed in relationship to the show's active engagement with an imagined *global* community. Despite its emphasis on various elements of "French" culture, a sharp awareness of this broader global framework permeated the entire discourse of the show. These transnational links were made particularly evident on the Friday night "primes," ostensibly marketed as transcending national borders. As one French television magazine put it, "On the nights of the prime, Star Academy welcomes stars from around the world and becomes one of Europe's largest variety shows" (Roque, December 15, 2007, p. 19). As MC Nikos Aliagas started the prime with greetings to the show's "international audience" or to "those who watch us from abroad," as he welcomed international stars onto the set as if he had always known them, and easily conversed with them (in five different languages) against a visual background of hybrid (trans)cultural references—gangsters in U.S. streets, samurai in full gear, Latin dancers—the show's narrative actively engaged the global. Just as the candidates (re)presented themselves to the viewers who would ultimately have a chance to "vote them off the island" (or, in this case, the academy), *Star Academy* (re)presented French national/cultural identity to an imagined global audience.

This reality TV version of "French" identity served to position France not only as a country reconciled with potentially contentious elements of its sociocultural context but also as a significant and benevolent global player. The emphasis on the global nature of the primes in the larger cultural discourse surrounding *Star Academy*, as illustrated in the quote above, positioned the show itself as a prized transnational cultural product. The often-mentioned fact that the show was able to attract celebrated international stars highlighted France's global cultural influence. If the likes of Madonna, Mariah Carey, Sting, and Ray Charles took time out of their busy schedules to perform in *Star Ac'*, France must have been on these artists' cultural radar. *Star Academy*'s idealized version of smoothly integrated French identity was portrayed as the subject of justified global admiration. For example, when Colombian rock star Juanes expressed his love for French culture and *Star Academy* in a short conversation in Spanish with Aliagas after performing with candidates, the host proceeded to translate as: "he says he loves France, can you blame him?" This exchange managed to simultaneously flaunt the "global" admiration for French culture ("he loves France") and secure Greek-born Aliagas' status as safely integrated ("can you blame him?").

Similarly, the show's narrative managed to *simultaneously* position its young candidates as French and global citizens equally at ease with iconic elements of French culture and with a vast array of globalized hybrid cultural forms. They could rap with 50 Cent and Passi,[8] rock with (Colombian) Juanes, (Australian) Kylie Minogue, and (French) Johnny Hallyday, sing duets with (Canadian) Celine Dion, (American) Beyoncé, (Barbadian) Rihanna, and (French) Michel Sardou. They wrote and performed their own songs in multiple languages and multiple genres and casually chatted with international stars. They emerged as perfect examples of 21st-century cosmopolitanism at its best. In fact, they were simultaneously *producing* "French" culture—as noted, *Star Ac'* candidates frequently go on to have successful singing careers[9]—and *positioning it as global*. In a culture insecure about its position in the world where every hint of continuing transnational influence is noted and celebrated,[10] *Star Academy* (re)assured its audience that France is not only alive and well, but also globally influential. Ultimately, it served to reconcile viewers with various contested arenas of France's contemporary socio-cultural environment and with globalization—all at the same time.

Jost (2007) argues that reality television claims to abolish the distinction between the "régions antérieures"—the "front stage" where social representation takes place—and the "régions postérieures"—the "back stage" where social actors would normally be protected from judgment. When inviting viewers into the back stage of popular music production in its daily broadcasts, *Star Ac'* also invited them into the back stage of "French" culture. Just as it constructed life at the academy as an "authentic" depiction of what goes on in show business and offered the candidates' everyday behavior as a reflection of their "authentic" selves—as opposed to the primes during which they were ostensibly asked to *perform*—*Star Academy* constructed the daily broadcasts as "authentic" representations of French culture. Viewers familiar with the "indigenous" practices and cultural heritage it celebrated were invited to enjoy them as insiders. The "front stage" of the weekly primes transposed these representations onto the global stage where "French culture" was performed through the candidates' interactions with the global and was ultimately offered for global consumption.

The show's distinction between the two—just as reality TV's claim to take viewers behind the curtain of celebrity construction—was, however, illusory. *Star Academy*'s idealized version of local/national "French" identity was not developed in opposition to the global. It was engaged in a symbiotic relationship with it. The front stage/global and the back stage/local are two sides of the same coin—one cannot exist without the other.

What Hybridity? Deconstructing the "Real"

The specific dynamics of this symbiotic relationship are worth briefly exploring before closing this chapter. In addition to illustrating the ways in which the local, national, and global are mutually constituted in contemporary cultural forms, the case of *Star Academy* in France points to the strategic nature of these constructions. As noted, *Star Academy*'s handling of race relations served to support an idealized vision of France as a color-blind nation where all citizens are treated as equally "French." This version of "reality," which powerfully contrasts with the racial tensions that permeate the French social-cultural landscape, served to suggest (to both local/national and global audiences) that France was living up to its promise of racial integration. The nature of the candidates' racial and ethnic identities was, however, frequently actively discussed in the larger cultural discourse surrounding the show. The Lebanese origin of one of the candidates generated intense online debate in the show's seventh season. Viewers sometimes supported a particular candidate because of her/his racial/ethnic makeup, or geographic origin. These discussions were neither denied nor confirmed (nor even acknowledged) by the show's producers or the candidates, but they illustrate the constructed and contested nature of *Star Academy*'s representations.

Similarly, because the show featured an equal number of male and female participants, it necessarily dabbled in gender constructions. In fact, *Star Academy*'s portrayal of male and female performers drew heavily on common gender (and racial) stereotypes. For instance, while the show's official website described Alice, one of the finalists of the eighth season, as "a pretty and graceful princess," Mickels, her male adversary who beat her in the last prime, was deemed "a good friend who knows how to help everyone get along" and who "easily adapts to communal life despite his assertive style." Yvane (aka Irie Kane), who is of mixed racial makeup, was characterized as "virile and with a real physical presence." However, just as there wasn't much talk about race in *Star Ac*, there wasn't much talk about what it means to be male or female—despite the fact that the show clearly provided some possible clues. This interestingly contrasts with the storm of controversies generated by the pan-Arab version of *Star Academy* (a dedicated *fatwa* was issued against it in Saudi Arabia) surrounding its representations of gender—which scholars argue served as a catalyst for public discussions of national identity, cultural authenticity, and the meaning of modernity (Kraidy, 2009a). The comparative lack of controversy in the French version of the show served, in contrast, to position France as a nation comfortably installed in the "posts"—postracial, postfeminist, postdiscrimination, postmodern.

Securing this position meant that *Star Academy* had to engage with the global rather selectively. For example, the show tended to position France as the leader of a (imagined) global francophone community defined almost exclusively in relationship to Quebec. This exclusion of much of the actual worldwide French-speaking population served to conveniently evade France's colonial past, the legacy of which is highlighted in the continuing influence of the French language in much of North and West Africa and parts of the Middle East. It also (over)emphasized France's influence in the francophone community by putting the focus on a relationship defined by a clear power differential, especially when considered in the context of the music industry where Quebecois artists are faced with the challenge of operating in a much smaller national market than their French counterparts.

This partial construction of the global francophone community is particularly interesting in light of the fact that the *Star Academy* format has been adapted with extreme success in the Arab world and Africa, often as a direct consequence of the success of the "original" French version (Kraidy and Murphy, 2008). One might think that producers could find an economic advantage in more assertively linking the French show to these varied global incarnations, especially since a large segment of France's viewing audience has strong cultural ties to the areas of the world they represent. The performances of Tunisian Nader Quirat and Saudi Arabian Abdul Aziz Abduhamid, respective winners of the fifth and sixth seasons of *Star Academy* in the Arab world, or that of Moroccan Hajar Hadnan who triumphed in *Star Academy* Maghreb in 2007, remained, however, outside the frame of the French version's imagined reality. Not all hybridity, in other words, was treated equally on the show.

This process of strategic negotiating of the local/national/global nexus is not unique to the French context. Kraidy's study of *Star Academy*'s pan-Arab version as a text that "confounds the boundaries between the 'domestic' and the 'foreign,' between what is 'Arab' or 'Islamic' and what is alien" (2009a, p. 111) points to equally contentious dynamics. A similar process is also at work in much Japanese popular culture (Ivy, 1995), particularly in television with its heavy emphasis on allegedly unscripted "live"[11] shows. When the five members of the popular all-male band SMAP perform (in different languages) on the stage of their variety show's studio with the most popular international star of the moment (as they have been doing every Monday night since 1996), when they sit down afterward for a short casual chat with their guest (through the intermediary of an interpreter), their performance is certainly reminiscent of that of *Star Academy*'s candidates on prime night.

Scholars have noted that the genre of reality television complicates the notion of reality by actively engaging viewers in its negotiation. Rather than simply pretending to straightforwardly "represent" reality, reality TV proposes to take viewers behind the curtain of its construction to create a "more 'knowing' relationship" with its audience (Kilborn, 2003, p. 60; see also Ouellette and Murray, 2004). They point to the audience's ability to deconstruct what is presented by producers as "real" through the recognition of processes of mise-en-scène, editing, and other forms of manipulation. They note that the search for "authentic" or emotional moments that escape producers' control—as when candidates fail to perform in accordance with the mediated selves they (and/or the producers) have carefully crafted—is an important and pleasurable subtext of the genre. Thus, it is important to keep in mind that viewers might actively engage with reality television and deconstruct its representations.

Scholars also argue, however, that reality TV's questioning and commodification of the real contribute to a decline in symbolic efficiency—in our ability to relate to things we cannot see with our own eyes—and to a trivialization of the banal, which "surfs on the idea that anything is possible, that the choices of some are as valid as those of others" (Jost, 2007, p. 100). The case of *Star Academy* in France demonstrates that there is danger in such relativism. Not all forms of hybridity are positioned as equally valid in globalized cultural forms. In fact, the show's active engagement with the global resulted in very specific, and political, characterizations of local, national, *and* global identities. In this particular case of the "local" adaptation of a "global" format, "local" differences—geography, race, gender—were actually quickly assimilated into an idealized version of a putative *national* identity constructed against the backdrop of a selectively envisioned "global" order. In this sense, the adaptation of *Star Academy* to the French market might be better described as a process of nationalization and assimilation—in line with French policies of racial integration—than one of localization. Whether or not viewers "bought" these constructions is beyond the scope of this chapter (the online discussions briefly mentioned above surrounding issues of race and ethnicity suggest that not all were sold on the show's characterizations).

At the very least, however, the case of *Star Academy* illustrates the dangers of conceptualizing globalized cultural forms solely in terms of how they intersect with reified "local" contexts. It encourages us to consider, instead, how local, national, and global dynamics are articulated in relationship to each other—as mutually constitutive elements—under specific conditions. This case study points, in particular, to the need to more assertively consider how the negotiation of the global/national/local nexus intersects with the construction of race, ethnicity, and trans-cultural relations in a contemporary era characterized by increased virtual interactions and permeated with a heightened awareness of processes of globalization—how these dynamics shape, in other words, the imagination of the global.

The next chapter further addresses this question. Employing a more broadly translocal lens as its analytical tool, it focuses on the news coverage of events that generated intense debate about race, ethnicity, and cultural/ national identity in each of the sites that constitute the focus of this book. It further explores how the three sites negotiated these particular dynamics in relationship to each other and to a broader imagined global community.

// TWO //

Holier-than-Thou: Representing the "Other" and Vindicating Ourselves in International News

All nations are, in the end, transnations, indelibly marked by the presence of the other nations for and against which they have diacritically defined themselves.
—Stam and Shohat, 2012, p. xiv

Unlike reality television, whose engagement with both the global and "the real" is often a point of contention, news ostensibly engages in an effort to "accurately represent" the global. It proposes to "bring the world" to its audiences—think of the "world" section of the *New York Times*, or the BBC's "world service." Thus, global news openly and necessarily engages in transnational comparisons. Chapter 1 began to explore the multidimensional ways in which the global/national/local are mutually constituted in contemporary globalized cultural forms, and pointed to the need to further address "the intersecting power lines" (Condry, 2006, p. 2) of this symbiotic relationship. This chapter continues this exploration through an examination of how the French, Japanese, and U.S. press negotiated the global/national/local nexus *in relationship to each other* in their coverage of dramatic global news events. It focuses on three events that generated heated debates about racial and/or cultural dynamics on each of these sites: Hurricane Katrina, the civil unrest that shook France in the fall of 2005, and the March 2011 Japanese earthquake and tsunami.

Considering how the press covered all three events in all three sites, this chapter reflects on how their engagement with "the global" intersected with these dynamics. Keeping in mind that "all national comparisons take place on transnational territory" (Stam and Shohat, 2009, p. 497), the chapter develops a broader reflection on how international news may contribute to a process through which "nation-states define themselves with and against other nations in a diacritical process of identity formation" (Stam and Shohat, 2009, p. 475).

Most of the coverage discussed here was drawn from major French, Japanese, and U.S. national newspapers—in particular, the *New York Times*, *Le Monde*, and *Yomiuri Shimbun*, even though others were also consulted and will occasionally be cited. These newspapers were chosen in part because of their similarities despite their different cultural origins: they are national "newspapers of record" of wide circulation with similar target audiences, and all adhere to ideals of objectivity, balance, and fairness. While, certainly, in an age of instant online communication these are not the only sources of information available to media consumers—and while the relative ability of these historically influential news organizations to influence an event's "prime definition" (Van Ginneken, 1998, p. 113) may be declining—they nevertheless enjoy significant name recognition. They also have the resources to send their own reporters to the scene of international events, and their websites tend to serve as aggregates of citizen footage and, occasionally, news from other organizations. Conversely, their pieces are frequently reprinted or reposted by other media outlets. Each consequently remains a significant and respected voice in the global cacophony that inevitably follows events of international magnitude.

Both opinion pieces and "hard" news stories were included in the analysis because I was interested in assessing the character of these newspapers' *overall discourse* about the events examined here. While the majority of articles mentioned were drawn from the international/national news sections of these publications—and were consequently presented to readers as "objective" works of journalism—more analytical pieces also contributed to the broader vision of the global/national constructed in their pages. The works of columnists, particularly high-profile individuals—for instance, Nicholas Kristof of the *New York Times* who frequently writes about global issues—cannot easily be removed from the larger framework in which they appear. They provide important additional context to the coverage of national and international events and influence the nature of the media's contribution to the global imaginary.

The next section provides contextual information on global news production and justification for the choice of this medium for a translocal/transnational analysis. The chapter then draws a series of parallels between the ways in which the three dramatic events were covered in the French, Japanese, and U.S. press. It illustrates how the three sites all engaged in a very similar process of employing transnational comparisons to downplay the implications of crises "at home," particularly as they related to racial tensions. It also demonstrates, however, that the French and U.S. discourse about the Japanese disaster further engaged in a process of "othering" Japan by consistently interpreting Japanese reactions to the event as illustrative of distinctive cultural/racial traits. A final section explores how the awareness of the global permeated the "local" coverage in all three sites.

News in a Global Context

Concerns over inequalities in global flows of news have historically generated much debate. In the 1970s, discussions within the United Nations Economic and Cultural Organization pointed to the disproportionate influence of the United States and European nations on transnational networks of news production and distribution. For a moment, these debates offered a glimpse at what a New World Information and Communication Order might look like if member nations were to agree to protect all nations' ability to develop their media organizations and cultural production. The United States and Britain's withdrawal from the organization in the mid-1980s after the release of the 1980 McBride Commission report, interpreted as an attack on freedom of the press and as a threat to these powerful nations' global business interests, put an end to the discussion. The era of extreme deregulation that followed eventually reached even those nations (including France) originally most opposed to treating news and other cultural products like any other commodities to be exchanged on the global market—and consequently more amenable to trade restrictions and/or government subsidies (McPhail, 2010). While Western European nations still tend to boast stronger public media than the United States, their media systems are undeniably commercial, and the relative influence of publically funded news organizations, whose continuing existence is often under question, is eroding.

As a consequence of these historical developments, U.S.-style commercial news is often taunted today as an admittedly imperfect yet worthy of emulation model of a relatively functional "free press." In a global context, news is typically not seen as a particularly problematic medium. Its claims of veracity are more easily accepted than those of, say, reality television. U.S. scholar William Hachten celebrates, for instance, the "growing acceptance of American news" (2005, p. 20) as a positive side effect of globalization. Similarly, while David Demers recognizes that global media "generally promote Western values," he does not see this as a problem, concluding that "the new global media order will be more liberating than disabling" (1999, pp. 166, 169). Organizations such as the Freedom Forum, which releases an annual survey of press freedom around the world, similarly tend to be more concerned with state control than with concentration of ownership or heightened commercialism, resulting in an overly positive assessment of "Western-style" commercial news.

Furthermore, even the most assertive efforts to critically consider the power dynamics of global news have tended to remain focused on issues of production, ownership, and distribution rather than on its significance as a *cultural* product. Early studies of transnational power struggles, whether supporting or critiquing the "cultural imperialism" thesis, have tended to focus on popular cultural texts as a more obvious site of U.S. ideological hegemony. Compared to Disney comics (Dorfman and Mattelart, 1971) or *Dallas* (Ang, 1985; Liebes and Katz, 1990), news has appeared relatively less problematic.

Finally, the crisis of identity brought about by the Internet and the development of blogging, "citizen journalism," and an increasingly fast-paced 24-hour news cycle has more recently led scholars to ponder whether journalism is still relevant. Faced with the decline of the most prestigious news organizations and with experts heralding the death of the newspaper, concerns over the survival of the press as an institution have taken precedence over transnational power struggles. Besides, the rise of Al Jazeera as a global player and the role of social media in the Arab world revolutions seem to suggest that a New World Communication and Information Order has indeed been achieved. How, specifically, this new order might function is, however, worthy of attention.

First of all, it is important to keep in mind that despite the often transnational ownership of news organizations, most news content is produced with a national or local audience in mind (Tunstall, 2008). Even the BBC *World Service* or the *International Herald Tribune*—which represent the exception rather than the norm in terms of the amount of resources they are able to allocate to international coverage—localize their content. National and local newspapers may be moving online, they may look less and less like the print publications we used to know, but they still exist—at least for the moment. On the other hand, the Internet's space-compressing abilities mean that even the most "hyperlocal" content has the potential to reach a broad international audience. The relationship between the global and the local in the production and distribution of news has acquired dimensions those involved in the NWICO debate could not have anticipated.

Celebratory accounts of the increased diversity of transnational news flows—whether originating from national institutions, multinational corporations, or local citizens—tend to downplay the negative impact of the spread of a commercial model of news production that financially benefits the most powerful global players. They also serve to distract from continuing questions of ideological biases at the national, regional, and global levels. Even the work of bloggers or citizen journalists is significantly influenced by the ideological context in which it is produced and distributed, if we are to accept Hall's definition of ideology as "those images, concepts and premises which provide the frameworks through which we represent, interpret, understand, and 'make sense' of some aspect of social existence" (Hall, 2011, p. 81).

Research suggests that such biases are likely to take on greater proportions when considered in a transnational context. Because international events are less likely to fit definitions of newsworthiness because of their geographical distance (de Beer and Merrill, 2008) and because they are more difficult and expensive to access, their reporting is particularly vulnerable to institutional and organizational pressures. Reporters struggling to make sense of a foreign environment in the limited time allotted to cover a story are also more likely to draw on familiar paradigms to interpret what they are witnessing. Studies of war coverage have shown, for instance, that reporting often loses all pretense of objectivity to separate the world into "us" vs. "them" camps regardless of the complex underlying nature of the conflict at hand (de Beer and Merrill, 2008).

Relatively recent events taking place in the three nations that constitute the focus of this book offered interesting opportunities to examine the process of ideological construction in news production. First, the coverage of Hurricane Katrina (which took a disproportionately heavy toll on African American victims in the southern United States in September 2005) and the racial unrest that shook France just a few weeks later following the deaths of two youths of African descent (electrocuted when they entered a voltage transformer while fleeing the police) provided a unique perspective on the internal negotiation of racial dynamics in relationship to the global. Aside from taking place within months of each other, these two events engendered similar debates over the structural inequalities of race and poverty on the socio-cultural landscape of the two nations in which they took place as well as in the heavy international coverage they received. More recently, the earthquake and tsunami that struck Japan's Northwestern region in March 2011, and the major nuclear disaster that followed, propelled Japan to the forefront of the international news scene, generating discussions over the nature of Japanese national and cultural identity both locally and globally. Considering how these events were covered in all three cultural contexts in relationship to each other gives us a chance to further explore the symbiotic relationship between the global, national, and local discussed in chapter 1 and how it intersects with the negotiation of racial and cultural dynamics.

General Patterns of Global News Coverage

It is clear that the protests that rocked France in the fall of 2005 were not as much of a "disaster" (except, perhaps for the political figures who had to deal with the situation) as a category 3 hurricane, or one of the most powerful earthquakes ever recorded—followed by a tsunami and a major nuclear accident. A number of common themes, however, quickly evolved in the coverage of these events, pointing to the standardized nature of news production and globally accepted definitions of newsworthiness. Early coverage focused on grim descriptions of the situation and on the rising estimated number of deaths or injured in all newspapers, regardless of where they were published and what event they described. Business reporters soon moved on to reflect on the possible economic implications of the situation. Critiques of the respective governments and institutions involved in trying to deal with these different crises naturally followed. More positive stories focused on the heroic acts of firefighters, doctors, military personnel, and private citizens in the face of adversity provided relief from the otherwise somber narrative and helped balance the newspapers' editorial mix.

Even the coverage of the unrest in the French banlieue (disadvantaged suburbs) was often eerily similar to descriptions of New Orleans in Katrina's aftermath. For instance, while *Le Monde* described New Orleans as a city "under siege" where "faced with looters, the national guards have received the order to shoot and kill" (Chaos en Louisiane, September 3, 2005), the *New York Times* noted that "a police station was ransacked, a garage was set on fire and a shopping center and two schools were vandalized" and that "Riot police have used tear gas and rubber bullets to repel the attacks" (Smith, November 5, 2005) after clashes near Paris.

Differences also quickly emerged, however, in the discourses the French, Japanese, and U.S. press constructed in reaction to these different events. On the most general level, and despite the heart-wrenching tales of devastation, death, and violence, the coverage of these tragedies tended to be proportionally more positive when the event took place "at home" than abroad. Thus, while tales of heroism were present in all the newspapers, they appeared most frequently in the *New York Times*' coverage of Katrina and in *Yomiuri*'s coverage of the earthquake, tsunami, and nuclear accident. Within this theme, the nature of the coverage was also different.

For example, an account in *Le Monde* of the struggle at New Orleans' Charity Hospital positively portrayed doctors keeping patients alive without electricity or water, but its portrayal of the police and military forces that ultimately came to their rescue was much less flattering. The article spoke of police boats and helicopters patrolling near the hospital who did not "seem to have any interest" in those inside: "I was wondering what they had to do that was more urgent than coming to get us. I would like to know who determined the emergency workers' priorities," said one of the doctors interviewed (Eudes, September 18, 2005). The article further noted that when a National Guard helicopter did arrive three days later, the soldiers' first action was to threaten to shoot doctors whom they had mistaken for looters. The report closed with three paragraphs on how the state subsequently tried to shut down Charity, described as the only hospital in New Orleans to treat uninsured and poor patients. In contrast, the *New York Times* offered an upbeat account of the same situation, noting that "morale was good" and that there was "plenty of peanut butter and cornflakes to go around" (Abelson and Feuer, September 1, 2005, 16A). The National Guard's rescue efforts were depicted as proceeding smoothly. A later follow-up story described doctors' heroic cleanup efforts and struggles with state legislators to keep the facility open (Nossiter, December 17, 2005).

Along the same lines, *Le Monde* described the New Orleans police department as made up of "some heroes . . . some people overwhelmed by the situation and some deserters" in an article headlined "The New Orleans Police: Between Devotion and Falling Apart" (Leser, September 4, 2005). The report portrayed the NOPD in such a state of disarray that it led officers to quit, commit suicide, or engage in violence and crime: "Journalists who witnessed violence against looters were threatened, and some photographers' materials were taken and destroyed. According to unverifiable rumors, some members of the NOPD would have become looters themselves and fled in vehicles full of their plunder." In contrast, while acknowledging the suicides and high number of officers who "simply walked off the job," the *New York Times* provided a more upbeat personal account of a sergeant who, "unlike some other officers who have succumbed to the pressure . . . said he was not going anywhere except into the streets to do his job" (Treaster and DeSantis, September 6, 2005, p. 21A).

Overall, the French and Japanese press provided a much more somber description of the situation in New Orleans—"There were bodies floating in rivers or abandoned on city streets. Makeshift refugee centers overflowed with people, yet there was no food, water or personnel to help them. Looting broke out as desperate people struggled to stay alive. A major city in the richest country in the world descended into anarchy," wrote the *Japan Times* shortly after the disaster (Katrina's Grim Reminder, September 7, 2005)—than the American newspapers where gloomy accounts of death and destruction were mitigated by these more positive descriptions of heroic acts.

A similar pattern was found in the Japanese press following the earthquake and tsunami, where less than a month after the disaster, numerous articles already focused on life returning to normal—from evacuees returning home (Final Miyakejima Evacuees Return Home, April 2, 2011) to the reopening of a tsunami-hit soy sauce factory (Mizuno, April 3, 2011) or of a local mall (Aeon Store Reopens in Disaster-hit City, April 1, 2011). Tales of sorrow were also more frequently mitigated by upbeat accounts with such headlines as "Giving kids something to smile about" (Yako, April 9, 2011) or "Hospital emerges as center of hope" (Takakura and Hinatani, March 28, 2011), tales of miraculous rescues—"Survivors fete miraculous return to life" (Uesugi et al., March 30, 2011), "'My grandma is inside!' Teen escapes rubble after 9 days" (March 22, 2011), "Miracle rescue, 9 days later" (March 22, 2011)—and tearful reunions—"Mother smiles again after being reunited with son" (Inoshita, April 16, 2011). A series of stories even detailed the miraculous rescue of a dog (Dog Rescued from Debris, April 3, 2011) and the process of reuniting him with his owner (Rescued Dog Reunites with Owner, April 6, 2011). A short 16 days after the disaster, an article already assured readers that eventually "the kids (and parents) will be all right," concluding that "with extra effort and care, a stressed child can be dancing and singing again for no other reason than feeling like it" (Mark, March 27, 2011).

Furthermore, while all newspapers questioned the response of their national government and/or institutions to the dramatic events taking place locally, the intensity of these critiques did not match the negative judgment they reserved for foreign officials: "Officials at every level of government—from the mayor of New Orleans to the president of the U.S.—bickered and stumbled from one moment to the next. The natural disaster was compounded by human failure. Although the storm's path was plain, New Orleans officials did not order the evacuation early enough; nor did they provide sufficient attention to the fate of those too poor to leave. State officials did not deploy the National Guard in time," wrote the *Japan Times* in the wake of Katrina (Katrina's Grim Reminder, September 7, 2005; see also Leser, September 4, 2005).

A few years later, the *New York Times* and *Le Monde* would similarly discuss the failures of the Japanese government's handling of its own crisis, with such headlines as "A political response without a compass" (Pons, March 17, 2011), "The tsunami forces Japan to rethink its political response" (Souyri, March 15, 2011), "Experts had long criticized potential weakness in design of stricken reactor" (Zeller, March 16, 2011), or "In Tokyo, a dearth of candor" (Tabuchi, Belson, and Onishi, March 17, 2011). One French report claimed that "the authorities offered confusing reports and avoided providing any details" and added that "the government shares responsibility for this indecisive communication with Tokyo's electric company" (Mesmer, March 16, 2011). Or, as one *New York Times* article simply concluded: "While national news media and opposition politicians have been quick to criticize Prime Minister Naoto Kan's handling of [the crisis], at least some residents said they *had low expectations of the central government to begin with*" (Fackler and Inoue, March 19, 2011, emphasis mine). French and American newspapers also occasionally critiqued the Japanese media *coverage* of the disaster, particularly as it related to the nuclear accident at the Fukushima power plant (see, for example, Bouthier, March 21, 2011; Onishi, June 25, 2011), suggesting in the process that they were doing a better job at providing detailed and accurate information.

In other words, no matter where it originated, the press tended to do a better job at identifying other nations' failures than at recognizing such failures "at home." While, certainly, all newspapers were at times critical of their national institutions—including the Japanese press (notwithstanding the French and U.S. newspapers' assertions otherwise)—these critiques did not reach the intensity they reserved for their assessment of tragic situations abroad. Most importantly, their interpretation of the nature and meaning of these failures significantly differed, a point to which I now turn.

What a Disaster! International Coverage and National Failure

In a nutshell, if press coverage of national events tended to blame individuals and/or institutions—George W. Bush, Nicolas Sarkozy, Naoto Kan, FEMA, TEPCO—for inadequately handling the situation, international coverage of these crises interpreted them as *national* failures.

For instance, Japanese and French newspapers portrayed the extreme damage caused by Katrina as an embarrassing reminder of the United States' declining global influence, a shameful indication of the failure of its outdated social system made obvious to the rest of the world by the international attention the disaster garnered. Noting that several commentators deemed the situation a national shame (Lesnes, September 4, 2005; Salle, September 8, 2005), *Le Monde* described the United States as a humiliated (Lesnes, September 4, 2005), humbled, and vulnerable nation (Vernet, September 9, 2005) forced to face its internal "social fractures" and loss of global power (Lesnes, September 3, 2005). As one article concluded a mere four days after the hurricane hit: "Americans witness with consternation this new demonstration of the vulnerability of their superpower. They also rediscover the growing presence of inequalities and misery in the United States" (Chaos en Louisiane, September 3, 2005). A few days later, another story bore the headline: "After Katrina, America wonders about the failures of its model" (Salles, September 8, 2005). The *Yomiuri Shimbun* suggested that the United States was "humbled by nature" and that "the hurricane highlighted the weak points of the superpower" (A Year of Natural Violence, December 29, 2005).

The U.S. and (to a lesser extent) Japanese coverage of the riots in France and the U.S. and French coverage of the Japanese disaster followed a similar pattern. For instance, fighting in the Paris suburbs led the *New York Times* to conclude that, "the civil unrest shakes *the foundation of the French republican ideal*" (Sciolino, November 10, 2005, emphasis mine). Noting that "France has been grappling for years with growing unrest among its second- and third-generation immigrants" (Smith, November 5, 2005, p. 1A), highlighting "France's failure to integrate immigrants into the country's broader society" (Smith, November 3, 2005, p. 11A), commenting on the "feelings of betrayal" experienced by generations of immigrants (Sciolino, December 12, 2005, p. 1A) or on the "scandalously high unemployment rate" in France's "crime-ridden housing projects" resulting from its "failed integration model" (While Paris Burns, November 8, 2005, p. 26A), the U.S. newspaper presented the riots as indicative of the demise of a clearly flawed system.

Likewise, the French and U.S. press portrayed disaster-struck Japan as a nation punished for its arrogant refusal to seek international help and in the process of receiving a lesson in humility—"The early disarray alarmed the United States government enough that it increasingly urged the Japanese to take more decisive action, and to be more forthcoming in sharing information. Making matters worse was Mr. Kan's initial reluctance to accept the help of the United States, which offered pump trucks, unmanned drones and the advice of American nuclear crisis experts," wrote the *New York Times* (Onishi and Fackler, June 13, 2011; see also Caramel, March 20, 2011). As an official interviewed in a *New York Times* article titled "For Japanese, learning to receive" put it, "It is very good for Japanese people to realize that Japan is not alone on the Earth" (Haberman, March 15, 2011). As suggested above, the crisis at the Fukushima power plant also led the French and U.S. press to reflect on the overall failure of Japan's political system: "Under Japan's electoral system, in which a significant percentage of legislators is chosen indirectly, parties reward institutional backers with seats in Parliament," wrote the *New York Times* (Onishi and Belson, April 27, 2011; for examples in *Le Monde*, see Pons, March 17, 2011; Souyri, March 15, 2011). Again, the "culture of complicity" (Onishi and Belson, April 27, 2011, p. A1) the U.S. and French press saw as characteristic of the Japanese context was not simply interpreted as indicative of a failure of Japanese business culture, but as a *national* deficiency—or, as Onishi and Belson put it, the result of an overly uncritical *national psyche* (2011, p. A1, emphasis mine).

This bleak assessment of other nations' total system failures powerfully contrasted with the portrayal these newspapers reserved for their own nation's reaction to disasters abroad. Whether pointing to the support of their national government and/or military (see, for example, Fackler, April 14, 2011; Fackler and McDonald, March 13, 2011, March 15, 2011; Fackler and Tabuchi, August 24, 2011), or the benevolent help of various private individuals and institutions—U.S. athletes (Clarey, March 20, 2011; Shpigel and Sandomir, March 12, 2011), "Japantown" restaurateurs (Gordinier, March 30, 2011)—their efforts to "localize" the story resulted in a highly positive assessment of their nation's willingness to pitch in in times of international crises. As the *New York Times* wrote:

> In Napa, Calif., residents planned a fund-raiser for Iwanuma, Japan, after seeing photographs of the damage caused when the tsunami swept over it. In Galveston, Tex., a group stitched blankets for the residents of Niigata to protect them against radiation that could fall with the snow and rain there. In Tuscaloosa, Ala., residents gathered money for Narashino, a city in Tokyo Bay. . . . It was an effort repeated across the United States, as towns big and small responded to the destruction and lives lost in their Japanese sister cities. (Wollan, March 20, 2011, p. 23A)

A few years earlier, article after article had similarly detailed the multiple ways in which Japan and France helped the struggling United States in the wake of Katrina (see, for example, Coles, September 29, 2005; Government to Send Researchers to Louisiana, September 6, 2005; Japan Government, Firms Join Relief Effort, September 2, 2005; Japan Ready to Double Hurricane Aid, September 7, 2005; Locals [sic] Musicians Support "Big Easy," November 21, 2005). Stories providing long lists of corporations donating goods and services (see, for example, More Japanese Firms, September 5, 2005), or highlighting the efforts of volunteers ranging from the Japanese self-defense forces to French members of Médecins sans Frontières (Goué, March 20, 2011; Japan NGO Members to Visit Houston, September 12, 2005) emphasized the generosity of local government agencies, corporations, and institutions against the backdrop of other nations' failures.

Recipients of this generosity were, naturally, portrayed as grateful. Shortly after Katrina, a U.S. envoy quoted in the Japanese press described Japan's "tremendous outpouring of support," adding that "it is very touching for an American to receive that kind of support because it just epitomizes the friendship that Japan and the United States enjoy" (U.S. Envoy Schieffer Thanks Japan for Hurricane Aid, September 9, 2005). An op-ed piece in *Le Monde* written by a U.S. citizen living in France noted that "Americans, once again, found the French on their side" and added that "Americans thank their French friends for their expressions of compassion and their help" (Stapleton, September 11, 2005). The *New York Times* would get its turn six years later to quote a Japanese official assuring the U.S. audience that "Everybody is very much touched by the sympathy and generosity of American people" (Haberman, March 15, 2011). Such coverage not only helped position other nations as struggling and humbled—as a French headline put it "After Katrina, the world holds out a helping hand to a humiliated America" (Lesnes, September 4, 2005)—but also served to position the giving nations as benevolent global citizens.

Holier than Thou: Racial Tensions at Home and Abroad

The presence of the kind of coverage described above is not particularly surprising considering the tendency across news organizations to attempt to localize international news stories and, perhaps, the natural human need to feel like one (or one's nation) is helping alleviate extreme misery in the face of disaster. The positioning of these powerful nations in relationship to each other through the reporting of tragic events also engendered, however, a more subtle and insidious discourse about race and culture both "at home" and "abroad." The issue of race arose most directly in the coverage of Katrina and of the riots in the French banlieues—which happened to take place within months of each other. The discourse surrounding the Japanese disaster ostensibly focused on cultural rather than racial issues. However, because definitions of Japanese cultural and racial identity are tightly intertwined both internally (Kondo, 1990) and globally—think of the "yellow peril"—questions of race remained close to the surface, particularly in international press coverage.

Race was undoubtedly a significant subtext of Katrina's global coverage. The French and Japanese press clearly characterized the hurricane's disproportionately heavy toll on the African American community as a *racial* issue— "The majority of the hurricane victims were poor African-Americans . . . The disaster areas became lawless and racial discrimination surfaced," wrote the *Yomiuri* (A Year of Natural Violence, December 29, 2005). They described how whites managed to leave while a vast majority of blacks remained behind (Eudes, September 4, 2005; Katrina's Grim Reminder, September 7, 2005; Leser, September 4, 2005). They suggested that the government's slow reaction had much to do with the color of victims' skin (Vernet, September 9, 2005). They included reports of race-related police brutality (Lesnes, January 18, 2006a), and spoke of accentuating racial tensions (Eudes, September 6, 2005; Lesnes, January 18, 2006b). As the *Yomiuri Shimbun* concluded in a report reflecting on the year's major events, "African-Americans suffered most as they lived in the hardest-hit areas. Some people say this highlighted the country's racial divisions and rich-poor gap" (Disasters Top This Year's News, December 30, 2005).

In contrast, only four *New York Times* articles in the sample of more than 500 read in detail for this analysis actually exhibited the kind of introspection America was, according to *Le Monde*, allegedly drawn into by the disaster (Salles, September 8, 2005). One column reflected on the "worsening poverty problem" caused by the Bush administration (Kristof, September 6, 2005, p. 27A). Another, in the sports section, used the advancement of two Americans to the U.S. open semi-finals to ponder the meaning of being American:

"Horrifying images since the storm have underscored the reality that there are multiple tiers of America and Americans. The images of death, desperation, hopelessness and poverty, flushed into full view, have made many of us wonder where this America was hiding" (Rhoden, September 10, 2005, p. 1D). An article titled "Across U.S., Outrage at Response" similarly reflected on the "deep collective national disbelief that the world's sole remaining superpower could not—or at least had not—responded faster" to the disaster and wondered about its impact on America's image abroad (Purdum, September 3, 2005, p. 21A).

These articles, however, fell short of directly addressing the issue of race as a contributing factor to the inequalities they recognized as a disturbing element of the American social fabric. While Kristof acknowledged that "an *African-American* baby in Washington has less of a chance of surviving its first year than a baby born in urban parts of the state of Kerala in India" (2005, p. 27A, emphasis mine), poverty's connection to race was not otherwise addressed in his column. Rhoden similarly failed to recognize that the "multiple tiers of America and Americans" (September 10, 2005, p. 1D) are, by and large, color-coded. Only one report, a collection of reactions from African American leaders, noted that "the disaster's impact underscores the intersection of race and class" (Gonzalez, September 2, 2005, p. 1A).

If race was the (often unspoken) subtext of stories about New Orleans neighborhoods, such articles tended to ostensibly address the issue of urban poverty rather than racial discrimination. Scholars have demonstrated that the issues of poverty and race are tightly interconnected in the U.S. news media, as black urban poor have come to dominate public images of poverty, unemployment, and welfare (Gilens, 1996). In this case, the focus on urban poverty allowed the *New York Times* to avoid directly confronting the issue of racism in U.S. society, despite the fact that its photographs of victims demonstrated that race certainly had something to do with how much individuals were impacted by the disaster. In addition, poverty could more easily be reduced to a personal rather than structural problem.

Indeed, a number of *New York Times* articles painted a rather negative picture of New Orleans prior to the hurricane as a crime-ridden (Dwyer and Drew, September 29, 2005; Herbert, September 8, 2005; Nossiter, November 10, 2005), corrupt (Dwyer and Drew, September 29, 2005), and chronically dysfunctional (Nossiter, November 4, 2005) city whose poor inhabitants lacked proper social skills and exhibited "extraordinary low expectations" (Herbert, September 8, 2005, p. A29). These articles implied that Katrina's poor victims were struggling not so much because of structural inequalities in education or wages, but because of personal and cultural deficiencies. As Brooks explained in an editorial,

In those cultural zones, many people dropped out of high school, so it seemed normal to drop out of high school. Many teenage girls had babies, so it seemed normal to become a teenaged mother. It was hard for men to get stable jobs, so it was not abnormal for them to commit crimes and hop from one relationship to another. (September 8, 2005, p. 29A)

Not surprisingly, Brooks' suggested solution was also a personal one: "culturally integrate . . . people who lack middle-class skills into neighborhoods who possess these skills and *who insist on certain standards of behavior*" (September 8, 2005, p. 29A, emphasis mine).

This discourse resonated with profiles of poor black victims, particularly those coming from the hard-hit Lower Ninth Ward. For example, a series of three stories published in the *New York Times* followed the trajectory of one family, the Jackson-Browns, from the New Orleans airport as they were being evacuated shortly after the storm, to the home of a couple in Pollock, Louisiana, who "embraced [them] as family" (Wilgoren, December 13, 2005, p. 1A), to a shack in a rundown section of Baton Rouge. After explaining that the Jackson-Browns' relationship with the "church going" Pollock couple had quickly soured after they asked to buy beer, and that the family was later tossed out of a shelter because Mr. Brown had yelled at a volunteer, the final article concludes: "This troubled, directionless odyssey is one of opportunities missed and squandered, of government money and charitable donations spent partly on a stack of DVD's and costume jewelry . . . of many days doing little more than waiting for someone to help" (p. 1A). A relatively more positive portrayal of another former Lower Ninth Ward resident nevertheless described how her mother abandoned her to her grandparents as a toddler and portrayed the family's attachment to a neighborhood "undermined by poverty and crime" as somewhat pathological (Sontag, November 5, 2005, p. 9A).

The frequent suggestion in the *New York Times* that a number of victims stubbornly attached to their community simply refused to leave despite orders to evacuate further reinforced this subtle rhetoric. As one article concluded, victims "refused to leave because they had survived earlier hurricanes, were worried about their property or pets, or were *simply obstinate*" (Dewan and Roberts, December 18, 2005, p. 1A, emphasis mine). Coupled with articles on white middle-class victims who had evacuated and on white middle-class neighborhoods allegedly ignored by the media—such as St. Bernard Parish whose citizens complained that they were "as hard hit as New Orleans . . . but got less attention" (Purnick, September 14, 2005, p. 21A)—this discourse ultimately implied that victimization was in part due to personal behavior. After all, as one headline put it, "The misery is spread equally" (Dao, August 31, 2005, p. 12A).

Thus, while the French and Japanese coverage of the hurricane presented its disproportionately heavy toll on African American populations as an indication of the (structural) failure of the American approach to race relations, the *New York Times* portrayed it as having much to do with the specific circumstances of the city of New Orleans and the personal life decisions of its inhabitants. In a pattern frequently observed by scholars (see, for example, van Dijk, 1991), the U.S. newspaper avoided directly addressing the larger structural dynamics of the racial tensions stirred by Katrina's destruction.

A similar pattern emerged in the coverage of France's racial tensions—except, this time, the roles were reversed. For example (and in stark contrast to its Katrina coverage), the *New York Times* dedicated its largest number of articles to racial issues in its strongly worded assessment of the French crisis. This led the U.S. newspaper to the same kind of conclusions about the failures of French society as those drawn about the United States by the French and Japanese press in the wake of Katrina. Noting that "France has been grappling for years with growing unrest among its second- and third-generation immigrants" (Smith, November 5, 2005, 1A), commenting on the "feelings of betrayal" experienced by generations of immigrants (Sciolino, December 12, 2005, p. 1A) and on the "scandalously high unemployment rate" in France's "crime-ridden housing projects" resulting from its "failed integration model" (While Paris Burns, November 8, 2005, p. 26A), the U.S. newspaper interpreted the riots as illustrating the fact that France had been wrong all along. As one article concluded:

> France clings to its cherished approach to immigration, which has been to declare that once in France, everyone is French and therefore equal, and that's that. The truth is that everyone is not French, nor equal, especially in an era of soaring immigration. (In Paris, Tough Talk Isn't Enough, November 4, 2005, p. 26A)

In a similar vein, the Japanese *Asahi Shimbun* concluded that the "shocking scenes of rioting in France showing shattered shop windows and cars on fire *leave us wondering if all this can be happening in an industrialized and democratic country*" (Shocking Scenes of Rioting, November 11, 2005, emphasis mine).

In an interesting rhetorical twist, this indictment of France's approach to immigration also served to shed a positive light on the United States' handling of racial tensions—much in need of positive reassessment in the wake of Katrina. Criticizing France's harsh denunciation of racism in the United States, the *New York Times* quickly moved to suggest that France's racial problem was even greater than that of the United States. As one article titled

"French lesson: Taunts about race can boomerang" defensively suggested: "The French news media were captivated by Hurricane Katrina, pointing out how the American government's faltering response brought into plain view the sad lot of black Americans. But this time the French, who have long criticized America's racism, could not overlook the parallels at home" (Tagliabue, September 21, 2005, p. 4A). The article goes on to describe France's failure to integrate black immigrants, adding that many "strike off for Britain, Canada and the United States, where they think they will find greater opportunities" (p. 4A, emphasis mine).

Descriptions of France's position on assimilation similarly suggested that American-style multiculturalism and affirmative action—rendered illegal by France's policy of color blindness discussed in chapter 1—were ultimately better, even if imperfect, solutions. A report comparing the British and French positions on immigration painted a positive picture of Britain's handling of racial crises, "that in some ways echoes America's response to its own urban racial disturbances," and which encourages Britons to "embrace ethnic diversity" (Cowell, November 20, 2005, p. 4D). As one article concluded, "In general, Europe, which has never developed an immigration culture, seems to have been less successful than the United States at integrating foreigners and giving them a stake in a new national identity" (Bernstein, November 8, 2005, p. 7A).[1]

In contrast (but in a move reminiscent of the U.S. coverage of Katrina), the French press focused on individual rather than structural issues in its coverage. The blame was placed on then minister of interior Nicolas Sarkozy for intensifying the violence with incendiary remarks and for creating tensions by supporting an increased police presence in poor neighborhoods (Bronner and Simon, November 2, 2005). The French government was criticized for failing to *fully implement* its integration policies. An article reflecting on Jacques Chirac's proclamation that "children of difficult neighborhoods" are "all daughters and sons of the republic" commented: "the problem is that the words and the actions of the government largely refute this beautiful proclamation" (Bernard, November 19, 2005).

Again, when addressing the problems of unemployment and poverty, *Le Monde*'s writers offered political reforms or personal solutions—such as Sarkozy's resignation (Blum, November 11, 2005), new urban and employment programs (Bronner and Kessous, March 23, 2006; Delberghe, November 6, 2005), and voter registration drives (Kessous, November 20, 2005)—but failed to consider an overall (re)assessment of France's approach to immigration and race relations. Even police brutality, widely discussed in both newspapers as a contributing factor to the violence, could, according to *Le*

Monde, be remedied with better training: "police officers [are] too young, without professional experience, and ill-equipped to deal with the problems faced by youths," stated one report arguing for reforms (Chaillou, January 17, 2006).

Furthermore, in a rhetorical turn similar to that taken just a few months earlier by the *New York Times* in its Katrina coverage, the French press addressed racial discrimination through descriptive and personal profiles rather than in broader analytical pieces considering its social and historical roots. While overall sympathetic to the protesters—as when portraying the pain of the two families who lost loved ones (Smolar, November 11, 2005) or deeming the disenfranchised youths' anger at the police and government largely justified (Bordenave and Kessous, November 8, 2005; Ceaux, November 4, 2005; Davet and Lhomme, November 11, 2005)—it nevertheless brought the issue of race back to a more personal level.

For example, while a profile featuring the family of a young man beaten by the police after he threw rocks at firefighters described the difficulties of integration encountered by his parents—"the condition of Algerian was not always easy to bear," the report notes (Chemin, November 16, 2005)—it also tells the more successful story of the young man's sister who "passed her baccalaureate at the Lycée Jacques-Brel in La Courneuve before registering at Paris-VIII University in Saint-Denis, where she is pursuing a bachelor's in communication," suggesting that integration, if difficult, is not impossible. Another report that focused on a group of youths condemning the violence quoted a Muslim leader as stating: "We have more rights here than in our country of origin" (Kessous, November 6, 2005), while other sources in the story blamed the unrest on children's failed education and parents' lack of care—"When a neighborhood is burning and you know that your kid who is 11, 12, even 15 isn't at home, what the heck is he doing outside?" Thus, in contrast to the U.S. and Japanese press's interpretation of the crisis as indicative of the failure of the French Republic's ability to adhere to its much-touted egalitarian (and, allegedly, color-blind) model, the French newspaper suggested that the ideals of *liberté*, *égalité*, and *fraternité* could be saved with a few political reforms and a healthy dose of personal determination.

Reflections on the Japanese National Psyche—or, How Those Japanese Are Not Like "Us"

Because of Japan's alleged racial homogeneity—which, as we will see later in this book, is actually a point of contention—the discourse surrounding Japan's natural disaster and the ensuing nuclear crisis focused less ostensibly on issues of race. The international coverage of the event quickly morphed, however, into a discussion of various aspects of Japanese *cultural/national* identity that eventually followed a pattern similar to that found in the coverage of the French and U.S. contexts. If reports of workers risking their lives to save the Fukushima plant were reminiscent of the coverage of Katrina's "heroes" a few years earlier, they differed in that the French and U.S. press characterized the behavior of these "heroes" as a prototypical Japanese cultural trait—notwithstanding much evidence suggesting that individuals in a different cultural environment would probably have done the same thing. In an article describing 50 workers who chose to stay at the Fukushima facility the *New York Times* noted, for instance, that "jobs in Japan confer identity, command loyalty and inspire a particularly fervent kind of dedication." Even after quoting a former senior operator at three U.S. power plants as saying that "he had no doubt that in an identical accident in the United States, 50 volunteers could be found to stay behind after everyone else evacuated from an extremely hazardous environment," the newspaper concluded: "But Japanese are raised to believe that individuals sacrifice for the good of the group" (Bradsher and Tabuchi, March 16, 2011, p. A1). One *Paris Match* front-page report even compared the plant operators to World War II kamikaze, quoting one of them as saying that he chose to stay behind for the good of his country (Byrka, April 8, 2011).

Scenes of life in shelters and individual profiles of victims were similarly replete with references to Japanese national and cultural identity. Titles such as "The Striking Self-Control of the Japanese" (Pons, March 15, 2011), "The Poignant Heroism of the Japanese" (Lachaud, March 17, 2011), or "The Japanese Could Teach Us a Thing or Two" (Kristof, March 20, 2011) suggested that there was something quintessentially Japanese about victims' responses to the disaster. Articles spoke of "the stoicism and self-sacrifice; the quiet bravery in the face of tragedy *that seems almost woven into the national character*" (Wines, March 26, 2011, p. A1, emphasis mine), of a "national obsession with self-restraint" (Belson and Onishi, March 28, 2011, p. A13), of a "national honor code" (Kristof, March 20, 2011), of "Japan's communal spirit," "tidy perfectionism," "proud cooperative spirit," and "strong sense of community" (Fackler, March 17, 2011, p. A12; March 24, 2011, p. A13). After characterizing pre-disaster Japan as "a country lulled by the reassuring rhythms of order and predictability" one *New York Times* report concluded that "the Japanese" were now "trying to uphold the ethic that they are taught from childhood: to do their best, persevere and suppress their own feelings for the sake of the group" (Belson, March 16, 2011, p. A1). As *Le Monde* put it: "The Japanese do not express pain or rebel against the inexorable. They suffer silently" (Pons, March 15, 2011).

While these reports were (initially) generally positive, at least when compared to the vitriolic assessments of the failures of the U.S. and French national systems described above, their sweeping generalizations about the nature of "the Japanese" deserve critical consideration. On the most obvious level, this focus on nebulous notions of an archetypal "Japanese spirit" is highly essentializing. It feeds common stereotypical visions of the Japanese population as homogeneous and of Japanese culture as both highly conformist and exotic—the New York Times just had to focus an entire front-page story on the fate of an 84-year-old geisha who escaped the tsunami (Onishi, April 5, 2011). Perhaps more disturbingly, this discourse powerfully resonates with common prejudiced characterizations of Asian racial identity as disciplined, conformist, traditionalist, submissive, and dreadfully non-assertive when compared to their "Western" counterparts—as when Kristof describes a Japanese game of musical chairs as "the most polite, most apologetic, and least competitive game of musical chairs in the history of the world" (March 20, 2011, p. 11) in an article titled "The Japanese could teach us a thing or two."

Indeed, behind the praise of the Japanese national spirit and the amazement at victims' ability to stoically endure lies the thinly veiled suggestion that the Japanese are fundamentally different from "us," the imagined (presumably majority white) "Western" audiences of these French and U.S. national newspapers. In other words, by emphasizing Japanese difference, the discourse of the French and U.S. press contributed to the normalizing of "Westernness" (as an imagined construct linking the two nations) and, by extension, whiteness (with which "Westernness" is typically associated) in a global context.

There certainly are cultural differences between Japan and France or the United States. There is also a grain of truth to the assertion that Japanese society is particularly well organized and community oriented—considering the population density of the country, it would be quasi-impossible to function otherwise. What was problematic, however, in the French and U.S. coverage of the disaster was the extent to which the trope of Japanese national identity/spirit became the only explanatory factor for all of the actions of tsunami victims—from their ability to organize themselves in order to survive (Fackler, March 24, 2011) to their desire to take a hot bath (Fackler, March 17, 2011; Wines, March 26, 2011).

In addition to feeding stereotypes about Japanese cultural/national/racial identity, this exclusive focus resonates with strategic acts of self-representation on the part of Japanese proponents of a nationalistic and conservative discourse about Japanese purity and uniqueness—the Nihonjinron (theories about the Japanese) discourse—which scholars have identified as highly problematic (Iwabuchi, 2002; McVeigh, 2004). As cultural anthropologist Dorinne Kondo reminds us, "Collective identities like 'the Japanese' or 'Japanese concepts of self' no longer seem . . . to be fixed essences, but rather strategic assertions which inevitably suppress differences, tensions, and contradictions within" (1990, p. 10). Incidentally, while Japanese writers sometimes contributed to such reports when those were published in the foreign press, sweeping generalizations about the nature of Japanese nation identity were virtually absent from the *Japanese* press, at least in the 1,200 or so articles examined for this analysis.[2]

Furthermore, as the coverage of the disaster shifted in focus from the tsunami and earthquake to the crisis at the Fukushima power plant, the tone of the French and U.S. press turned more negative. In the face of a nuclear breakdown requiring that extreme measures be taken to avoid a potentially global disaster, the alleged collectivism, self-restraint, and lack of combativeness of "the Japanese" quickly became a liability. In stark contrast to initial reports of a highly organized nation reacting to tragedy with civility and discipline, efforts to avert nuclear disaster were described as "frantic," "desperate measures" on the part of a nation "scrambling" to avoid a major meltdown "at any cost" (for examples, see Belson, Tabuchi, and Bradsher, March 19, 2011; Le Hir and Morin, March 19, 2011; Sanger and Wald, March 14, 2011; Sanger and Broad, March 18, 2011; Tabuchi and Wald, March 13, 2011, March 14, 2011). The lack of transparency on the part of the Japanese nuclear industry and possible breaches in safety measures were, once again, attributed to specifically Japanese socio-cultural traits and interpreted as national failures.

For instance, one *New York Times* article compared the Japanese nuclear industry to a Japanese village where "*Just as in any Japanese village*, the like-minded—nuclear industry officials, bureaucrats, politicians and scientists—have prospered by rewarding one another with construction projects, lucrative positions, and political, financial and regulatory support" (Onishi and Belson, April 27, 2011, emphasis mine). Another story suggested that the highly disciplined Japanese population was easily manipulated by its authorities, concluding, "As the Japanese continue to search for answers to the disaster at the Fukushima Daiichi plant, some are digging deep into the *national psyche* and examining a *national propensity* to embrace a belief now widely seen as irrational" (Onishi, June 25, 2011, p. A1, emphasis mine; for a similar example in *Le Monde* see Mesmer, March 19, 2011). Some reports more broadly addressed the negative consequences of the Japanese failure to challenge authority: "Japan's ethic of uncomplaining perseverance—gaman, in Japanese—may . . . explain why the country settles for third-rate leaders" wrote Kristof (March 20, 2011, p. WK11). Finally, in a rhetorical twist reminiscent of the U.S. newspaper's coverage of the riots in France, the *New York Times* columnist went on to link racial discrimination and racially motivated violence to *Japanese* cultural traits:

Japan's tight-knit social fabric can lead to discrimination against those who don't fit in. Bullying is a problem from elementary school to the corporate suite. Ethnic Koreans and an underclass known as burakumin are stigmatized. Indeed, after the terrible 1923 earthquake, Japanese rampaged against ethnic Koreans (who were accused of setting fires or even somehow causing the quake) and slaughtered an estimated 6,000 of them. So Japan's communitarianism has its downside. (Kristof, March 20, 2011, p. WK11)

From a hurricane in the United States, to riots in France, to an earthquake, tsunami, and nuclear disaster in Japan, the media coverage had come full circle.

The Whole World Is Watching: Transnational Comparisons and the Awareness of the Global

In their discussion of transnational comparisons Stam and Shohat (2009) note that nation-states tend to "project repressed historical memories onto the screens of other nations and to search for comparisons that flatter rather than those that shame or embarrass" (p. 476). This process was evident in the transnational coverage of the three events described here. While the coverage differed at times due to the specific circumstances under which each event took place, its most remarkable feature was the striking *similarities* that emerged in the rhetoric employed in all three sites when discussing events taking place "at home" vs. those taking place "abroad."

"Local" coverage followed patterns familiar to media scholars. In the coverage of hurricane Katrina and the riot in France, this included, for instance, the linkage of poverty to race (Gilens, 1996), the subtle "blaming of the victim" (Meyers, 2004), the tendency to link minorities to crime and violence (Sommers et al., 2006), and the failure to fully address and the "explaining away" (Van Dijk, 1991, p. 16) of the structural underlying causes of the problems at hand. "International" coverage, on the other hand, readily identified *other nations'* problems as indicative of a total system failure—of a failure at the *national* level.

The racial subtext of this discourse was particularly striking, supporting Stam and Shohat's suggestion that "cross-national race-related comparisons have been instrumental in extremely diverse ways, emphasizing contrasts, similarities, or complementarities" (2009, p. 487). Just as *Star Academy*'s active engagement with the global resulted in political characterizations of local, national, and global identities, transnational comparisons in press coverage of international events served to reconcile "local" audiences with the politics of race and to strategically position each nation in a broader imagined global order.

Indeed, the coverage of all of these events clearly took place against the backdrop of a global system of news production and distribution that reporters in each cultural environment were obviously aware of. In addition to sharing resources—as when the *New York Times* started streaming NHK coverage of the tsunami on its website—different news organizations commented on each other's coverage and frequently detailed, often with much concern, how the international press was representing their respective nations (see, for example, Bernstein, September 4, 2005; Leser, November 15, 2005; Purdum, September 3, 2005; Yamada, March 28, 2011).

While the translocal comparison provided here demonstrates how the three sites negotiated these dynamics in relationship to each other, it is worth noting that the discourse of the press also interestingly served to set these three powerful nations apart *as a group* from nations where, the coverage suggested, this kind of failure might be routinely expected. A *New York Times* article contrasted, for instance, the "trained population" of Japan to "the much less experienced Southeast Asians, many of whom died in the 2004 Indian Ocean tsunami because they lingered near the coast" (Glanz and Onishi, March 12, 2011, p. A1). Another report noted that "it is sobering that such calamities could so badly hurt Japan, a *technologically advanced nation* that puts great emphasis on disaster mitigation" (Japan's Multiple Calamities, March 15, 2011, p. A34, emphasis mine).

The coverage suggested that the scenes of dead bodies floating in New Orleans, of cars burning in the French banlieues, or of workers frantically attempting to avert a nuclear disaster were so shocking and humiliating because they were reminiscent of scenes one might encounter in "less developed" nations—as one source put it in a *New York Times* report, "It really makes us look very much like Bangladesh or Baghdad" (Purdum, September 3, 2005, p. A1). Whether describing New Orleans as a city "converted into a Third World city" (Lesnes, September 3, 2005), or images of the refugee camps of the Tohoku region as "not so different from those we can see in developing countries" (Caramel, March 20, 2011), the coverage of these events set up a clear dichotomy between powerful nations (where these kinds of things are not supposed to happen at all) and less powerful ones (where these kinds of thing are expected to happen routinely). If the comparison with less economically powerful nations served to illustrate that "the North . . . discovered Souths on its own territory" (Mattelart, 2005a, p. 104), it also served to suggest that such circumstances were unusual and the result of exceptional events—illustrative of a system failure, but of one that was potentially temporary, as opposed to that of a "third world" characterized as chronically defective.

It is the comparison with other "technologically advanced" nations, however, that ultimately made the vision of the global emerging from the pages of these highly respected news organizations particularly powerful in its ability to reconcile readers with the potential failures of their own local/national systems. If even other highly economically developed nations could be shown to have failed to adequately respond to their respective crises, readers could be reassured that—no matter how badly they might think their nation was doing in dealing with its own issues—it was still doing better than virtually *anyone else in the world.*

This translocal comparison of news coverage illustrates the sheer complexity and multidimensional nature of the representations of "the self" and "the Other" in a globalized media environment. It demonstrates that the process of localization of dramatic news events taking place "at home" served to move the media's lens away from the national level to cast these events as the result of individual rather than structural flaws. In stark contrast, disasters taking place "abroad" were most frequently interpreted through a national prism—as a result, in other words, not only of the failure of other environments' local institutions or political leaders, but of their failure *as a nation.* Transnational comparisons were a crucial component of both of these processes as the French, Japanese, and U.S. press negotiated the global/national/local nexus in relationship to each other. This case study also points (again) to the centrality of dynamics of race in the definition of national identities.

Finally, while the similarities between the three sites were striking in their swift identification of other nations' failure and corresponding tendency to ignore the structural dimensions of "local" crises, there were qualitative differences in the nature of the three sites' relationship to each other. France and the United States were particularly quick to identify each other's failures. Their respective newspapers of record spent much time and resources producing highly critical reports concentrating on the other nation's race problem and inability to properly handle it. This suggests that the comparison with another "Western" nation was a particularly powerful means to reconcile "local" audiences with the contentious dynamics of race "at home." It also suggests, as noted in this book's introduction, that we need to more carefully attend to the ways in which nations traditionally defined as "Western" negotiate their national identities in relationship to each other, and not just to "the Rest."

The French and U.S. press also engaged, however, in a process of "othering" Japan by consistently interpreting Japanese reactions to the 2011 earthquake and tsunami as illustrative of distinctive cultural/racial traits positioned in opposition to those of "the West." This essentializing discourse on Japanese national identity/psyche/spirit served, in turn, to subtly normalize whiteness in the global imaginary by emphasizing the fundamental "difference" of the Japanese (racial) "Other."

The possible "on the ground" consequences of this process of positioning are explored in the next chapter. Employing globalized fashion magazines as its empirical starting point and turning to Japan as a site of reception, it considers how Japan's status as a "non-Western/non-majority white" social context might shape its relationship to "the global." It also develops a more focused critique of gender and class dynamics, by examining how the Japanese negotiation of race interlocks with these dimensions in globalized cultural forms and their local negotiation.

THREE

Talking about *non-no*: (Re)fashioning Race and Gender in Global Magazines

Fashion, movies, music, we're influenced from everything in Japan. We might have our own opinion or own identity, but still, we are influenced one way or another by these things.
    —Chieko, 23

Things are fast now. Now the world has become small. . . . now with the mass media, everyone knows about the new styles immediately.
    —Takako, 48

Comparing to when I was young, there are many more opportunities now to be exposed to the media, to get information from the media. So the young tend to follow the ideas promoted in the media.
    —Horie-san,[1] 47

The last time we went to Harajuku to go shopping, most of the people around there were from the countryside. They all had magazines and maps and were looking for the shops. . . . I think that magazines have a strong effect on the young, like "I want this" when they're looking at magazines.
    —Oda-san, 52

[When I was young] there were magazines with white models but they were the magazines that were from foreign countries, like *Elle* or *Vogue* that were imported to Japan and I read those.
    —Takako, 48

The quotes above illustrate the extent to which global media have entered individuals' daily lives in an increasingly fast-paced world that "has become small." We have seen, however, that the hybrid cultural forms that emerge from our coincident engagement with the global, national, and local are frequently contentious and permeated with power struggles, particularly as they intersect with the dynamics of race both locally and globally. This chapter turns to Japan as a site of reception to investigate how the global dynamics of race and culture intersect with a local context frequently positioned as a cultural/racial "other" in relationship to Europe and the United States. It considers both how the global/national/local is discursively negotiated in Japanese textual representations and how this global imaginary might shape local subjectivities. Focusing on the highly gendered and consumer-oriented medium of fashion magazines, it also reflects on the gendered and class dimensions of this negotiation.

After a brief description of the history and continuing influence of fashion magazines in a global context, the chapter turns to a more specific exploration of the multiple ways in which culture, race, gender, and the global are articulated in Japanese texts. It then moves beyond textual constructions to explore how Japanese women negotiate these representations in their media consumption. The conclusions drawn in this chapter are based on insights gathered throughout my 18-year engagement with the small Shikoku community described earlier in this book, and particularly through ethnographic research specifically focused on women's engagement with mediated representations of beauty and fashion conducted over an 8-month period in 1998–99 and followed up with additional series of formal interviews and participant observation in 2009 and 2011.

Fashion Magazines as Global Texts

By 1915, the American *Vogue* already had a British edition. Its French edition followed ten years later and, aside from a brief interruption in production due to Nazi occupation (Peterson, 1964), has been published ever since. *Elle*, created in 1945 by French journalists and writers Hélène Gordon Lazareff and Macelle Auclair, now counts 42 international editions in more than 60 countries, including Slovenia, Turkey, India, and Thailand, and reaches some 23 million readers around the globe (Elle: About Us, n.d.). Its Japanese edition started in 1969 (Hafstrand, 1995). *Cosmopolitan*'s 58 international editions published in 34 languages are distributed today in more than 100 countries (Cosmopolitan, n.d.). It first appeared in France in 1973 and was exported to Japan in 1980.

Scholars have demonstrated the historical and cultural significance of such magazines in various cultural contexts, pointing, in particular, to their role in constructing and perpetuating cultural ideals of womanhood and in establishing a female cultural space readers are encouraged to engage in through consumption (see, for example, Kitch, 2000; Dollase, 2003, 2008; Sakamoto, 1999). Magazines' function as global texts has not, however, yet been as fully explored.

This is in part due to the fact that, as Australian media scholar Jinna Tay contends, "Fashion magazines are one of the most successfully 'glocalized' or adapted media in the world" (2009, p. 245)—a fact that to some extent serves to veil their global status. Indeed, in a manner reminiscent of reality television programs (but with a much longer history), globally successful fashion magazines heavily rely on formatted content and editorial formulae applied transnationally to different international editions in order to "conform to certain structural rules which allow their target readership to find them" even if their actual content "may be textually different around the globe" (Tay, 2009, p. 245). Like reality television, their content is, in turn, carefully localized. Hamid Mowlana points, for instance, to "a growing demand for editorial and financial control over imported publications" in such places as Japan or Mexico, adding that "Japanese publishers may not only press for greater financial control of the imported U.S. . . . magazines, but insist that only 50 percent of the content of such magazines be of original U.S. copy" (1986/1997, p. 56).

As a result, fashion magazines' cultural origins easily dissolve into the global scape of fashion, glamour, and beauty. As global media scholars David Machin and Theo Van Leeuwen note in their comparative study of international editions of *Cosmopolitan*, despite differences in language and style between localized versions, the magazine ultimately "clearly contributes to increased global cultural homogeneity" (2005, p. 588). As they conclude, "Although local versions adopt [the *Cosmo* style] in their own specific ways, overall it is a *global* style. The local languages may differ, but the identities and values conveyed by the style do not" (2005, p. 598, emphasis in original). While the status of fashion magazines as heavily "glocalized" texts has long been recognized, the practical implications of this global homogenization of style—the significance of fashion magazines as global texts—are more difficult to assess. The fact that the global style promoted in magazines is influenced by many magazines' European and North American origins is particularly significant, as a closer look at the Japanese context illustrates.

White Models and Hybridity in Japanese Fashion Magazines

Whenever I accompany students from the United States to Japan, their surprise at seeing Caucasian faces on billboards or the covers of magazines reminds me of my own reaction in early January 1995 when I first stepped out of the ferry in the small Shikoku village that was to later become my field site. At the time, the face of the white woman advertising facial cream on a small rusted metal sign hanging, probably since sometime in the 1950s, outside a long-gone general store, or that of Harrison Ford on the window of the local liquor distributor, seemed oddly out of place. Now that I have developed a greater familiarity with the many Japanese celebrities used in advertising and spent years studying different aspects of the Japanese media, foreign faces seem to naturally fit into the hybrid mix that constitutes Japanese popular culture. Their presence, however, is not devoid of implications.

Of course, the large number of non-Asian models and celebrities on the Japanese media market can be explained in part by the global nature of fashion magazines and of the advertising they carry, which constitutes a large portion of their content. Thus, advertising scholars Mariko Morimoto and Susan Chang's discovery, in their analysis of four magazines published in Japan, of a congruency "between the use of models from different cultural backgrounds and the origins of the publications and the advertisers" (2009, p. 184) is not particularly surprising. What is more interesting is their finding that while the Japanese editions of the French *Marie-Claire* (*Marie-Claire Japon*) and of the American *Harper's Bazaar* (*Harper's Bazaar Japan*) exhibited a higher percentage difference in their use of "Western" vs. "Asian" models (94 percent and 6 percent respectively) than the "domestic" Japanese fashion magazines included in their study, the latter still featured a much higher percentage of "Western" models than "Asian" ones (63 percent vs. 37 percent).

I had reached a similar conclusion when I first turned to the study of Japanese magazines in the late 1990s (Darling-Wolf, 2000a). At the time, I found that 41 percent of the models featured in advertising in the bi-monthly *non-no*—one of the oldest and most influential Japanese women's magazines, launched in 1971 by the prominent publisher Shueisha (Sakamoto, 1999)—and 33 percent of those found in editorial content were white. The numbers for the equally popular *an-an* were 31 percent and 33 percent respectively. This despite the fact that both magazines, as suggested in the quotes opening this chapter, are generally perceived as employing fewer non-Japanese models than their counterparts of foreign origin.

A more recent unpublished analysis of the French, U.S., and Japanese editions of *Elle* conducted in 2009 revealed an even more striking pattern. Only about 8 percent of the models featured in the Japanese edition appeared to be of Asian descent, while almost 89 percent were Caucasian. These percentages remained higher, however, than in the other two editions of the magazine, where only 3 percent and 1 percent of the models appearing respectively in the U.S. and French versions of the magazine were of Asian descent. In other words, the transnational culture of beauty, fashion, and upper-class consumption represented in the pages of global fashion magazines still remains white dominated. In addition, while *Elle Japan* tended to be more inclusive toward the rest of Asia than its U.S. and French counterparts—it included, for instance, a spread on fashion in Paris, London, New York, Milan, and Seoul—these different geographic environments were all visually integrated into one deterritorialized urban context lacking cultural specificity. Whether in Paris or Seoul, models were posed in similar urban scenes, consuming the same kinds of globally distributed products.

The equation of white "Westerners" with physical attractiveness and luxury is further accentuated by the fact that "Western models tend to be featured more frequently in ads for product categories associated with appearances, while Asian models tend to be featured more in ads for services or practical products" (Morimoto and Chang, 2009, p. 180). This points to a situation in which Japanese producers and consumers find themselves negotiating their position as racial and cultural minorities on the global fashion scene. As cultural anthropologist Dorinne Kondo suggests, "fashion provides us with an exemplary site for examining the constitutive contradictions of Japanese identity at a moment when Japan has assumed an acknowledged place as a global economic power" (1997, p. 55).

Even Japanese magazines employing relatively fewer non-Asian models engage in the construction of an imagined global landscape that intersects with racial and gendered representations. The hybrid deterritorialized consumer culture they promote draws from a wide array of cultural influences. In a comparative study of non-no and Men's non-no (its counterpart targeted at men launched in 1986) I found that Men's non-no's representations of masculinity drew from a seemingly limitless variety of (mostly "Western") cultural contexts (Darling-Wolf, 2006). Cowboys appeared in numerous fashion spreads and in ads (of both Japanese and U.S./European origin) for whiskey, jeans, cigarettes, and beauty products. (Presumably) "European" dandies were depicted as ideals of sophistication in Japanese advertising for French and Italian products—a recurring ad promoting the beauty salon "Dandy House" juxtaposed a clean-shaven Asian man in a tailored suit with photographs of a Caucasian model getting a facial. Androgynous (racially Asian) British punks posed against the Union Jack and posters of popular British bands. Hip-hop-inspired spreads shot in gritty urban environments featured gangster-like Asian models and popular Japanese DJs photographed from a low angle to make them look more intimidating.

Furthermore, as the same models took on multiple racial identifications—a black "gangsta" on one page might turn into a Latino lover on the next—racial and cultural identities were not only deterritorialized but also disembodied in the magazine's discourse. This process is facilitated by the fact that several of the models Men's non-no regularly employs (they are identified by name and familiar to frequent readers) are of mixed racial heritage. Posed alongside less familiar Caucasian or black models in "culturally neutral" urban environments they serve to further integrate Japanese and gaijin (the term used to refer to foreigners, literally meaning "outsider") into the same global environment of capitalist consumption. This strategic integration of racially hybrid "Japanese" models into a symbolically constructed global fashion scene ultimately reduces race, ethnicity, and culture to a series of playful identifications for Japanese consumers to enjoy (Darling-Wolf, 2006).

While such racial representations disturbingly fail to acknowledge the global implications of the politics of race/culture by reducing them to things one wears or consumes they also help to complicate racial identification. In particular, by positioning racially hybrid models as culturally Japanese, *Men's non-no* underscores the constructed nature of race in Japan. In a nation where discourses about racial purity have often historically intersected with constructions of national identity (Iwabuchi, 2006), this is a potentially destabilizing discourse.

When Gender and Race Intersect

Interestingly, and in sharp contrast to U.S. publications targeted at a male readership, *Men's non-no* also displays a rather playful and irreverent attitude toward constructions of gender. In keeping with representations of masculinity found throughout the Japanese popular cultural environment (Darling-Wolf, 2004) *Men's non-no's* models and the celebrities it features—Gackt, Takuya Kimura, Yôsuke Kubozuka, Jun Matsumoto—are frequently highly androgynous. The magazine further minimizes gender distinctions through a process of "masculinization" of its female models included in fashion spreads, who often appear dressed in androgynous attire and posed in similar poses as their male counterparts (for specific examples, see Darling-Wolf, 2006—or browse the magazine online at http://www.mensnonno.jp). Again, such representations serve to complicate and deconstruct fixed and essentializing constructions of gender by pointing to its socially determined and artificial nature. Just as with race, ethnicity, and culture, however, the magazine's equation of gender-bending with consumption mitigates the potentially empowering elements of its representations, as expensive fashion becomes the ultimate gender equalizer.

Furthermore, *Men's non-no's* fluid constructions of race, ethnicity, and gender powerfully contrast with those found in *non-no*, its sister publication targeted at a female readership. Unlike *Men's non-no's* almost exclusively visual discourse (the men's magazine offers very little textual contextualization to its fashion spreads) of multiple and ambiguous gendered, racial, and cultural identifications, *non-no's* discourse is highly gendered. While men are occasionally mentioned or quoted in *non-no's* editorial content, they are almost completely visually excluded from its pages—male models never seem to appear, for instance, in fashion spreads—resulting in a discourse that, despite a good amount of talk about love, sex, and boyfriends, privileges female-to-female relationships.

The fantasy non-no constructs is one of exclusive female friendship forged through the sharing of beauty, fashion, and dieting advice, or through dressing up for parties or excursions in the park. This friendship is presented as highly pleasurable, as evidenced by the body language of the female models laughing, holding hands, or grabbing each other's neck (Darling-Wolf, 2006). Noting that magazines such as non-no or an-an emerged in the 1970s as new kinds of publications that promoted a single lifestyle—by assuming, for instance, that women had a room of their own to decorate—focused on female pleasure, Japanese media scholar Kazue Sakamoto points to the subversive potential of such representations at a time when the idea of "young women living alone in Tokyo ... was quite revolutionary" (1999, p. 181).

The gender identities emerging from this discourse are, however, overall far less fluid than those found in the men's magazine. In contrast to Men's non-no's vast array of possible "masculinities," non-no's constructions of femininity draw exclusively from the "cute" (kawaii) ideal of mixed innocence and (sexual) maturity evident throughout the Japanese popular cultural environment (McVeigh, 2000). In the issues I examined, for instance, the ideal woman was described as doll-like (oningyou), girly (gâri), thin (hosoi), yet mature/adult-like (otona-ppoi) and attractive/popular (moteru).

Body monitoring is also a significant subtext of the "girl culture" non-no constructs for its readers. In the summer months, women in bathing suits posed to accentuate their extreme slenderness appear in almost every spread. Articles offer dieting advice or toning exercises. Ads for weight loss programs full of "before and after" pictures are a recurring feature both in non-no and in other Japanese women's magazines (Darling-Wolf, 2000a). Finally, while Men's non-no's discourse is mostly descriptive, non-no's is highly prescriptive—readers are told exactly what to do to achieve the ideal look (for examples, see Darling-Wolf, 2006). These findings are in keeping with linguist and anthropologist Miyako Inoue's identification of early Japanese women's magazines, and the advertising they carry, as instrumental in developing a "chatty" and "personable" speech that "came to be normalized as a generic speech style of modern Japanese women" and inaugurated "the birth of a new consumer body disciplined corporeally to respond to advertisement's hailing" (2007, pp. 537, 544; see also Horioka, 1993).

Most significantly, non-no's racial and cultural representations are much less diverse than those found in Men's non-no. All models featured in non-no's editorial content in the issues I examined appeared to be Asian and were positioned as culturally Japanese—even if they were frequently subtly "whitened" through makeup and lighting in a process commonly used in Japanese publications (Darling-Wolf, 2000a). While female readers are encouraged to embrace their Japaneseness in the magazine, physical features typically associated with a Caucasian racial identity are clearly emphasized—as evidenced by the numerous articles explaining how to create the illusion of rounder eyes and whiter skin and the ads for eye glue or cosmetic surgery. All models adhere to the same standard of beauty: light skin, round eyes, straight nose, ultra-slim body. While other possible identifications can certainly be found elsewhere in Japanese popular culture—particularly since hip-hop gained popularity among young Japanese women—and while white skin has long been a standard of beauty in Japan, non-no's representations of race and culture powerfully contrast in their limited scope with the racial diversity and cultural hybridity of *Men's* non-no's male models.

Furthermore, whereas *Men's* non-no's hybridity rests both on the racial ambiguity of well-known models and the assimilation of outsiders of varied ethnicities into its overall visual discourse, the latter strategy is missing from non-no. Models of different races/cultures (mostly white) are present, yet clearly separated from the magazine's cast of familiar (presumably) Japanese models. The complexity of this simultaneous process of racial/cultural dichotomizing and integration is particularly striking in non-no's representations of female sexuality. Ideals of childlike/innocent but sexy/knowing Japanese sexuality (non-no's readers are clearly assumed to be sexually active) most powerfully contrast with the magazine's more sexually aggressive representations of *gaijin* (foreigners/outsiders). It is also evident in non-no's frequent portrayal of kimono-clad Japanese models enjoying "traditional" Japanese activities. While, arguably, the *yukata* (summer kimonos) sold today as popular fashion items in Tokyo's trendiest department stores have relatively little to do with their original incarnation, these representations again contrast with *Men's* non-no's complete lack of direct references to more "traditional" elements of Japanese culture (despite the fact that men do frequently wear *yukata* to summer festivals).

Thus, while encouraging readers to engage in globalized consumption, non-no's gender representations also link femininity to nostalgic definitions of Japanese cultural/national identity that serve "to establish national identity-building binaries: *our* cultural heritage/*your* practical things . . . Japan/the West; and the Japanese/the rest" (McVeigh, 2000, p. 4, emphasis in original). More generally, non-no's discourse illustrates gender's powerful intersection with the negotiation of the global/national/local. As feminist anthropologist Susan Ossman puts it, "As women alter their skirts in synch with international fashion, their sartorial choices are also asked to stand for national or ethnic or religious identities" (2011, p. 21).

In her analysis of former Miss World and Bollywood superstar Rai Aishwarya, Parameswaran suggests that Rai's hybrid form of Whitened/Westernized beauty merged with ethnic/traditional upper-class femininity serves to "absorb the West in a new transnational economic order" (2011, p. 78). The "Westernized" Japanese models in *non-no* are similarly portrayed as managing to "exceed Western standards of beauty" while simultaneously protecting their "native" cultural identities from "the contaminating influences of Western commodity and entertainment culture" (Parameswaran, 2011, p. 80). Cast in the role of "keepers of tradition," expected to strive for an impossible-to-attain "Westernized" physical look, yet encouraged to remain "behaviorally" Japanese, *non-no*'s female readers face a particularly complex set of expectations.

Contextualizing Magazine Reading: Negotiating the Global in Everyday Life

Japanese fashion magazines demonstrate how the negotiation of the local/national in relationship to the global intersects with the politics of both race and gender in popular culture. Scholars have warned, however, that focusing solely on magazines' discursive elements does not fully do justice to the medium's complex intertextual connection to diverse aspects of consumer culture. They have called for more contextualized considerations of magazine reading taking into account "other modes of the subject's relation with media texts" (Inoue, 2007, p. 525)—for a more complete analysis, in other words, of the "circuit of culture" (Du Gay, 2013, p. xxxi) shaping this cultural form and of the ways in which it is articulated. My countless conversations on the subject with Japanese women validate the need for such an analysis.

First, we must keep in mind that, as numerous studies of media audiences have demonstrated, the *act* of consuming popular culture is often as important as the content of the texts itself. In the three-generational families that have participated in my research I have often found that mothers, daughters, and sisters enjoy the opportunity to sit down with a magazine together, discuss fashion and beauty choices, or go shopping for the perfect outfit. Using magazines as a connecting tool, mothers might leaf through the publications brought home by their daughters—as Izumi, the then-39-year-old mother of two high school girls, explained in 1999, "I wouldn't buy those by myself, but my daughters buy them so I read them sometimes"—or enjoy reminiscing about their own engagement with global fashion trends: "When I look back at when I was young we did the same things," she added.

Furthermore, while the younger women that constitute fashion magazines' main target audience often express feelings of alienation toward the glamorous culture of global consumption portrayed in their favorite publications they nevertheless display a very practical attitude toward them. They might purchase a specific issue because it features a style they want to imitate or a particularly appetizing diet, or use them for inspiration before getting a haircut, or buying or making a new outfit. The publications young women frequently spontaneously brought to interviews were often missing photographs here and there, where hair or clothing styles had been cut out. When recalling why they had avidly read fashion magazines in their high school years, two women in their 20s noted that they did it "to find out the clothes I wanted to wear, or for the hairstyles, I imitated the hairstyles," or "for the small things, accessories, to know what I wanted." When asked why they read magazines more frequently in the past, one of them responded: "I didn't know much then!" The other explained: "before, I was reading them for research." This conception of magazines as practical sources of information—common throughout the Japanese media where "how to" guides range from specific descriptions of how to perform dance steps in hip-hop magazines to the detailing of which boots and goggles are needed to become a biker (and which stores to find them at)—often creates frustration toward the relatively less prescriptive style of the Japanese editions of U.S. and European publications. As one reader in her 20s put it, "Western magazines don't give us much information. In Japanese magazines, they have a lot of information. They have just regular people and give us information about them. Maybe that's why there are so many people wearing these clothes, they say where to find these clothes in the magazines and how to wear them."

Young rural women of relatively lower socio-economic status tend to be particularly resourceful in their attempts to create a fashionable identity at a fraction of the price of that sold in the magazines they read. After identifying a style they like, their next step is to try to find clothes that are similar to those featured in the magazine but that they "can buy." If that proves impossible, they might resort to sewing or knitting the outfit or accessory they are longing for—or, in the case of the youngest informants, to having their mothers do it for them. Their favorite kinds of clothes are, as a 16-year-old explained to me one day, "Clothes that are cheap, but look expensive." Women old enough to have a credit card might employ it to make clothing purchases—as a woman in her 20s explained: "If it's too expensive, I just give up, but if I feel that I can save the money in about two or three months, then I charge it and pay later."

Thus, as Oda-san's quote opening this chapter illustrates, fashion magazines serve as cultural maps guiding their young readers through the complex maze of physical self-definition—"I don't want to be a dope about fashion, or many other things, so [magazines are] my information source" explained one reader. Also illustrated in the quotes above is the fact that these guides are particularly precious to young rural women who otherwise feel removed from the urban culture of beauty and fashion promoted throughout the Japanese media: "The young in the countryside often imitate the fashions in the magazines," noted Oda-san who was 52 years old when I interviewed her in 1999. As an older women recalled, "When I was young, only the young who lived in the city, in Tokyo, would have that kind of fashion. So the only way I could know about new fashion was by seeing people from Tokyo when they came back here. Otherwise, I couldn't know what was popular in urban areas," to which her daughter-in-law added, "When I was young, for example, it took one or two years for the fashion and clothing from Tokyo to reach this area." In other words, for rural readers, fashion magazines serve as a source of global cultural capital that helps reduce the cultural gap they experience toward more urban settings where forms of globalized consumption are more readily available.

But if this increased and faster access to globalized information is often appreciated—especially by younger readers of relatively higher socio-economic status who feel particularly pressured to conform to the upper-class ideals of urban sophistication promoted in the magazines—it can also be interpreted as encouraging young rural women to engage in homogenized less-than-desirable cultural practices: "the young in the countryside start to imitate [urban fashion styles] all at once," noted one older woman "Now, it seems that most of the women on television have the same personality," commented another. Deeming urbanites "entirely different," her friend concluded: "They're scary!"

In either case, while they may still occasionally consult magazines when needing a haircut or a special outfit (or in an effort to bond with their daughters), older women tend to exhibit a much more detached attitude toward the culture of fashion and luxury they promote. As Izumi explained, "If I were younger I might be interested in these . . . but now I can't find anything I would really wear." Or, as 44-year-old Abe-san more forcefully put it, "I don't like to read these kinds of magazines. . . . They're all about diets or fortune telling and all about what celebrities wear, so I'm fed up with them. That's all they have in there, diets!" Similarly, while Izumi's daughter Mie and her best friend Madoka avidly read *Cutie* or *Zipper* (Japanese fashion magazines targeted at a younger audience) when they first started participating in my research as high school students, the two young women, now mothers themselves and in their late 20s, told me in a 2009 interview that they read *Orange Page*—a cooking and homemaking magazine that, incidentally, they had deemed a publication for "obaasan" (slightly pejorative term used to refer to middle-aged women) when 16. They still cared about fashion, however, and displayed the same kind of ingenuity in finding alternative ways to engage in the global culture of consumption promoted in magazines that they had 10 years earlier. When I commented in 2009 on the small Louis Vuitton bag Mie carried around (which I knew she could not afford on her salary as an "office lady"), she responded, clearly admiringly, that her mother-in-law had managed to find a used one and given it to her as a gift. It is also important to note that despite the rise of the Internet in this 10 year period, these young women still read print magazines, even if different ones (the continuing strength of the Japanese magazine industry suggests that they are not the only ones).

These examples illustrate the importance of keeping in mind the ways in which media consumption intersects with various aspects of the sociocultural context—class, geography, age, race, gender—in which it takes place. This does not mean, however, that media consumers' negotiation of global and/or globalized cultural forms is impervious to the realities of global power dynamics. In the case of fashion magazines, their racial and class-specific subtexts are particularly crucial elements of this negotiation.

White Models Just Look Better in the Picture

When asked about the evolution of cultural perceptions of female attractiveness in Japan, the women I interviewed quickly identified globalization as a significant factor in their construction (Takako's "the world has become small"). They pointed to a shift in cultural ideals of beauty coinciding with "the time when women changed from kimono to Western clothing" (Izumi, 39). As 81-year-old Toyoda-san explained, "Before the war there weren't any white models, but after the war we started to think that American things were better than Japanese things, we got the media, these kinds of things." They generally recognized and critiqued the historical legacy of "Western"[2] media influence on contemporary Japanese culture—a legacy 24-year-old Mako characterized as "the Western thing" still haunting the Japanese and resulting in a situation in which, as she put it, "Western movies, Western culture, Western anything, it's all good."

Older women reminisced about the postwar invasion of "Western" actors (Audrey Hepburn, Gregory Peck, Grace Kelly, Alain Delon, Danielle Darrieux, John Wayne), movies (*Casablanca, King Kong, Planet of the Apes, Roman Holiday*), singers (Elvis Presley, The Beatles, Paul Anka), and models on the Japanese popular culture scene: "When I was young 'Twiggy,' do you know? the model . . . Twiggy, she had come to Japan, she wore a mini skirt, that kind of thing . . . This Twiggy, this model was very popular among young people. She was very thin and I wanted to be like that" (Takako, 48). Forty-seven-year-old Horie-san fondly recalled watching French and American films on television as a child "because of the different lifestyles, the different clothes, and [because] people admire the way of thought of Westerners." Toyoda-san remembered the time when "a teacher told us students that it was OK to have a hairstyle like Audrey Hepburn," adding that "the hairstyles and makeup styles were very popular."

Younger women admitted not having given much thought to the presence of white models in Japanese publications, which, as a group of 16-year-olds put it, they were "accustomed to seeing" and found "natural." As 23-year-old Chieko explained, "For us, we've always seen these things, it's been natural to see Western movies and listen to Western music since we were children." The global nature of magazines outlined above combined with the popularity of "Western styles" were frequently offered as a possible explanation for U.S. and European models' popularity: "I think some magazines are originally made in Paris or New York. Like *Frau*, *Elle*, that's originally in France, that's one reason. The other reason is like I said before . . . we want to be like Western people," explained 24-year-old Mako.

Japanese media consumers also pointed to the exoticized subtext of representations such as those found in *non-no*, which they often found pleasurable: "I can enjoy a different world without leaving Japan, a different culture" (Takako, 48), "We can see people in a different world" (Kiyomi, 23), "They are people living in a different world" (Mako, 24). As 68-year-old Tanaka-san concluded, "Maybe we admire foreign culture or foreign ways of thought because we are different from that in Japan." They recognized, in other words, that such imagery was part of the broader process of imagining the global in Japan—a pleasurable fantasy of globalized engagement readers could "long for" and "dream about": "There is a kind of admiration. Maybe these are not about being close or familiar, these are a little 'high class' [in English]. They represent the kind of image of what we want to be, it's a kind of admiration" (Kiyomi, 23). Or, as Mako put it:

> Things like this magazine [picking up the Japanese magazine *Spring*], this is not real life. We want to be like this stuff, but this is actually not our life, it's kind of apart from our real life. In that kind of thing, we don't want to see real life, like, you know, some short fat girl wearing these clothes, that doesn't look good, right? And we keep thinking that . . . and then . . . we are not Western people but it's OK, because this is not our real life.

The women I interviewed nevertheless expressed ambiguous feelings of combined distancing and yearning toward exoticized representations of (mostly white) "Western"[3] models. Comments such as "They look good, but they are difficult to be close to, to marry, or to be good friends with. . . . it's difficult to be good friends with them, but we want to be good friends" (Miko, 24) and "They look so good, but they are not . . . maybe close in feelings. They are just out there. They are the people who are living in a different world, but they look good. We don't feel familiar with them" (Mako, 24) illustrate the mixture of admiration, longing, and alienation this imagery generated. Partly as a result of such feelings, young women often strongly asserted their personal preference for Japanese models they could feel "closer to"—"there are too many Westerners in the Japanese media" (Emiko, 28)—and noted that they did not "like the way the society is [admiring Westerners]" (Takie, 28).

Deeming efforts to imitate Caucasian models a painful exercise in futility—as 44-year-old Abe-san noted, "Japanese women might think that they can look nice in these kinds of things, but they can't"—they rebelled against the alienating nature of their presence in Japanese publications: "If I wear the same clothes, I'm not going to be like them!" (Mako, 24); "I personally think that it's funny that they would have white models in [Japanese magazines]. It is Japanese women who read these magazines, and Japanese women try to wear those clothes. . . . Mostly they don't give me good advice about fashion or makeup" (Horie-san, 47); "Westerners and Japanese have completely different [body] styles, so if I try to wear these kinds of clothes, they generally don't fit me, so I feel angry. I feel like I'm being deceived" (Chieko, 23). As a result, they frequently called for the inclusion of easier-to-emulate Japanese models in Japanese magazines. As 23-year-old Kumiko put it, "[White models] look nice and they have good styles, so they're beautiful. But I want the magazines to have Japanese models. Japanese models have a different style from these white models. I just can't imagine myself wearing these kinds of clothes."

If they frequently disapproved of the use of Caucasian models, the women who participated in my research also ultimately argued, however, that their presence in Japanese publications made business sense *because they are more beautiful than their Japanese counterparts.* As Horie-san explained: "They have good appearance, good [body] style. They are nicer than Japanese, they are more beautiful than Japanese, they have better styles than Japanese, so they look nice in the new fashion and makeup."

In interview after interview they expressed their admiration for "Western bodies"—that is, physical traits most commonly associated in Japan with a Caucasian racial identity: "Westerners have a very nice [body] style, they look good, their fashion is neat. So basically, many Japanese people admire Western styles of fashion. Westerners look better, they have longer legs, they are taller" (Takako, 48); "They have a good [body] style, they're pretty" (Sachiko, 68); "They are tall, so they look good" (Fujida-san, 64); "They have good appearance, big eyes, high noses" (Reiko, 16); "Westerners are more beautiful, they are tall, have high noses, big eyes, and a good sense of style" (Nishimura-san, 46); "Compared to Japanese women, they are more elegant, they look more excellent than the Japanese" (Chieko, 23); "We admire Western people, it's true, I think. The one reason is that they are tall, they are taller than we are" (Aya, 16); "They have good [body] style, you know, compared to Japanese models, they have nice breasts, nice hips, longer legs" (Abe-san, 44); "Compared to the Japanese, they have better style and better appearance, they have smaller faces, they're taller" (Takako, in a different interview); "They have good body styles, good proportions of the body. Maybe we like the way white people look" (Miko, 24); "They represent the kind of image that we want to be, it's a kind of admiration" (Chieko); "They have everything that Japanese people want to have" (Madoka, 16); "They're beautiful, that's the kind of beauty we pursue" (Toyoda-san, 81). Or, as Izumi (39) concluded, "When we were young, we admired [white Westerners], because they have what we don't have."[4]

Some ultimately came up with a racial taxonomy placing whites at the top, Japanese at the bottom, and "halves"—individuals of mixed Asian and Caucasian ethnicity—in between. For instance, talking about the evolution of models' racial origin in Japanese women's magazines, Horie-san explained in 1999: "When I was young, *an-an* used lots of halves. *Non-no* had only Japanese models. Maybe at the beginning, when they started to be published, these magazines, like *an-an* or *non-no*, they couldn't get many white models, so they used halves instead. They were more beautiful than the Japanese so they were used as models." Attempting to explain the popularity of Hollywood in Japan, Abe-san similarly noted, "The Japanese feel inferior to the white, so Japanese tend to follow or imitate what is popular in America.[5] And the Japanese feel superiority to the blacks and to the South East Asians, so even though there are black or Asian movies, they don't become popular in Japan."

Hip-hop's spread through mainstream Japanese popular culture has since then further complicated this racial hierarchy and raised the status of blackness as an object of admiration—hence the greater racial diversity in *Men's non-no's* more recent issues. However, as the comparison with *non-no* demonstrated, hip-hop has generally had a stronger impact on mainstream representations of masculinity than femininity.[6] If hip-hop-inspired magazines such as *Woofin' Girl* have started to tap the female market and stars like Amuro Namie have made identification with blackness more popular among women,[7] mainstream Japanese women's magazines remain, as Morimoto and Chang (2009) have recently shown, largely white-dominated.

Furthermore while informants interviewed both in 1999 and in 2009–11 recognized hip-hop's influence on Japanese popular culture and often expressed admiration for African American stars—Mariah Carey frequently came up—their dichotomized categorization of Japanese/Asian vs. Western/White-Black and the combined feeling of admiration and alienation occasioned by representations of "Westerners" (be they white or black) in the Japanese media remained largely unchanged. Asked about her image of "Westerners," Mie commented in a 2009 interview, "I feel admiration," to which Madoka immediately added, "it's an unknown world."

Gender and Race and Female Beauty in a Global Order

The ambiguities in readers' reactions to the (omni)presence of white (and, to a lesser extent, black) models in Japanese fashion magazines point to the complexity of individuals' local engagement with a patriarchal, white-dominated, global capitalist order. Constructions of feminine beauty in Japan are caught in the multifaceted interplay between gender, globalization, nationalism, race, and class to a greater extent than constructions of male attractiveness.

Women around the globe confront the difficult task of negotiating their gendered identities in the face of media standards of attractiveness increasingly removed from the biological realities of actual female bodies (for a detailed discussion of this process see Darling-Wolf, 2000b). This task, however, takes on an additional dimension for "non-white" (please pardon the short-cut in this description) media consumers as they contend with "beauty's asymmetrical relations with differently raced bodies" (Parameswaran, 2011, p. 75).

Despite their frequent rebellion against the presence of "Westerners" in Japanese magazines, despite their requests for more racially appropriate models, and despite the feelings of alienation this imagery frequently occasioned, the Japanese media consumers that I interviewed did not challenge the validity of global standards of feminine beauty modeled—at least initially (Leslie, 1995)—after a Caucasian ideal. While they generally recognized the potentially harmful nature of admiring physical attributes characteristic of a different race and forcefully called for healthier representations, they did not question whether such traits were actually worthy of admiration. Despite their insightful critiques of U.S. and European media's historical influence on their own popular cultural environment, they failed to identify the equation of "Western/white" (and, occasionally, black) femininity with globalized glamour, beauty, and success as a racist legacy (Moeran, 2010). As Mako—whose assessment of such representations as a pleasurable fantasy was quoted earlier—concluded shortly after deeming the presence of white models in Japanese magazines problematic: "I just think that white people are greatly beautiful. Just to see the white women, they are so beautiful. Not just the face, but the [body] style. We are short, our legs are short. But they have long legs and . . . that's much better in the picture."

The Japanese women who participate in my research are no more cultural dopes than their counterparts in other parts of the world—who resort to cosmetic surgery, dieting, and other painful practices to fit media ideals of beauty at an equally disturbing rate (Worldwide Plastic Surgery Statistics, 2010). Their specific situation, however, provides a valuable illustration of the multidimensional ways in which dynamics of race, gender, class, geography, and national identity formation interlock with the awareness of the global that characterizes globalization. My informants' engagement with "global culture" shapes not only how they imagine the "Other," but also how they imagine what it means to be Japanese-rural-lower/upper-class-Asian-female[8] (and vice versa)—how they experience, in other words, their own locality. For them, the process of imagining the global is mired in particularly complex identity politics. It illustrates how, in a globalized world, the production of locality is "more than ever shot through with contradictions" (Appadurai, 1996, p. 198). While this process is not unique to women in their position, their experience does significantly differ from that of individuals whose (white) racial identity is more easily "naturalized" in a global context or that of individuals whose experience of race is shaped by their status as "minorities" at the local/national level. It also differs from that of their male counterparts. It demonstrates how the local/national/global are mutually constituted not only in globalized popular cultural forms but also in individuals' media consumption. It points to the extent to which the imagination has become "a form of negotiation between sites of agency (individuals) and globally defined fields of possibility" (Appadurai, 1996, p. 31).

The different empirical examples examined so far in this book illustrate the complex interplay of "the global" with various local and national dynamics. They point to the often-political nature of processes of representation and positioning against the backdrop of an imagined global community and to their possible consequences on individuals' daily lives. The similarities and differences between the ways in which these processes take shape in the French, Japanese, and U.S. media also point to the need to develop new theoretical models that move beyond essentialized characterizations of large areas of the world to more carefully tease out globalization's intersecting and constantly shifting power lines. Developing such a model is made difficult, however, by the fact that a myopic process of positioning similar to that found in reality television, news, or magazines permeates much academic work on globalized cultural forms. The next two chapters address the problematic consequences of this positioning in intellectual discourses, which, just like popular cultural texts, "are never insulated from the national and global environment in which they develop" (Kraidy, 2005, p. 17).

Having established the centrality of dynamics of gender, race, and class in the negotiation of the local/national/global nexus, we now turn to a genre in which these dynamics are particularly contentious. The next chapter explores what turning a translocal lens to hip-hop as a *global* phenomenon can teach us about the politics of representation of race, class, and gender not only in hip-hop itself but also in the heated scholarly debates surrounding it.

FOUR

Disjuncture and Difference from the *Banlieue* to the *Ganba*: Embracing Hip-hop as a Global Genre

As a global phenomenon, hip-hop illustrates the transoceanic crossings of diasporic cultures. As an international lingua franca, rap is performed not only in French and Portuguese but also in Hindi, Chinese, Arabic, Amymara, and Yoruba.
   —Stam and Shohat, 2012, p. 146

Hip-hop's mixing of musical influences from a variety of cultural contexts, its simultaneous assertions of global universality and local authenticity, its intricate articulation of multiple identities, and its extreme commercial success (ironically built upon claims to represent subaltern voices) powerfully illustrate the complex nature of the global "mediascapes" that Appadurai (1990) claims are built upon the disjunctures between globalization's different dimensions. Approaching hip-hop from a translocal perspective, this chapter considers what we can learn from the genre's global popularity about the politics of representation of gender, race, and class not only in the genre itself, but also in academic discussions surrounding its contested definitions of authenticity and of cultural, racial, ethnic, and gender identities. In keeping with this book's focus, the examples employed throughout the chapter will most heavily draw from the French and Japanese hip-hop scenes.[1] The chapter will demonstrate how these two environments can productively be compared to each other and to the way hip-hop is approached in the United States. The French context provides a particularly relevant example, as France stands as the second largest consumer and producer of rap music in the world after the United States (Molinero, 2009).

   The next section explores the ways in which the global and the local are mutually constitutive elements of hip-hop's multiple incarnations. The chapter then illustrates how the complexity of hip-hop's engagement in the local/national/global nexus is not always fully addressed in academic discourse about the genre. It starts with a discussion of how the frequent positioning of hip-hop as an African/Latino/a American genre in U.S. scholarship leads to problematic characterizations of hip-hop's global dynamics. It also considers how a focus on U.S.-style race relations may not do justice to the global politics of race permeating the genre in a transnational context. It then turns to an examination of how definitions of authenticity/in-authenticity along issues of commercialism and integration within mainstream society serve to perpetuate the cycle of oppression that rappers are challenging in their artistic productions. Finally, it addresses how academic discourse about hip-hop, as a global phenomenon, has yet to fully address the genre's contentious gender dynamics.

Rapping in Local Languages: Hip-hop's Global/Local Articulations

"Hip-hop has the ability to live on legends maintained by all its members," writes French sociologist Hughes Bazin (1998, p. 14). As U.S. cultural anthropologist Ian Condry puts it in his study of the Japanese context, the genre provides "a way for hip-hoppers to imagine themselves as part of a global cultural movement" (2006, p. 217).

Thanks to Afrika Bambaata's Zulu Nation, to the popularity of break-dancing (which often preceded other elements of hip-hop culture in its transnational reach), and to the increased interconnectedness of cultural forms that characterizes globalization, hip-hop started to spread throughout the world sometime in the 1980s. While the movement was initially frequently dismissed as a passing fad emanating from U.S. transnational power (Boucher, 1998; Condry, 2006; Marti, 2005), history shows that Zulu Nation's influence quickly receded, and rap promptly morphed into varied (sub)culturally specific forms with impressive lasting power (Boucher, 1998). Today hip-hop is widely recognized as a global movement (see, for example, Dyson, 2007; Rose, 2008).

Hip-hop's continuing influence rests in part on its ability to shape individuals' imagination of the global by drawing transnational connections that give producers and amateurs of the genre a sense of belonging to "a mythical, utopian, and idealized world" (Boucher, 1998, p. 306). This symbolic community is maintained through cultural practices shared transnationally and through transnational and/or transcultural intertextuality. References to the practice of "the dozens" (in which two individuals insult each other until one of them gives up) might serve, for instance, to link French rappers to their counterparts in the United States while creating a feeling of community among amateurs who catch the references. As French cultural critics George

Lapassade and Philippe Rousselot explain, for instance, in reference to the French group NTM: "While it is true that NTM means 'The North transmits the message' [*le Nord Transmet le Message*] (where North refers to Department number 93), all French B-boys know that NTM also means 'Nique ta Mère' [fuck your mother]. This polysemy . . . is allusive, and only the initiated know that it is the fraternal echo of the American motherfucker" (1990, p. 22). Similarly, rap's symbolic connection to African American street culture is perpetuated in the works of international rap artists—as when French rappers speak of French "ghetto culture" (Prévos, 1998, p. 68). The practice of sampling huge international hits further establishes the genre's global intertextuality. Audiences' enjoyment of the music rests, in turn, on their possession of enough global cultural capital to "get" these intertextual allusions.

Hip-hop's symbolic connections are also enacted through the sharing of a stated set of "universal" values (Zulu Nation's love, peace, and unity, "keeping it real") and of a tradition of social activism. African American studies scholar Halifu Osumare speaks of "Hip-hop's connective marginalities," that she defines as "social resonances between black expressive culture within its contextual political history and similar dynamics in other nations" (2001, p. 172). The fact that black rappers living in France "claim a tradition of activism (*tradition revendicatrice*) linked to black American culture" (Bazin, 1998, p. 14) and that Japanese hip-hop "draws inspiration from African American struggles while generating distinctive approaches to race and protest in Japan" (Condry, 2006, p. 29) illustrate this process.

These connective marginalities, however, are not solely constructed in solidarity with impoverished African Americans who are often credited (at least by French and Japanese rappers) with having "given birth" to the genre in the U.S. ghetto. They are both recontextualized in each "local" environment where hip-hop develops, and "(re)universalized" to be applied transnationally across racial and/or ethnic differences to create "a new cultural politics of affiliation . . . that eschews national distinctions in favor of thinking about transnational connectedness among different groups" (Condry, 2006, p. 47).

Finally, on a more basic level, hip-hop's ability to participate "in a symbolic network that circulates globally" (Tickner, 2008, p. 121) is predicated on the availability of transnational networks of cultural production and distribution. These include major multinational corporations that have learned to capitalize on rap's commercial potential and are now dominating the music market—allowing, for instance, French rapper MC Solaar to sell 250,000 copies of his double platinum second album outside of France (Beau, 1996). They also take the form of more informal networks of independent producers that, while previously available, developed an immediate global reach with the growth of the Internet starting in the mid-1990s. As one Japanese producer put it in a personal conversation about the influence of social networking sites on the Japanese hip-hop scene: "before . . . it was very difficult to promote Japanese music to the world because we are isolated . . . but now it's very easy, now I find it's very easy to connect with music business people so I find that maybe we can promote Japanese artists" (personal conversation, June 6, 2009).

The potentially immediate global reach of the Internet may, in turn, feed into the symbolic vision of a global hip-hop culture both originated and spread throughout the world beyond and above national and ethnic boundaries. As the Japanese producer continued, "So what I do is maybe not focus on nationality or identity but I do the label to enjoy seeing that global dynamism changing and to connect global people in all edges of the world." Or as Coma-chi, a popular Japanese female rapper, put it, "I can connect globally, anywhere in the world. I can quickly update my music, express directly how I feel right now" (personal conversation, June 10, 2009). Thus, hip-hop is a significant contributor to the process of imagining the global that characterizes globalization.

Hip-hop's success also rests, however, on its asserted link (actual or imagined) to highly local contexts. It is a genre, in other words, where the mutually constitutive nature of the global (hip-hop as a transnational movement) and the local (hip-hop as "authentic representative" of individuals' experiences of oppression) is ostensibly recognized. As ethnomusicologist and cultural anthropologist Thomas Solomon explains in his study of hip-hop in Istanbul:

> Istanbul hip-hoppers adopt and adapt the widely circulating discourses of rap and hip-hop and use them as resources for constructing locally specific meanings. Through their own study of the internationally circulating media texts of hip-hop . . . originating outside of Turkey, Istanbul hip-hoppers understand that the discourse of rap characteristically includes the practice of representing . . . one's place. (2005, p. 8, emphasis in original)[2]

In the case of French rap, this process of local representation takes place in conversation with the strong lyrical tradition of the French chansonniers (Liu, 1997)—the much-celebrated singer-songwriters who provide political and social commentary often drawing inspiration from current events. Thus, while recognized as an adaptation of "a musical current born in the Bronx,"[3] French rap is also seen as engaging in a process through which it "measures itself against the model of French song" (Pecqueux, 2007, p. 46; see also Boucher, 1998; Molinero, 2009).

French rap artists frequently point to the legacy (and at times sample the

works) of such cultural icons as George Brassens, Jean Ferrat, Maxime le Forestier, and Serge Gainsbourg[4] to frame their anti-establishment lyrics within
the context of a larger French tradition of socially engaged artistic expression.
In 2000, some of France's best-known rappers released an album covering
the songs of Charles Aznavour, Francis Cabrel, Serge Gainsbourg, Renaud,
George Brassens, Jacques Brel, and other celebrated singers (*L'Hip-Hopée*,
2000). Hip-hop artist (and actor) Oxmo Puccino's rendition of Brel's *Ces gens
là* even earned him for a moment the nickname of the "Black Jack Brel." A
year later, an anthology titled *Hexagone 2001, Rien N'a Changé* [Hexagon (i.e.,
France)[5] 2001, nothing has changed] offered rap versions of Renaud's[6] most
socially engaged titles. The album's title referred to the highly popular singer-
songwriter's 1975 song "Hexagone" that bitingly critiqued France's cultural
arrogance. In a similar vein, the title song of French rapper Joey Starr's[7]
(2006) first solo album *Gare au Jaguarr* [Watch for the jaguar(r)] humorously
transposed the events described in Brassens' famous song "Gare au gorille"
[Watch for the gorilla] from an urban zoo to the street culture of French housing projects.[8]

French rap is indeed further geographically and symbolically localized in
the culture of the French banlieue—the suburban areas of Paris and other major cities (particularly Marseilles) that "have come to symbolize the excesses in
violence, drug consumption, social dislocation, and delinquency encountered
in financially strapped urban neighborhoods" (Prévos, 1998, p. 67). While
not all French rappers actually grew up in such neighborhoods (just as not all
U.S. rappers grew up on the streets of the Bronx or LA), the banlieue serves
as a symbolic space that rappers propose to "represent." As French historian
Pierre-Antoine Marti puts it, "[Rappers] are all inhabitants of this imaginary
banlieue that haunts the national consciousness" (2005, p. 96; see also Stam
and Shohat, 2012, p. 147).

References to the RER (Paris' suburban rail system), stores such as Tati
where low-income families shop, or to specific zip codes—as when the group
Ministère AMER rap about the 95200 zip code (of Garges-Sarcelles in the
northern banlieues of Paris)—clearly establish this geographical and cultural
anchorage in the *cités* (low-income housing projects). "I lived the banlieue version [of hip-hop] [*moi j'l'ai vécu version banlieue*]" rap the group Sniper (2006)
in a song titled "Retour aux racines" [Back to the roots]. Through allusions
to the Front National extreme-right party or to various politicians—as in
La Fouine's *Jacques Chirac*, titled after the former French president and Paris
mayor (released online in 2012)—rappers assertively engage in local and national politics. For instance, in 2004 Rohff, a rapper who immigrated to the
Paris suburbs from the Union of the Comoros as a child, responded to then
minister of interior Nicolas Sarkozy's characterization of banlieue youths as

"scum" (racaille) with a song titled "Méssage à la racaille" [message to the scum] (Montaigne, 2006).

Finally, French rap is more generally steeped in references to the broader French popular cultural context ranging from television shows such as the Club Dorothée that most children growing up in France in the late 1980s and 1990s spent their Wednesdays[9] watching, to famous television commercials or literary texts—"Gavroche is back, it's not Voltaire's fault" [Gavroche est de retour, c'est pas la faute à Voltaire] rap the group IAM in their song "Achevez-les," referring both to Victor Hugo's famed novel Les Misérables and to the musical of the same name.[10] Because of the globalized nature of contemporary popular culture, these references naturally include "imported" elements. Thus, American television series such as Starsky and Hutch, Dallas, The A-Team, or MacGyver regularly come up in the works of French rappers—"I show up quick like Starsky" [J'débaque sec à la Starsky] rap IAM (2003). So does Japanese animation, which, as we will see in chapter 5, has been hugely culturally influential in France since the late 1970s. One popular group is even called the Saïan Supa Crew after the "super Saiyan" fighters of Dragon Ball. Bollywood has more recently made its entry into rappers' large repertoire of globalized references (Sniper, 2012).

Once again, however, these references to elements of the "global" cannot be fully understood without taking into account their intersection with "the local." For instance, the generation that watched the Club Dorothée on Wednesdays also remembers watching Starsky and Hutch every Sunday afternoon on TF1 (the same channel that broadcast Star Academy) at a time when most French TV viewers only had access to four channels (one of which was local). The series happened to be scheduled after a program focusing on hip-hop (Marti, 2005). Similarly, when Saïan Supa Crew mention Dragon Ball, Captain Tsubasa, or San Ku Kai (all Japanese texts) in their song "J'avais" (2001), what they nostalgically recall is getting up to watch these shows on Wednesday mornings (a French practice): "It's the time . . . when on Wednesday you wake up for Dragon Ball" [C'est l'époque . . . Ou l'mercredi tu t'réveilles pour Dragon Ball]. When mentioning these global texts, French rappers simultaneously point to French cultural practices.

These examples illustrate how hip-hop's significance cannot be fully captured with a lens too broadly fitted to its global dimensions or too narrowly focused on its localized incarnations. Unfortunately, scholars' (and, to some extent rappers' and consumers') ability to clearly articulate the multiple ways in which the global and the local are mutually constitutive elements of hip-hop's (trans)cultural influence is often limited by the politics of representation permeating hip-hop's discourse (and discourses about hip-hop), and, more generally, by the politics of academic production. The limitations of current academic work on hip-hop when considering the genre as a global phenomenon are further explored in the following section. A discussion of how a translocal perspective might help overcome these limitations is also provided when appropriate.

Rap as an (African) American Genre

While scholars often recognize hip-hop's hybrid transcultural roots and the significance of both African American and Latin American influences on the genre, academic work on hip-hop in the United States has historically focused on the politics of race as they relate to African American experiences in a U.S. context. This results in a situation in which "rap music and black culture become entwined and mutually construct each other" (Condry, 2006, p. 31). For instance, in her widely acclaimed study of hip-hop in the United States, professor of Africana studies Tricia Rose (1994) defines hip-hop as "an Afrocentric cultural form which attempts to negotiate the experiences of marginalization, brutally truncated opportunity and oppression *within the cultural imperatives of African American and Caribbean history*" (p. 21, emphasis mine; for other examples see Dawson, 1999; Holmes-Smith, 1997; Krims, 2000). Similarly, editors Murray Forman and Mark Anthony Neal note in their introduction to *That's the Joint! The Hip-Hop Studies Reader* that among "a growing number of progressive black thinkers . . . there is general concurrence that hip-hop represents an extension of specifically African American cultural tradition" even if it "also poses challenges and introduces ruptures to prevailing notions of an unbroken cultural continuum" (2004, p. 3). Certainly, considering the crucial importance of African American cultural production in the United States, the complex politics of its negotiation must be critically examined. Rose's (and others') work usefully contributes to this task. Defining hip-hop as *solely* or, at least, *most significantly*, a black American[11] (emphasis on both terms) genre (or even as a black American/Latina/o/Caribbean genre) becomes problematic, however, when applied to the study of hip-hop as a *global* phenomenon—a fact that, incidentally, Rose (2008) aptly recognizes in her more recent work.

On the most basic level, the historical fact of hip-hop's spread to other cultural and/or linguistic contexts frequently remains unnoticed. For example, when professor of Black and Puerto Rican studies Juan Flores notes in an essay on the development of Puerto Rican rap in the United States that "by the early 1990s hip-hop had finally broken the language barrier" (2004, p. 69), he fails to acknowledge that French rapper Dee Nasty released his first French-language album *Paname City Rappin'* in 1984, or that Japanese DJs such as Crazy A or DJ Krush were performing in Japanese every Sunday in Yoyogi park around the same time. When writer David Samuels describes rap's early spread "from New York to Philadelphia, Chicago, Boston, and other cities with substantial black populations" (2004, p. 148), he similarly fails to recognize that the genre quickly spread transnationally as well (and simultaneously reinforces hip-hop's position as an African American genre).

Even when this history is acknowledged, however, viewing hip-hop as essentially an "American" cultural practice results in an oversimplification of transcultural dynamics along U.S. vs. "the Rest" lines, in which the study of the genre's global incarnations involves "studying the appropriation of rap and hip-hop as an essentialized, endemically African American cultural form" (Mitchell, 2000, p. 5). For instance, in an article on global hip-hop, Osumare describes rap as "the most invading of black music," a homogenizing force that has "affected nearly every country on the map" (2001, p. 171). After a discussion of Senegalese rap, she concludes that "an age of increasing complexity has been created by juxtapositions of local cultures and exported postmodernity *from the primary global power, the continental United States*" (2001, p. 174, emphasis mine).

This positioning frequently translates into a summary dismissal of all forms of hip-hop generated outside the context of African American/Latino/a culture as necessarily inauthentic. In an article titled "Getting real about global hip-hop" U.S. cultural critic Yvonne Bynoe (2002) concludes, for instance, that foreigners simply do not (and cannot) "get it." Making racial emulation the central argument of her discussion of Japanese rap, Osumare similarly portrays the latter as a bad copy of the American original, noting that "Global commodification promotes a vacuous 'jigger-like'[12] cultural appropriation that can only be termed imitation though conspicuous consumption" (2001, p. 177). Even less critical analyses of hip-hop in different parts of the world tend to position hip-hop's global spread as a fairly straightforward process of localization of an African American cultural form (see, for example, Bennett, 2004; Mitchell, 2001).

In his ethnographic analysis of the Tokyo hip-hop scene, cultural anthropologist Ian Condry demonstrates, however, that the politics of race in Japanese hip-hop are much more complex than might appear at first sight and must be considered within Japan's "differently configured racial context" (Condry, 2006, p. 39; see also Condry, 2000, 2001) where notions of "black" and "white" are entangled in Japan's relationship to the foreign Other and, more, generally, its imaginary of "the West." As he warns, "we in the United States may need to rethink a common American ethnocentrism that tends to equate foreign interest in U.S. popular culture with a desire to be American or, by analogy, Japanese interest in black culture with a desire to be black" (Condry, 2006, p. 47).

Conceptions of "the global" as a U.S.-dominated totalizing whole to be opposed to local environments are not particularly useful heuristic devices when considering hip-hop as a transnational phenomenon. Its translocal connections are much more complex and interesting than that. Scholars have pointed, for instance, to the significance of postcolonial relationships in rap's transnational spread (Davies and Bantahila, 2006). Thus, Senegalese rappers may arguably be more influenced by such figures as MC Solaar, one of France's most famous and internationally known rappers,[13] who was born in Senegal (a former French colony that gained its independence in 1960) of Chadian parents, than by U.S. artists. Solaar and other French rappers more generally exert a powerful influence on the francophone hip-hop community that, again, at times supersedes that of their U.S. counterparts (Low, Sarkar, and Winer, 2009). As one Montreal rapper explained, "When I heard Solaar do it in French I said, 'Damn! A'right!'" [*Quand j'ai entendu Solaar le faire en français j'ai dit, 'Damn! A'right!'*]. Another Quebecois rapper described the "declic IAM" [the IAM turn on] as a significant turning point in francophone rap: "Everyone sounded like [IAM lead rapper] Akhénaton" [*Tout le monde sonnait comme Akhénaton*] (cited in Low, Sarkar, and Winer, 2009, p. 66).

When the French group IAM choose to title their song "Do the raï thing" (2003) they are making translocal references not only to Spike Lee's globally distributed film of U.S. origin *Do the Right Thing*, but also to French rap's connection to a form of Algerian popular music—raï finds its roots in Western Algeria in Bedouin music, and its contemporary form is "a mixture of melodic traditional Algerian melodies and coarse French pop" (Orlando, 2003, p. 401)—from which it draws inspiration and, more generally, to the significance of North African postcolonial identities in the French hip-hop scene. References that dynamics considered solely on a local vs. global axis (in which American rap stands for the global) cannot easily address.

Thinking translocally helps us realize that hip-hop has taken multiple and unexpected paths in its global voyage, including ones that may not necessarily lead back to the United States. Approaching hip-hop from a different point of entry, scholars conducting research on non-U.S. cultural environments tend to portray the genre differently than their U.S.-focused counterparts. While generally positioning the movement as having African American origins, they see it as quickly evolving beyond this cultural context into multiple and equally "authentic" culturally diversified forms drawing "from almost all musical horizons" (Marti, 2005, p. 20; see also Barrer, 2009; Condry, 2006; Mitchell, 2000)—Low, Sarkar, and Winer (2009) speak of rap's histories (plural). As Bazin puts it, "while it is possible to describe the cultural roots and social anchorage of its beginnings, hip-hop cannot be reduced to fixed cultural traits, or to a unique social membership . . . it's a constantly evolving form" (1998, p. 10).

Moving away from characterizations of the United States as hip-hop's most globally significant cultural center, Pecqueux questions the "constant genealogy" that interprets French rap as the natural godchild of American rap. Noting that it is hard to imagine that "the rappers are more familiar with the griots and the dozens than Brassens or Aznavour," he challenges what he calls the "crossing of the Atlantic" version of French rap's history that interprets early French rap as an imitation of an American form "as if nothing in French cultural history could prefigure the particular development of this artistic practice." "While one cannot seriously deny the fact that French rap is linked to a musical practice born in the Bronx," he concludes, "we still must problematize its Crossing of the Atlantic" (2007, pp. 34, 35, 35, 34, 42).

Rap as a transnational phenomenon becomes "a narrative tool which complements and merges with localized social discourses concerning inequality and critical political reflection" (Barrer, 2009, p. 252). It moves definitions of authenticity away from the question of whether foreigners can "get" hip-hop's meaning in an African American context to the necessity of developing culturally specific texts that meaningfully relate to "local" issues and power relations (Clarke and Hischock, 2009; Mitchell, 2000). From such a perspective, U.S. rap may even—in an interesting reversal of Bynoe's (2002) characterization—be regarded as "less authentic" than rap in other cultural contexts (by scholars and rappers alike) because its commercial success and widespread global distribution move it further away from its original context of production (Boucher, 1998; Marti, 2005; Molinero, 2009). Reflecting with nostalgia on the development of the genre, Rose (2008) recognizes this possibility in the introduction to her biting critique of contemporary commercialized hip-hop in the United States: "A few artists *elsewhere around the globe*, along with some who have slipped into American radio rotation and others in the so-called underground, reflect the extraordinary life force that remains" (p. x, emphasis mine).

In a similar vein, rapping in English may be considered an impediment to developing "authentic" (i.e., culturally specific) rap because of the transnational dominance of English-language U.S. hip-hop—as when French sociologist Manuel Boucher suggests that British rap has had difficulties finding its own voice because of the "handicap" of "using the same language as those from hip-hop's birth place" (1998, p. 37).

In a global context, hip-hop's local incarnations may even be developed *in opposition* to U.S. cultural production: "I have nothing to do with American rap" [*Je n'ai rien à voir avec le rap Américain*] raps MC Solaar in his 1998 hit *La vie n'est qu'un moment* [Life is but a moment]. Rap's development in France was ironically aided by the country's transcultural power struggle with the United States. Because it is in the French language, French rap benefits from France's protectionist cultural policies that require radio stations to include 40 percent (35 percent in the case of radios targeted at a youth audience) of francophone production in their music programming.[14] As former DJ and program director of Paris' Radio Nova, Loïc Dury explains, "We started playing rap in 88, but today, they force you to blast [*bastonner*] French rap, because of the quotas" (cited in Bocquet and Pierre-Adolphe, 1997).

More generally, French rap is frequently positioned both as a local antidote to American "cultural imperialism" and as an important vector of French global influence. Solaar has been acknowledged as "one of the important figures in the exportation of French culture" (Liu, 1997, p. 329, emphasis mine).[15] Rap artists have received some of France's most prestigious music awards, including the "Victoires de la musique." A 1996 *Nouvel Observateur* article titled "*Le Rap? Il parle la France*" [Rap? It speaks of France] placed Solaar along other internationally prominent French icons including Jacques Derrida, Phillipe Starck, and Pierre Boulez (Loupias, March 1996).[16] Ten years later, the same news magazine deemed French rappers "the children of hip-hop and of Derrida" (Vigoureux, May 18, 2006).

Thus, we must resist the temptation to position the United States as hip-hop's sole "authentic" cultural representative—or hip-hop as a symptom of U.S. cultural imperialism. A translocal perspective demonstrates that hip-hop spreads through different points of entry. It helps us come to terms with the facts that Cuban rappers pursue their careers in France (Fernandes, 2003) and that Turkish rap "started not in Turkey, but in Germany, practised by members of the Turkish 'guestworker' [*Gastarbeiter*] community especially in, but not limited to, the cities of Berlin and Frankfurt" (Solomon, 2005, p. 3). It encourages us to see how the processes of cultural production that Condry (2006) describes in the context of the Japanese *genba*—the actual place of cultural production—may be more similar to those taking place in the French banlieue than in the American ghetto (and vice versa). It severs the easy correlation of the United States with "the global" and even "the West." It also complicates our understanding of the politics of race in a global context.

U.S.-Style Racial Dynamics in a Global Context

U.S. hip-hop, which is frequently positioned as the voice of an oppressed racial minority, cannot easily be dissociated from the politics of race in the United States. Thus, analyses taking U.S. hip-hop as their point of entry tend to be couched in U.S.-influenced conceptualizations of race relations where transnational hip-hop intersects with critiques of the global commodification of "black culture" (Bynoe, 2002, p. 83). Scholars have pointed to the essentializing nature of the suggestion that there is such a thing as a unified "black culture" and to the danger of positioning hip-hop as its global representative (Rose, 2008). More generally, such interpretations fail to fully problematize the politics of race in a global context. As Shome notes, "rarely is the connection between the production and management of the domestic 'ethnic' inside the U.S. and larger globalized racial politics addressed in 'domestic' race research. Rarely is it acknowledged that minorities within the U.S., when we consider a larger global scale, make up a 'privileged' minority" (2006c, p. 8).

Indeed, as U.S. citizens, U.S. rappers hold a relatively privileged global position. At the very least, this position gives them access to transnational networks of production and distribution not available to all. In his analysis of rap in Zimbabwe, Australian cultural critic Tony Mitchell notes, for instance, that African rap, which developed in part "in opposition to a perceived U.S. cultural imperialism in rap and hip-hop" (2000, p. 42), has found it difficult to successfully break into the global market. Pointing to the fact that non-American African rappers are generally marginalized in the United States, he suggests that the global dominance of African American rap developed at the expense of other transnational African voices. Mitchell also describes Zimbabwean rappers' discomfort with black Americans' use of African practices such as hair beading. He concludes that rap in Zimbabwe "challenges the standard rhetoric about the Afrodiasporic and Afrocentric aspects of American rap and hip-hop" (2000, p. 42).

In a similar vein, U.S. hip-hop's power to influence global definitions of "black culture" and "black experience" in line with a culturally specific American experience has yet to be adequately addressed. So is its power to impact the global imagination of Africa through its construction of a U.S.-style Afrocentricism based on "a very particular way of looking at the world that, far more than it expresses any exilic consciousness of Africa, betrays a distinctively American understanding of ethnicity and cultural difference" (Gilroy, 2004, p. 89). Noting that "only thirty-seven percent of the blacks who live in the Western hemisphere live in the United States" British cultural critic Paul Gilroy points to the dangers of globally accepting such "Americocentric" (2004, pp. 88, 91) positions.

A translocal perspective demonstrates that racial dynamics may be negotiated differently in different places, including through connections that bypass the United States altogether—or that race may simply not be a significant subtext of hip-hop's discourse in some cultural contexts (see Barrer, 2009; Solomon, 2005, for specific examples). As Shome and Hegde remind us, the U.S.-style "narrative of 'difference' despite all its political value and theoretical potency, becomes unsettled in complicated ways in globalization" (2002, pp. 175–76).

Interesting parallels exist, for instance, between the politics of race in

Japanese and French hip-hop. Some Japanese rappers engage in a critical deconstruction of what it means to be Japanese by challenging the hegemonic notion that Japan is a racially homogeneous nation, and point to the racial subtext of the country's history of imperialist aggression toward its Asian neighbors (Condry, 2006). Their message powerfully resonates with that of French rappers who challenge France's position of "color blindness" to celebrate *métissage* (mixing) and construct "frenchness" as a multiethnic and culturally diverse identity shaped by France's colonial past. The "local" culture of the banlieue described above is indeed steeped in the translocal experiences of immigration, diaspora, and (post)colonialism: "To each his/her nostalgia, mine was the colonies" [*À chacun sa nostagie, la mienne c'était les colonies*] raps Solaar (1998; for other examples see Sniper, 2001, 2011). Or, as Stam and Shohat put it, "At times, French rappers perform a percussive version of what in an academic context would be called postcolonial critique" (2012, p. 148).

As a consequence of this postcolonial position, French rappers who often "carry a genetic link to Africa" (Stam and Shohat, 2012, p. 146) as second-generation immigrants might find it difficult to engage in a U.S.-style Afrocentricism that may "not refer to present-day Africa, but to an older, somewhat mythical place of origin" (Dennis, 2006, pp. 281–82; see also Gilroy, 2004). Fully aware of Africa's present-day realities—raï became popular among rappers, for instance, as an expression of solidarity with two well-known raï singers who were gunned down in Algeria in the 1990s (Orlando, 2003)—and of the fact that they do not "fit" any better in their parents' (often African) "home" lands than in middle-class French society (Marti, 2005; Stam and Shohat, 2012), they have "a closer physical and therefore less mythical relationship . . . to the '*pays d'origine*' [African homeland] than [rappers] in the U.S." (Cannon, 1994, p. 164). As rapper La Rumeur (2007) puts it in a song titled "Là où poussent mes racines" [Where my roots grow]:

> I don't like the warm water, the exoticism [*Je n'aime pas l'eau tiède,*
> *l'exotisme*]
> On the village/homeland [*Sur le bled*]
> Between you and me [*De toi à moi*]
> This cult of black Africa [*Ce culte de l'Afrique noire*]

While expressing solidarity with the plight of racial minorities in the United States, French rappers do not see U.S.-style racial politics as a particularly useful model when applied to the French context—as one rapper put it in reference to the pro-black movement in France: "It's a fad, it's bullshit; three quarters of the people who claim to be pro-black don't know anything, haven't read anything *and refer too much to Americans*" (Little MC, quoted in

Boucher, 1998, p. 185, emphasis mine). They are also skeptical toward African American conceptualizations of Islam, particularly as defined by The Nation of Islam, which they see as too racially exclusionary. As another rapper explained, "The problem of Islam in France is very different from the problem of Islam in the United States. In the U.S., when you say Islam, it's a religion for black people, you can't enter it. In France, anyone can enter, there is a universality to the message" (Abu, quoted in Boucher, 1998, p. 194; see also Swedenburg, 2001).

Thus, if hip-hop's attraction rests in part on the movement's ability to capitalize on transnational solidarity, the complexity of its racial dynamics as a global phenomenon requires us to move beyond the limitations of U.S.-style identity politics. As Condry concludes in the case of Japan, while "Japanese hip-hop does deal with race issues," it is "often in ways that contrast with hip-hop in the United States" (2006, p. 46).

Rappers Stay Pure, or the Problematics of Authenticity

Unfortunately, the politics of race in hip-hop (and in academic scholarship about hip-hop) are further complicated by their entanglement with issues of representation and authenticity. Indeed, despite its hybrid nature, hip-hop is generally positioned as *representing* specific (sub)cultures or ethnic/racial/class identities. While its various incarnations suggest that it may mean different things to different people in different places, the notion of authenticity remains one of its significant recurring subtexts. A frequently discussed marker of authenticity in hip-hop is the common distinction between "commercial" and "underground" positions. While scholars have noted that the two are necessarily engaged in a symbiotic relationship—a large underground scene feeds a smaller commercial production business where artists, once signed by a major record company, are brought to stardom (Boucher, 1998; Condry, 2006)—and while they recognize that underground rappers generally strive for commercial success, the two categories frequently remain strictly dichotomized in analyses of hip-hop's socio-cultural impact (Molinero, 2009). As the voice of the disfranchised, rap loses credibility with commercial success.

Discomfort with rap's commodification is understandable in light of the trajectory of other forms of subaltern expression, which have historically been caught in a situation in which "black artists were prevented by the exclusionary forces of racism from taking command of their intellectual property" (Basu and Werber, 2001, p. 243). Cultural critics Dipannita Basu and Pnina Werbner note, however, that hip-hop has not necessarily followed this too-familiar pattern. Contrasting the genre's commercial development to that of earlier musical forms, they argue that black entrepreneurs have managed to retain greater control over its process of commercialization to successfully "make a dent in the white domination and appropriation of the music industry" (2001, pp. 243–44). Or, as sociologist and public intellectual Michael Eric Dyson puts it, "thousands of young black professionals eat from hip-hop's table" (2007, p. 54).

Commercial success is nevertheless frequently portrayed, both in academic work and in the larger cultural discussions surrounding hip-hop, as compromising a rapper's authenticity. In his study of French rap, Boucher suggests that in order to be commercially successful, rappers must learn to "compromise" and avoid the more violent or political positions that "could frighten the larger public." He criticizes Solaar for practicing a "reassuring" and "acceptable" rap steeped in literary references, and IAM for appearing on television as "nice boys, human, and close to the people" despite their "B-Boys look" (1998, p. 123). French historian Pierre-Antoine Marti (2005) similarly notes Solaar's "ambiguous position in the world of French rap" due to his extreme commercial success, and maintains that "the greater public naturally turns to more festive or calm rap. It is less attracted by its more militant and activist dimensions" (2005, p. 47). Paradoxically, Boucher later argues that more "authentic" groups who "refuse to compromise with the system" have achieved financial success because expressing rebellion has become fashionable and because, to the business world, "any 'product' that can make benefits is potentially interesting" (1998, p. 126). Clearly, scholars themselves hold an "ambiguous position" toward rap's commercialization.

While it is valid to question rappers' ability to represent the plight of the financially marginalized once they have become millionaires—and while we should maintain a critical eye toward rap's co-option by large transnational companies—equating rap's commercial success with an automatic loss of authenticity introduces new tensions in the negotiation of its relationship to class, ethnic, racial, and/or national identities. First, reducing the definition of an "underground" (i.e., "authentic") artist to one who "doesn't shift many units" (Neate, 2004, p. 19) perpetuates the cycle of truncated economic opportunities rappers are denouncing in their songs by suggesting that rappers must (ideally) remain poor in order to remain authentic.

Dichotomized conceptualizations of underground vs. commercial rap also more generally perpetuate the cycle of marginalization along racial and/or ethnic lines. Much ambivalence toward hugely transnationally popular MC Solaar, for instance, rests on the perception that he is too fully "integrated" within the French cultural context to remain "authentic" as a rapper. Noting that "Solaar is often compared to Gainsbourg and that critics like to inscribe him in the noble tradition of "French song" [*la chanson française*]," Marti "takes his defense" by suggesting that "[this] is *not fully justified: Solaar has remained a* rapper" (2005, p. 46, emphasis mine). This powerfully contrasts with Solaar's (1998) own assertion that he is "representing the French rhyme" [*Je représente la rime hexagonale*].

While Marti marvels at rappers' attachment to French republican values—"Could rappers reveal themselves to be more republican than the Republic? It may be a bit excessive to say so, but they all display a profound attachment to some of its values. The republican motto 'Liberté, Égalité, Fraternité' is not without its appeal [*n'est pas sans leur déplaire*]"—he nevertheless describes them as "French on paper, a little less in the soul" (2005, pp. 235, 201). Similarly, while professor of French and Francophone literatures Valérie Orlando (2003) acknowledges rappers' desire to be considered French—she cites a rapper as saying, "I'm French, formed by the Republican School system. I'm a young Maghrebian who mixes two languages, Arabic and French. Voilà! I'm a Muslim Made in France!" (2003, p. 402)—she nevertheless concludes that "the Beurs[17] seek to negotiate new identities for themselves somewhere *between French and Other*" (2003, p. 413, emphasis mine). By refusing to consent to rappers' assertions of French identity, these scholars theoretically reproduce the process of exclusion from full participation in French society hip-hop artists are denouncing in their work. In stark contrast to France's official policy of color blindness, they subtly suggest that one cannot *truly* be French and black, brown, and/or Muslim (despite the fact that Islam is the second most widely practiced religion in France after Roman Catholicism).

The racial undertones of this positioning are indeed difficult to miss. For instance, after criticizing Solaar for using "turns of phrase that are poetic and 'close to home' [*bien de chez nous*]," Boucher cites Fanon—"Nothing more sensational than a black expressing himself correctly, since, really, he assumes the white world" (cited in Boucher, 1998, p. 123)—to suggest that Solaar's self-positioning as representative of French culture (*I represent the French rhyme*) compromises his black male identity. Boucher celebrates, on the other hand, the more "hard core," "violent," and "pure and hard [*pure et dur*]" rap of those who "want to keep their 'authenticity'" (Boucher, 1998, pp. 120, 123, 124, 124). This results in a gangsta rap-inspired characterization of "authentic" ethnic/black identity as violent, threatening, and refusing to "integrate" that ultimately resonates with the discourse of ultra-conservative politicians and journalists who paint the banlieue as a site of social strife threatening France's core identity. Scholars in the United States have pointed to the deeply essentializing nature of a similar process of definition in U.S. rap that "denies and silences a wide range of black urban ghetto experiences and points of view" and ultimately serves as "a cover for perpetuating gross stereotypes about black people" (Rose, 2008, pp. 139, 141).

Associating authenticity with violence and street credibility also positions rappers as cultural representatives of a limited conceptualization of ethnic/racial/banlieue/ghetto identity that condemns them to a "a continuous representation of the self" [*présentation de soi en continu*] (Hennion, 2005, p. 122) from which they can only deviate at the risk of being accused of ethnic treason. Like Spivak's subaltern speech (1988), from the moment it gains recognition (economic and otherwise) rappers' discourse loses credibility as the voice of the oppressed and compromises their position as members of subaltern culture. In order to stay "pure"—Boucher describes 'underground' rap as "a step toward *the myth of found again purity*" (1998, p. 134, emphasis mine)—rappers must remain on the margins. Challenging such characterizations, Dyson suggests that we work to "acknowledge that it's not a simple either/or—either you sell out to white corporate interests and get exploited, or you stay pure and black and at home and undistributed and unable to cross over" (2007, p. 56).

French sociologist Anthony Pecqueux (2007) further warns that scholars' desire to validate "underground" rap's political message often leads to a paradoxical idealization of rappers' socio-cultural position as "representatives of the street" that results in a suspension of critical judgment regarding the genre's violent, misogynist, and potentially racist subtexts (see also Gilroy, 1993). This, I contend, is often the case in analyses of hip-hop's global spread, particularly as they relate to representation of gender.

Sexism: Global Rap's Lost Dimension

"Gender and sexuality are central to the study of music's cultural and emotional resonance, often referred to as authenticity, in popular music studies," writes Vincent Stephens (2005, p. 23) in his analysis of the intersection of gender, homophobia, and race in Eminem's music. Scholars in the United States have powerfully critiqued U.S. hip-hop's gendered constructions (see, for example, Calhoun, 2005; Conrad, Dixon, and Zhang, 2009; Dyson, 2007; Peterson et al., 2007; Rose, 2008). Numerous others have explored the genre's productive potential for feminist artists and scholars (for examples, see Haugen, 2003; Oware, 2007; Pough, Richardson, Durham, and Raimist, 2007; Reid-Brinkley, 2008; Skeggs, 1993). Robust critiques of hip-hop's misogynist subtext are, however, largely absent from analyses of the genre's global spread.

For instance, while she acknowledges that female rappers often find it difficult to "reconcile their identity as rappers with their identity as women," French sociologist Stéphanie Molinero (2009, p. 173) does not elaborate on why that might be the case in her analysis of rap's reception in France. Her observation that rap's public is mostly male and that female consumers tend to prefer more commercial rap leads her to problematically conclude that women are uncritical media consumers who "remain dominated" (2009, p. 194). Similarly, in his otherwise excellent analysis of hip-hop in Japan, Condry usefully acknowledges the presence and influence of female rappers on the Japanese hip-hop scene, yet fails to fully address the broader gender politics permeating the genre transnationally—including, but not limited to, the objectification of female bodies, the use of the "virgin/ho" stereotypical dichotomy, or the equation of "authentic" masculinity with violence and domination in some hip-hop texts.

Most frequently, analyses of gender in hip-hop's different global incarnations ultimately fall in line with a too familiar cultural narrative that recognizes hip-hop as a historically male-dominated genre but suggests that the situation is slowly improving. Little empirical evidence supports this picture—at least when one looks at the more recently commercially successful forms of hip-hop. In fact, Rose convincingly argues that the relatively recent commercial success of gangsta rap has actually led to a sharp *increase* in hypersexism as the genre panders to "America's racist and sexist lowest common denominator" (2008, p. 2). As a young artist involved in both the American and Japanese hip-hop scenes explained when asked whether she felt hip-hop today was still male dominated: "Yes, more than in the 90s, more than ever . . . [In the 90s] we got to see all different types of women. . . . I saw women with negative messages, but I saw women with more positive messages, and I saw women working together, and that really shaped me as far as how I think about women in hip-hop and in culture, in terms of what we can have. *But that was all taken away*" (personal conversation, June 10, 2009, emphasis mine).

Scholars' failure (or unwillingness) to fully address global hip-hop's gender dynamics stems in part from the suspension of critical judgment discussed above and from scholars' attempts to position themselves as "decoders" of rappers' messages (Pecqueux, 2007). Thus, rappers' talk of sexual domination—as when Ministère AMER raps about retaliating against the police by having sex with and/or sodomizing their wives and daughters in *Brigitte (Femme de Flic)* (1992)—is interpreted solely as an act of rebellion against the establishment (Boucher, 1998; Marti 2005). Rappers' suggestion that women should wear the Chador is seen as an act of provocation: "when Ministère AMER claims the Chador, it is first an act of provocation: *Le tchador? C'est pour enerver les français!* [the Chador? It's to bug the French!]" writes Boucher (1998, p. 229). There is no denying that these acts are, at least in part, meant to provoke. The fact, however, that this provocation is constructed through the vehicle of women needs to be critically addressed. Wearing the Chador is not necessarily oppressive, but it should be a choice *women* make, not one dictated by male rappers. As Dyson reminds us, "Just because 'the white man's foot is on your neck' doesn't mean that your foot can't in turn be on a black female's neck" (2007, p. 106).

This excusing of misogynist acts and/or lyrics as a form of subaltern expression also serves to locate sexism as an integral part of subaltern and/ or minority identity—as when Boucher notes that "dominated social actors can easily develop . . . a form of segregation toward young women" (1998, p. 225). As Rose puts it when pointing to similar arguments in the U.S. context: "It's as if black teenagers have smuggled sexism and homophobia into American culture, bringing them in like unauthorized imports" (2008, p. 8). Such discussions not only construct "dominated social actors" as particularly sexist, but also—by defining hip-hop as an expression of dominated identity while it is, mostly, an expression of dominated *male* identity—normalizes masculinity in definitions of ethnic/racial identities. This results in a situation in which "black women simultaneously grapple with their disgust at black female representation in black popular culture and their fear of the possible ramifications for publicly attacking black men" (Reid-Brinkley, 2008, p. 249). As Rose concludes, "As long as the equation between attacking sexism in hip-hop and attacking black men remains in place, little critical commentary can occur within hip-hop culture, and women and men will continue to be viewed as traitors for challenging it and for demanding less exploitative expression" (2007, p. 157; see also Dyson, 2007; Morgan, 2004).

Thus, while it is important to acknowledge the contribution of female rappers and recognize the fact that some artists (and scholars) have managed to re-appropriate and redefine elements of hip-hop's misogynist subtext to form their own (feminist) cultural forms (Armstead, 2008; Báez, 2006; Pough, Richardson, Durham, and Raimist, 2007), we must also continue to more broadly critically explore hip-hop's intersection with gender dynamics in a globalized world.

Among other things, doing so requires us to carefully locate rap's misogyny within "the broader cultures of violence, sexism, and racism that deeply inform hip-hop, motivating the sales associated with these images" (Rose, 2008, p. 28). After all, is Ministère AMER's 1992 evocation of sexual activity with a "femme de flic" fundamentally different (even if perhaps more direct) than that of Brassens (1955/2005) some 37 years earlier, and to which the rappers playfully refer? Indeed, the works of the celebrated artists French rappers are frequently referring to point to a long tradition of rather less-than-empowering characterizations of female sexuality in popular French music. Brassens' "Le Gorille" (1952/2004)—which French rapper Joey Starr (2006) refers to in "Gare au Jaguarr"—portrays women lusting after a large gorilla and suggests that an elderly woman would enjoy his sexual attention: "Bah, sighed the hundred-year-old woman / that someone might still desire me /

that would be extraordinary / and to be honest, beyond my wildest dreams [*Bah, soupirait la centenaire / qu'on puisse encore me desirer / ce serait extraordinaire / et pour tout dire inespéré*]." In case the nature of the sexual attention the gorilla might bestow on his prey is not clear enough, the term "rape" comes up later in the song: "Suppose that one of you might be / Like the ape forced to / rape a judge or a very old woman / which of the two would you choose? [*Supposez que l'un de vous puisse être / Comme le singe, obligé de / Violer un juge ou une ancêtre / Lequel choisirait-il des deux?*]."

In a similar vein, "Je suis un voyou" [I'm a ruffian], sung by both Brassens in 1955 (1954/2002) and Renaud in 1996 (1996/2004), undermines the famous "no means no" rape education slogan by suggesting that women enjoy unsolicited sexual advances, even if they say they don't. After descriptions of sexual activities ranging from biting the lips of the song's heroine to tearing up her dress through "picking forbidden fruit in her blouse" the song repeatedly concludes: "She told me in a severe tone / 'What are you doing?' / But she let me go on / Girls are like that [*Ell' m'a dit, d'un ton sévère / 'Qu'est-ce que tu fais là?' / Mais elle m'a laissé faire / Les fill's, c'est comm' ça*]."

One does not even know where to start with Gainsbourg, whose entire repertoire is famously permeated with characterizations of women as purely sexual objects: "There I take the girl and then pschtt (as in the sound made by a carbonated drink being opened) / I take my flight [*Crac je prends la fille et puis pschtt / J'prends la fuite*]" he sings in his onomatopoeia-filled 1973 song "Sensuelle et sans suite" (a play on words literally meaning "sensual and without follow up"), followed by: I'm a hero, for these little ones / Quick they're on their back and me pschtt / I take advantage of it [*J'suis un crac, pour ces p'tites / Crac les v'la sur l'dos et moi pschtt / J'en profite*].

Of course, these often light-hearted songs are not meant to be taken literally—"Le Gorille" was intended as a biting attack on the death penalty (the gorilla ultimately chooses to rape the judge who screams like the man he had had executed that very morning)—and Gainsbourg's bad boy image was an integral part of his media persona as he worked to shock French society into discussing its greatest taboos.[18] The same could be said, however, of much of rap's content (Dyson, 2007).

Like the works of rappers they inspired, these songs' representations of sexuality stirred much controversy in their own time even if they were to ultimately become celebrated pieces of French cultural heritage—"Le Gorille" was banned from the airwaves for two years after its release due to its "pornographic content."[19] Thus, rap's tendency to treat women as sexual objects may be more productively addressed in relationship to this long legacy of similar representations in French popular music than as a symptom of subaltern (non-white/lower class) masculinity having to assert itself at women's expense. While the examples provided here draw from the French context, scholars in other cultural environments have made similar observations (see, for example, Dyson, 2007; Rose, 2008).

Questioning such a characterization would also help us more effectively address hip-hop's potential contribution to the global spread of racial and cultural stereotypes, through its association (particularly in U.S. gangsta rap) of African American masculinity with violence and misogyny. While this association has been to some extent problematized in the United States, it is not always as assertively addressed in studies of hip-hop as a transnational phenomenon. The spread of conceptions of authenticity "frequently defined by ideas about sexuality and patterns of interaction between men and women that are taken to be expressive of essential, that is, racial difference" (Gilroy, 2004, p. 89) takes on new dimensions in a global context. As Gilroy puts it, "when these things come down the transnational wire to us in Europe and to black folks in other parts of the world, they become metaphysical statements about what blackness is" (2004, p. 90). In turn, these statements might resonate, for non-black global audiences, with common stereotypes about black masculinity and/or U.S. culture as particularly sexist and violent (Condry, 2006; Cornyetz, 1994), which can then be opposed to the situation "at home." As Japanese female rapper Coma-chi explained when asked what she thought about the representation of women in U.S. hip-hop: "In Japan, mainstream hip-hop does not do that, they respect women. . . . *I think it's related to Japanese culture*" (personal conversation, June 2009, emphasis mine). Recognizing that rap's misogynist and violent subtext resonates with various aspects of global and local culture—not just those attributed to African American voices—might help complicate this notion.

No One Is Pure: Hybridity as Hip-hop's Productive Potential

Because of the tensions that inevitably arise when subaltern voices attempt to gain recognition within the environment responsible for their domination, hip-hop has long been mired in identity politics. Its global spread has, however, rendered its politics of representation exponentially more complex. Hip-hop's claims to authenticity are, for better or for worse, as varied as the different cultural environments to which the genre has been adapted. As Condry suggests, whether or not one accepts these claims is based on one's location and is, to some extent, arbitrary. Thus, assertions of hip-hop's "true" essence, if useful in helping us "understand conventions of inclusion and exclusion" (Condry, 2006, p. 35), are problematic at best, particularly when considering hip-hop as a globally influential genre.

But just because hip-hop has come to mean different things to different people in different places does not mean that it has lost all meaning, or its productive potential. One of the most positive side effects of hip-hop's commercial success and its transnational spread is the multifaceted nature of the tensions it has introduced into notions of political engagement vs. commodification, into constructions of racial, ethnic, national, cultural, and class identities, and into the relationship between the global, the national, and the local. Global hip-hop's productive potential rests, in other words, in its (ethnic, racial, cultural, (trans)national, commercial, underground, linguistic, regional, and so on) *hybridity*, which, rather than granting individuals ownership over essentialized identities, destabilizes boundaries. It rests on its ability to produce a "different notion of authenticity" that "affirms the value of mixing and what might be called creolization" (Gilroy, 2004, p. 91)—a form of authenticity, as Gilroy concludes, "premised on the notion of flows" (2004, p. 91).

In this sense, the most "political" aspect of Japanese and French rappers' intervention into their respective socio-cultural contexts is perhaps their potential to ignite a discussion—at the local, national, and transnational level—about what it means to be Japanese and/or French. When Japanese rappers point to the plight of *burakumin, nikkeijin*,[20] or Korean immigrants and their descendants, when they ask their audience to acknowledge the legacy of Japan's imperialist history, they challenge hegemonic constructions of Japan as a racially and ethnically homogeneous nation[21] and engage in a "transnational cultural politics of race by critiquing the enduring racism among right-wing Japanese toward their Asian neighbors" (Condry, 2006, p. 45).

Likewise, when French rappers claim their position as both representatives and producers of "French culture" while simultaneously addressing the legacy of colonialism and celebrating hybridity, they help destabilize culturally and racially essentialist notions of what it means to be French and "create other cultural forms that will become new references for French society and will be reappropriated within [France's] cultural heritage" (Boucher, 1998, p. 366). While France's institutions may be slow to change, scholars have pointed to the profound effect hip-hop has had on conceptualizations of French cultural identity (see, for example, Orlando, 2003; Stam and Shohat, 2012, p. 146). "Contemporary French hip-hop culture's music and films demonstrate," Orlando argues, "how the urban multiethnic communities of France are being reconstructed to bring the voice of the disconnected into the mainstream. As these artistic modes exemplify, France's identity is no longer rooted in the tenets of assimilationist theory which marginalize ethnic minorities on the peripheries of *Français-de-souche* culture" (2003, p. 412).

Even the notion of *français-de-souche*, however, is deconstructed by French rappers—as when French solo artist Passi (2000) (formerly of the group Ministère AMER), raps in his second solo album: "Our first steps were in

Africa five million years ago / if you put A+B together you will see we are all immigrants" [*Nos premiers pas c'était en Afrique il y a cinq millions d'années / si tu fais A+B tu verras qu'on est tous des immigrés*]. Or, as the French group KDD (1998) suggests, "We must remix France with our couscous sauce"[22] [*Il faut remanier la France à notre sauce couscous*]. It is by claiming a hybridized identity as black/beur/from the banlieue (etc.) *and* French *à part entière* [fully French] that French rappers are being most political. As the group Sniper concludes in their 2001 song titled "La France" [France]: "France to the French (referring to a commonly used ultra-conservative slogan) / as long as I'm here / that will be impossible [*La France aux français / tant que j'y serai / ce sera impossible*]."

As a genre that, from its inception, was built upon both claims of authenticity (at least symbolically) based on individuals' material engagement with (hyper)local contexts *and* links to an imagined global community, hip-hop provides a particularly useful terrain from which to explore the mutually constitutive nature of the local/national/global nexus and its intersection with the politics of race, ethnicity, class, and gender. This chapter demonstrates that hip-hop, as a global phenomenon, cannot be adequately understood with a lens too broadly aimed at the political economic dynamics of its global spread or too narrowly focused on its local identity politics. It is only by considering hip-hop as a *translocal* genre built upon local-to-local connections within a global context—rather than as a global, local, or even localized phenomenon—that we can fully tease out its complex dimensions. Perhaps most importantly, a translocal perspective helps us critically assess which boundaries remain untouched both in artists' conceptualizations of global hybridity and in scholarly discussions surrounding the genre. It helps us move beyond the recognition of hip-hop's hybrid nature to begin to tease out *which* hybridity gets privileged and *how* it matters. It helps us grasp, in other words, "*how* power works in concrete local settings" against the backdrop of global processes (Kraidy and Murphy, 2008, p. 351, emphasis in original). This case study demonstrates, in particular, that while recognizing hip-hop's productive potential, we must work to more fully address its possible contribution to globally distributed hegemonic conceptualizations of masculinity, femininity, and sexuality that powerfully intersect with racial, ethnic, and national identities on multiple levels.

The complex translocal dynamics permeating hip-hop's worldwide spread also illustrate the need to move beyond characterizations of transnational cultural influence couched in a simplistic dichotomy between the United States as the most influential global cultural producer and a homogenized "Rest." In order to further deconstruct such conceptualizations, the next chapter turns to Japan as a site of global cultural production. Comparing Japanese animation's powerful and complex impact on the French popular cultural scene to its trajectory into the U.S. context, it illustrates how analyses too narrowly focused on the U.S. experience result in dangerously essentializing characterizations of both "the West" and "Japan." It demonstrates the productive potential of decentralizing the United States' position as both a global cultural *producer* and as the taken-for-granted representative of "the West" in the *reception* of global culture.

// FIVE //

What West Is It? Anime and Manga according to *Candy* and *Goldorak*

Lord Ko, le dinosaure, deux balafres comme Albator

[Lord Ko[ssity] the dinosaur, two scars like Albator]
 —French rapper Lord Kossity, *Gladiator* (2001)

Japanese "cool" is traveling popularly and profitably around the world and insinuating itself into the everyday lives and fantasy desires of postindustrial kids from Taiwan and Australia to Hong Kong and France.
 —Allison, 2006, p. 5

If Japan's rise to economic superpower dominated U.S. academic discussions in the 1980s, the last 15 years or so have been marked by an intense fascination, both in academic and popular discourse, with the country's perceived increase in global cultural influence (see, for example, Faiola, 2003; Talbot, 2002). As *Pokémon* and *Hello Kitty* invaded U.S. TV screens and supermarket aisles at a time when, paradoxically, Japanese economic influence was on the decline, U.S. scholars (and a good number of Japanese officials) started to point to the emergence of a new kind of Japanese superpower. The discussion shifted from Japan's Gross National Product to its "Gross National Cool" (McGray, 2002). The characters in Japanese animated cartoon series (animation or *anime*) and in the related genre of *manga* (Japanese-style comic books or graphic novels), along with their videogame cousins, came to symbolize a new order in millennial capitalism characterized by a decline in U.S. cultural hegemony and the fragmentation of global powers (Allison, 2006). Thus, Japanese animation provides a logical starting point to an analysis aimed at decentralizing the role of the United States as the world's most significant global cultural producer.

This chapter will demonstrate, however, that while intending to point to Japan's growing influence and to a concomitant relative decline in U.S. power, the academic and popular discourse about Japanese animation's "global" popularity has paradoxically resulted in the re-centralizing of the United States as both a global cultural producer and a consumer of globalized cultural forms. Turning a translocal lens to the genre's transnational spread, this chapter illustrates the multiple ways in which this discourse is problematic. Throughout the chapter, the names of a few scholars will frequently reappear. These scholars are most assertively critiqued here not because their work is particularly problematic but, on the contrary, because they have produced the most comprehensive and sophisticated studies of Japanese animation and/or comics. Their works have become seminal texts in the academic study of Japanese popular culture in general and have greatly contributed to our understanding of its influence in the U.S. context. The chapter's deconstruction of these scholars' characterization of global processes is offered in an effort to illustrate the productive potential of a more translocal approach. It does not invalidate their otherwise positive contributions to the field of Japanese studies.

The chapter starts with a critique of the tendency to merge the United States with "the West" in studies of Japanese animation's global spread. It then turns to an analysis of the genre's voyage to France—drawing both from historical evidence and from interviews with media consumers—to illustrate the multiple ways in which its powerful intersection with the French popular cultural context differed from its influence in the United States. It concludes with a reflection on what we can learn theoretically from these differences about the nature of the global imagination and its significance for media consumers. It points, in particular, to the relatively unique position of the United States in relationship to "non-native" globalized popular cultural forms.

The Japanese term "anime" will frequently be used in the chapter as a shortcut for "Japanese animation." The Japanese term "manga" will be used to refer to Japanese comic books and to differentiate these texts from their European counterparts, generally known as *bandes dessinées* (or the abbreviated "BD"), and from U.S.-style comic books.

The West according to the United States

The academic discourse on Japanese animation's impact on "Western" cultural environments tends to remain dominated today by the works of U.S. critics—most of them cultural anthropologists, Asian studies scholars, and/ or individuals with a long-term engagement in the genre's fan subculture— and (to a lesser extent) by scholars of Japanese origin operating within an Anglo American academic setting. This is due in part to the fact that cultural studies in the United States and Britain has raised the status of popular culture to a higher level than in other academic contexts, resulting in a situation in which Japanese academia has yet to fully enter the conversation (Choo, 2008). The historical significance of Japan's relationship to the United States also partly explains this situation. While these works have contributed to our understanding of anime's cultural meaning in the Japanese context (see, for example, Napier, 2005, 2007; Poitras, 2008; Schodt, 1983, 1996, 2007) and of the significance of its entry into U.S. culture, their tendency to position the United States as representative of *all* of "the West" limits their usefulness when considering Japanese animation as a *global* genre (Berndt, 2008).

"America" and "the West" are frequently used interchangeably in discussions of anime's "global" spread. For example, after noting that the genre must convince "*American* children to adapt to its aesthetics," U.S. cultural historian Gary Cross continues with the observations that "*Western* children may embrace Japanese animation because it is 'foreign' and thus 'cool'" (2006, p. xviii, emphasis mine). In his description of its search for "an appreciative *Western* audience" cultural critic Shinobu Price notes that "anime has been appearing on major *U.S.* television networks since the 1960s" but that "the true crossover boom came in the early 80's when a new generation of *Americans*" began to appreciate it (2001, p. 160, emphasis mine). After observing that "Japanese animation was initially very hard to come by in the *West*," professor of Japanese literature and culture Susan Napier adds that "a few series . . . crossed into *American* television, but they were almost always *Americanized* beyond recognition" (2007, p. 134, emphasis mine).

More generally, these works tend to uncritically equate the cultural and historical trajectory of U.S. consumers' engagement with anime and/or manga with that of the rest of "the West." For example, when popular author Gilles Poitras suggests that "adult Westerners" are not familiar with Japanese animation and later contrasts Japanese texts to "the cartoons of their youth" (2008, p. 48), he is ignoring the fact that a rather large number of "adult Westerners" outside of the United States actually grew up on rather heavy doses of Japanese animation, as this chapter will soon demonstrate. Similarly, while Napier sets out to analyze the cultural significance of Japanese influence *in the mind of the West* (as suggested by the title of her book), her conclusion that "unlike the fan cultures existing around *Star Trek* or *Star Wars*, non-Japanese fans of anime are coalescing around a *non-domestic* fan product that *until quite recently did not even appear in English*" (2007, p. 136, emphasis mine) implies that the "non-Japanese" fans she is describing are in fact both American (*Star Trek* or *Star Wars* as "domestic" products) and English speakers.

These slippages on the part of U.S.-based scholars studying Japanese cultural production are understandable considering the fact that a similar merging between "the West" and "America" frequently happens in Japan. Unfortunately, this results in the development of a genealogy of Japanese animation's entry into "Western" cultural territory based on a rather limited and not particularly "representative" set of circumstances. This genealogy almost exclusively equates "Western" animation with Disney in its comparisons with Japanese productions (see, for example, Napier, 2005; MacWilliams, 2008; Poitras, 2008; Price, 2008), focuses only on the relatively small portion of texts that "made it" to the United States, and pinpoints Japanese animation's initial entry into "the West" to the 1960s (with such texts as *Speed Racer*, *Astro Boy*, and *Kimba, the White Lion*) but sees its apogee as taking place in the late 1980s and beyond (Patten, 2004).

While this genealogy may paint an accurate portrait of Japanese animation's relationship to U.S. popular culture and of the significance of U.S. fans' engagement with these texts, it fails to take into account the genre's different trajectory into other "Western," particularly non-English-speaking, environments, as well as in other parts of the world. This "crossing of the Pacific" version of anime's spread to "the West" must be problematized. A translocal comparison with the French popular cultural context helps us accomplish this goal.

A Different "West"

Contrasting anime's entry into the U.S. cultural context to its influx onto the French popular cultural scene quickly reveals differences that allow us to start deconstructing notions of the United States as representative of "the West." Most broadly, Japan's relationship to France is premised on a different set of historical circumstances than its relationship to the United States steeped in the legacy of its World War II defeat, of the psychologically marking events of the nuclear bombings of Hiroshima and Nagasaki, and of a postwar period marked by American occupation and concomitant cultural influence. The full details of the complex cultural outcome of these historical events have been outlined by numerous scholars (see, for example, Gordon, 1993; Iriye, 1967) and are beyond the scope of this book, but suffice it to note that the United States' shift from enemy to protector in the mind of the Japanese public followed a necessarily tortuous path that continues to mark these two nations' relationships. Similarly, Japan's economic rise in the 1980s was experienced differently in the United States than in other parts of the world. Anxieties in the United States over Japan's economic success—over the possibility that Japan may have after all "won the war" or "beaten America at its own game"— were so strong not only because they threatened the United States' global economic domination but, more profoundly, because they challenged the very core of American identity as the world's leader (Napier, 2007).

Japan's relationship to France has, in contrast, been relatively less antagonistic. If dread of the "yellow peril" certainly spread to France during World War II—and resurged to some extent in the 1980s—Hitler's Germany represented a much more immediate and alarming enemy whose presence on French soil powerfully contrasted with the remoteness of the war in the Pacific. Thus, as French cultural critic Anne Garrigue puts it, "Asia is today . . . a region that a majority of French nationals approach in a less confrontational or desperate manner than Africa, the Middle East or the United States" (2004, p. 15). It is a region, she adds, that "has always occupied a special place in *our imaginary*" (2004, p. 26, emphasis mine).

France's relationship to Japan is indeed marked by a long history of transnational borrowing epitomized by the *Japonisme* of 19th-century French writers and artists whose "fan culture" (they gathered over Japanese food and sake to admire woodcut prints, which many of them collected, and wrote sonnets of *haiku* inspiration) is reminiscent of the anime and manga fan activity Napier (2007) describes—a fact that, incidentally, she aptly recognizes. If this admiration for all things Japanese was tinted with Orientalism, it nevertheless had a remarkable impact on the development of French visual culture, an impact that set up the stage for the later influence of the highly visual genres of anime and manga.

Furthermore, because of the circumstances of its historical development, the French media landscape provided a much more amenable terrain to early anime's entry than the U.S. context. The destruction of the French infrastructure caused by World War II bombings and the German occupation resulted in a relatively later development of domestic television production and a later spread of television to a majority of French households. In 1950, television broadcasting only covered about 10 percent of the French territory, and French households owned a total of only about 3,500 sets. France's second television channel was inaugurated in 1964, its third (a local channel that did not cover the entire territory) in 1972, its fourth came only in 1984. All non-pay channels were public until 1986, and cable and satellite did not have a strong penetration until the late 1990s.

This resulted in a situation in which French television consumers growing up in the late 1970s and throughout the 1980s (the time, as we will soon see, of Japanese animation's intense penetration of the French media market) had access to a more limited set of viewing choices, mostly provided by the two largest (then) public channels, TF1 and Antenne 2, than viewers in the United States. If "by 1968 Japanese animation had become virtually unsalable in America" because "American studios were creating an increasing quantity of TV cartoons better tailored for American audiences" (Patten, 2004, p. 54), Japanese animation encountered little such "native" competition on the French market. France's comparatively weak position as a global cultural producer has meant that it has long been flooded with all sorts of foreign imports. The fact that quotas are still in place today to guarantee French cultural products a mere 35 to 40 percent share of the French audiovisual primetime landscape powerfully illustrates the scope of this foreign penetration.

Thus, despite the common stereotype of France as "a country not known for its generosity to non-native cultural products" (Napier, 2005, p. 5), French consumers are actually quite familiar with "non-native" fare. In addition to "native" texts such as French comedy films or Franco-Belgian comic books (*bandes dessinées* or BD's) and to the usual globally distributed Hollywood and Disney blockbusters, the media consumers I interviewed in France reminisced about growing up with (British) Enid Blyton books—as a man in his 40s put it, "my entire childhood was shaped by Enid Blyton"[1]—American and Australian TV series—"*Little House on the Prairie*, oh my, how I cried watching *Little House on the Prairie!*" (41-year-old woman)—Italian Westerns, German cop shows, and, of course, Japanese or Euro-Japanese animation.

Texts as diverse as the Japanese *City Hunter*, *Captain Tsubasa*, *Princess Sarah*, *Heidi* (both animated series), *Dragon Ball Z*, and *Power Rangers*, the Franco-Belgian *Asterix*, *Tintin*, *Boule et Bill*, *The Smurfs*, and *Largo Winch* (the comic book version), the French *Barbapapas*, *Mickey Magazine*, *Hélène et les Garçons*, and *Tom Tom et Nana*, the American *Batman*, *Scooby-Doo*, *MacGyver*, *Lost*, *X-Men*, *House, M.D.*, *CSI*, *Desperate Housewives*, *The A-Team*, and *Shrek*, and the Swedish *Pippi Longstocking*, along with Tim Burton and Miyazaki films (to mention just a few), all repeatedly came up in interviews. Older viewers might add *Candy*, *Goldorak*, *Ulysse 31*, *Saint Seiya*, *The Wild Wild West*, *The Avengers*, *Zorro*, *Maya l'Abeille*, *L'Ile aux Enfants*, and Woody Allen and Wong Kar-Wai films to the mix. A highly nonscientific survey conducted in early 2010 of the vast DVD aisle of the supermarket near the small town where I conducted fieldwork counted 18 non-French titles in its "top 20" recent DVDs. The DVD release of *Avatar* was quite an event for several weeks a few months later. In other words, the fact that France "in the mid 1990s carried over 30 hours a week of Japanese cartoons" (Napier, 2005, p. 5) rested in large part on these cartoons' intersection with an already hospitable cultural terrain and on a differently conditioned engagement with global popular cultural production than is found in the United States.

In addition, French media consumers' attitude toward Japanese cultural texts is shaped in part by France's complex relationship to U.S. popular culture whose highly popular nature raises the specter of cultural imperialism. In an essay comparing the cultural policies of the United States, Europe, and Japan, political scientist Harvey Feigenbaum reminds us of the relatively unique position held by the United States vis-à-vis transnational cultural influence. Noting that "every member of UNESCO voted in favor of the Universal Declaration on Cultural Diversity, with the sole exceptions of the United States and Israel"

(2007, p. 374, emphasis mine), he suggests that "for Europeans, and others, the ubiquity of American popular culture is at best a mixed blessing, and to most represents one of the major liabilities of globalization" (2007, p. 375). Thus, as Garrigue contends, engagement with Japanese anime or manga can serve as "a form of resistance to American cultural hegemony" (2004, p. 114) on the part of French media consumers.

Anime's Voyage to France

The differences between France's and the United States' historical and cultural relationships to Japan (and to each other) have resulted in tangible differences in the way anime and manga came to influence these two contexts. First of all, while Napier suggests that the 1989 release of Katsuhiro Otomo's *Akira* "in many ways can be seen as the film that started the anime boom in the West" (2005, p. 41), the first major wave of culturally influential Japanese animation—France's "anime boom"—actually hit France a full 10 years earlier. It came with the broadcasting of two highly influential texts: Toei Animation's *Goldorak* (*UFO Robot Grendizer* in Japanese) first aired on July 3, 1978—less than 18 months after it finished airing on the Japanese Fuji TV—and the hugely globally popular *shôjo* (girl) anime *Candy* (*Candy Candy*) on September 18 of the same year, before it finished airing on NET TV (now TV Asahi) in Japan. Both were broadcast as part of (the French public channel) Antenne 2's children's program *Récré A2*. Both were inspired by popular manga (the *Candy* manga was published in France in 1982).

Due in part to the scarcity of programming targeted at a younger audience on French television at the time, these two texts enjoyed an immediate phenomenal success. *Goldorak* was so popular that it landed on the cover of the French news magazine *Paris Match* under the heading *La Folie* Goldorak [The Goldorak Madness] on January 5, 1979. Both programs were constantly rerun through the mid-1990s, and their cultural significance cannot easily be overstated (Hermelin, 2000). As a male informant in his 40s recalled: "*Goldorak*, I knew it was Japanese because everyone talked about it when it first came out." To this day, the generation who grew up in the late 1970s and early 1980s is frequently referred to in France as "la génération *Goldorak*" [the Goldorak generation] (Garrigue, 2004). When the digitally re-mastered unedited version of the first 12 episodes of the series was released on DVD in late May 2013, it quickly made it to the number 1 slot in national sales despite its rather steep price tag of €34.99.

Regardless of their age, the French media consumers I interviewed were all familiar with these two texts. When reminiscing about this first wave of Japanese animation, and some of the other series that quickly followed, their

Fig. 1. *Goldorak* was the best-selling video throughout France in early June 2013 (photo taken by the author at a local supermarket).

typical first reaction was to burst into a rendition of their theme songs—I can myself still recall all of the lyrics of the French version of *Candy*'s opening song (titled *Au Pays de Candy* [*In Candy's Country*—which, incidentally, refers to the United States]) as well as those of other classics. Those who had been part of *Candy*'s and *Goldorak*'s original target audience remembered them as the most influential programs they had watched in their youth: "our generation, it's *Candy* and *Goldorak*" explained a 40-year-old woman. "If I must cite one [show] that made me, ah! . . . that provoked emotions in me, it's *Candy*! I watched the whole thing . . . from when they find her baby in the basket until . . . when she's a nurse afterwards. Yes, from the beginning to the end."

These media consumers, now in their mid-30s to early 40s, fondly reminisced about *Goldorak*'s powerful "fulguropoing" [which might be loosely translated as *lightningfist*]—"Goldorak was great! The lightningfist! (33-year-old man). "Goldorak, yes, the lightningfist!" (40-year-old woman)—and the transforming robot's other numerous impressive attributes: "There was the lightningfist, his fist shot off, that was really something! He transformed into a space ship . . . and you could buy the figurine that you put into the space ship and there was the head, Goldorak's head that stuck out. Goldorak, I'm telling you, that was quite a machine, not your average kitchen appliance!" (37-year-old man).

They also identified these shows as significant contributors to their cultural identity. As the man quoted above concluded: "*Goldorak*, it's universal. You can ask my brother, you can ask all the kids I lived with [his family was a host family for disadvantaged children in the summers], that's it . . . the glue at the base of culture. Because in the end, that's what we're talking about here, culture." Other scholars' discussions with French media consumers have prompted similar comments—as when a young woman explained in an interview with Garrigue: "*Candy* and *Goldorak* marked my generation. When I was six years old, I followed these almost traumatizing, dramatic, intense stories with passion. In our eyes it was much stronger than Walt Disney" (2004, p. 126).

These shows' success quickly led to a genuine tsunami of Japanese shows, particularly those produced by Toei Animation, on the French popular cultural scene. In 1980, the space pirate *Albator* (mentioned by rapper Lord Kossity in this chapter's opening quote) possibly surpassed *Goldorak* in popularity, particularly among the female audience, with his flowing long hair, "virile attitude" (40-year-old woman), and the famous scar—"he was beautiful with his scar" (32-year-old woman)—that marked his angular facial features. He was quickly followed by *Capitaine Flam* (*Captain Future*) in 1981 and countless others too numerous to mention. While some of these early imports were "Goldorakesque" science fiction shows, others—including Isao Takahata and Hayao Miyazaki's *Heidi* (*Arupusu no Shôjo Haiji*), which started airing in France in December 1978, Yoshihirô Kuroda and Fumio Kurokawa's *Bouba le Petit Ourson* (*Seton Dôbutsuki Kuma no ko Jacky*) in 1981, and Osamu Dezaki's *Remi sans Famille* (*Ie Naki Ko Remi*) based on a well-known French novel by Hector Malot, and Hiroshi Saitô's *Tom Sawyer* in 1982—drew from different corners of Japanese anime's vast repertoire. Yet others, such as *San Ku Kai* (broadcast in 1979 in both France and Japan) and *X-Or* (broadcast in Japan in 1982 and in France in 1983), while not animated (they featured live Japanese actors) resonated with the early science fiction animation in their themes and overall aesthetic.

From then on, different waves of Japanese texts were to follow, each marking a generation of French youths in slightly different ways. Thus, following "the Goldorak generation" of those growing up in the late 1970s and early 1980s, Garrigue (2004, p. 124) identifies the "Chevaliers du Zodiaque (*Saint Seiya*) generation" (late 1980s) and the "Dragon Ball Z generation" (1990s and beyond). In line with this characterization, the French satellite channel *Manga* advertised in late 2009 its upcoming programming of *Albator*, *Flo et les Robinson Suisses* (The Swiss Family Robinson), *Ranma ½*, *Olive et Tom* (Captain Tsubasa), and *Dragon Ball Z* by claiming that it "remains the channel of all generations."

Aside from their relatively early arrival when compared to the spread of culturally influential anime and manga to the United States, these texts are significant in that they differ from the texts typically identified as the "seminal" texts of Japanese anime's voyage to "the West"—*Speed Racer*, *Astro Boy*, and *Kimba, the White Lion*, followed, for a later generation more consciously engaged with the genre, by *Akira*, *Ghost in the Shell*, *Neon Genesis Evangelion*, the later Miyazaki films (*Princess Mononoke*, *Spirited Away*), and the lighter *Pokémon* and *Yugi-oh*. In fact, many of these shows—including *Goldorak* and *Candy*—were not shown as full stand-alone series in the United States[2] and are, consequently, generally ignored by U.S. scholars who fail to recognize their influence not only in France but also throughout Europe, Africa, and Latin America.[3] Discussions of the works of the extremely popular (among scholars as well as audiences) Hayao Miyazaki typically fail, for instance, to mention—other than occasionally in passing (see, for example, Drazen, 2003, p. 257)—that he was involved in the *Heidi* project along with his current Studio Ghibli partner Isao Takahata.

Equally disturbing is the fact that U.S. scholars frequently miss these texts' significance in the *Japanese* context. In May 2009, a TV Asahi special claiming to have 10,000 respondents ranked *Heidi* number one "favorite childhood anime" among Japanese female viewers (Cooper-Chen, 2010). In 2005, the Ghibli museum in Tokyo had a major exhibit on the show that detailed its creation, included many of its early drawings and sketches, and featured photographs of Takahata and Miyazaki posing near the house that served as the inspiration for the home of Heidi's grandfather during a research trip to Switzerland—all this despite the fact that the show was produced for another animation studio. Heidi and her friends from the series were even given their own postage stamps by the Japanese postal system (Arupsu no shôjo Haiji no kitte [Girl from the Alps stamp], 2013) in January 2013.

Like their French counterparts, the Japanese media consumers I interviewed fondly recalled watching *Candy Candy*, *Captain Tsubasa* (*Olive et Tom*), *Captain Harlock* (*Albator*), *Heidi*, and the numerous other shows that were part of the Nippon Animation "World Masterpiece Theater" (*Sekai Meisaku Gekijô*) series. Lasting for 28 seasons from 1969 to 1997 and resumed in 2007, the series features works inspired by famous European and North American literary texts, including (in addition to *Heidi* and *Remi sans Famille*) such classics as *Little Princess* (*Shôkôjo Sêra/Princess Sarah*), *Tom Sawyer*, *Anne of Green Gables* (*Akage no Anne*), *Little Women* (*Ai no Wakasu Monogatari*), and *A Dog of Flanders* (*Furandâsu no Inu*). They, too, frequently broke into song when reminiscing about their childhood engagement with these texts.

Like their French counterparts, those old enough to have been part of the "*Candy* generation" identified it as a cultural reference point: "When I was young, there was *Candy Candy*, the manga. There was also the anime" (41-year-old woman). When I explained to one of them that I was going to ask her about the shows she watched while growing up, her response was "All the way from *Candy Candy*?" Another wanting me to clarify (in a different interview) what I meant by "shows she watched while growing up" asked, "like *Candy Candy*?" Even those too young (or too male!) to remember watching *Candy* often nevertheless had a relationship with it: "It was popular when I was very small. And *Candy Candy* had a special box in the show and my mother bought me that box. That's what I remember. I was too young to remember the show" (30-year-old female); "In my house, my older sister watched it, so I've seen it a few times" (39-year-old male). Again, the cultural significance (global and otherwise) of these texts is difficult to overstate.

From *Candy* to *Totally Spies!*: Localizing Japanese Texts (and "Japonizing" French ones)

These differences between the French and U.S. cultural landscapes have more generally resulted in anime's influence being negotiated quite differently in these two contexts. While scholars in the United States identify Japanese animation as progressing from relatively "culturally odorless" texts (Iwabuchi, 2002)—such as *Speed Racer* or even the early version of *Pokémon* from which references to Japan were carefully erased—to more culturally marked products consumed at least in part for their "Japaneseness" (Allison, 2006), anime and manga in France were quickly localized on different axes and in particularly complex ways. Or, to put it differently, they developed a different kind of hybridity.

While the early seminal texts of anime's entry into the French cultural context may be seen as fairly culturally neutral, at least as far as Japanese culture is concerned—Candy is a young *American* girl, Goldorak is a war machine and his pilot is, technically, an alien, Albator wanders somewhere through space in his pirate ship—these texts unmistakably adhere to the highly marked aesthetic of classic Japanese animation. Candy flaunts a prototypical 1970s *shôjo* (girl) *manga* look, while Goldorak draws from the equally recognizable tradition of Japanese robot/transformer/superheroes from outer space (his "color scheme" and "facial features" are reminiscent of Ultra Man's, and he is constantly fighting dragon-like robotic monsters). In other words, while these texts are not ostensibly set in a Japanese context and do not propose to "represent" aspects of Japanese culture—there are subtle references to Japanese daily life in *Goldorak* (such as when the characters eat onigiri) but these are mixed in with loads of references to other cultural environments—they are strongly *visually* marked as Japanese or, at least, different. As one French media consumer in her 20s explained, "*Goldorak* and all that, they didn't have the same look [*pas la même tête*] as the other cartoons" or, as a 46-year-old woman similarly recalled, "I think that we started to realize where cartoons came from when the Japanese entered the production scene [. . .] First of all, it was a new graphic style, and also, a new generation of cartoons that didn't look like what we had seen until then."

French media consumers came to associate these texts' visual features—color scheme, lines, editing—with their Japanese origin. As a 40-year-old female informant recalled, "I think that I knew that when they had big eyes, it was Japanese, because there was a particular drawing style [*un graphisme particulier*]. . . . Yes, *Candy*, *Goldorak*, I knew it was Japanese. . . . It was in relationship to the graphic elements that we could recognize that." Thus, as French cultural critic François Hermelin puts it, "For years, starting at the end of the 1970s, the Japanese cartoon series [*séries de dessins animés japonais*] that poured onto the European airwaves prepared the younger generation for the stereotypes of the Japanese genre" (2000, p. 142). These distinctive features are still easily identifiable today—as a 19-year-old man explained, "They don't have the same eyes . . . They have big eyes, the Japanese [characters] they have big round eyes"—even though they have been adapted to a variety of non-Japanese texts: "Now [the animated series] *Totally Spies!*, they do the same kind of thing, even though it is French"[4] (40-year-old woman).

Furthermore, because of limited production budgets, visual elements pointing to anime's Japanese origins could not always be erased when the genre first entered the French cultural context. As a *Goldorak* viewer in his 40s recalled, "When they went places . . . it was written in Japanese, and that is something that impressed me, because if they went to a store and picked up a can or something, it was written in Japanese on it." Japanese writing in kanji and kana (the two sets of characters used to write Japanese) appeared in titles, credits, or in the opening scenes of these early shows. As a 42-year-old woman explained, "In the ending credits you had [Japanese] characters. Even in the titles, there was writing in Japanese underneath [the French translation], I remember . . ." Songs in Japanese punctuated *Heidi*'s most emotionally charged moments. In a particularly interesting twist for French viewers, the maps of *France* used in *Remi sans Famille* to follow the hero and his companions' travels throughout the country were labeled in katakana (the Japanese set of characters used to identify words of foreign origin). These subtle references to the Japanese cultural context created a form of visual and aural hybridity independent of the texts' (often already quite hybrid) scripted narrative.

These texts' status as cultural phenomena also rested, however, on their successful integration into the broader French cultural context. This was accomplished in part through a process of localization that involved the inclusion of opening and ending songs in French marketed as separate texts and sung by well-known artists. Chantal Goya, who marked a generation of French children with her cheery pop songs (many of them written by her famous singer-songwriter husband Jean-Jacques Debout), performed the theme songs of *Capitaine Flam* (*Captain Future*), *Bouba le Petit Ourson* (*Seton Dôbutsuki Kuma no Ko Jacky*), and *Les Quatres Filles du Docteur March* (*Ai no Wakasu Monogatari/Little Women*). Dorothée (a close friend of Goya's) performed a reworked version of *Candy*'s opening song when the show re-ran on her program *Club Dorothée* in 1987. As a result, informants too young to recall *Candy*'s or *Goldorak*'s initial entry into the French media market frequently commented in interviews that they "remembered the music better than the show."

These singers' performances served to intertextually link Japanese animation to other elements of the French popular cultural scene. Perhaps most significantly, Dorothée hosted Antenne 2's *Récré A2* (the show that brought *Candy* and *Goldorak* to the French market) from 1978 to 1987, when she moved to TF1 to host *Club Dorothée*. Thus, as illustrated in the songs of the French rappers discussed in chapter 4, most media consumers growing up in France between the late 1970s and the late 1990s (*Club Dorothée* went off the air in 1997) encountered Japanese animation through the culturally specific experience of watching one of these shows.[5] It is an experience they recall with much fondness, as in the exchange below worth quoting at length as it illustrates both Dorothée's importance and anime's omnipresence.

When asked to recall the shows that were most important to them when growing up, three women and one man, all in their early 20s, replied:

BRIGITTE: *Dorothée.*

CHRISTINE: That's exactly what I was going to say!

ANNE: The *Club Dorothée*. I was a member of the club so, at the end, when they ran the credits, at the end they put on the birthdays . . .

DAVID (SPEAKING AT THE SAME TIME): The birthdays!

ANNE: And so, my birthday went on . . .

CHRISTINE: No way! . . .

BRIGITTE [TO ME]: Because she had registered.

ANNE: Yes, I was registered with the club and I had received their letter and after each episode at the end of the *Club Dorothée* they put the names of all the participants and the date of their birthdays and they put my birthday on.

DAVID: Yes, the birthdays! The ending credits lasted forever!

FABIENNE (TO DAVID): Did you watch *Club Dorothée?*

DAVID: Of course, they showed *Dragon Ball*[6] and *Olive et Tom (Captain Tsubasa)*.

BRIGITTE: Oh yes! *Olive et Tom!*

CHRISTINE: I watched *Princess Sarah*.

ANNE: Oh yes! Me too!

DAVID: Nicky Larson [from the manga Shitîhantâ—City Hunter].

BRIGITTE: I watched *Princess Sarah, Sailor Moon*.

CHRISTINE: Me too, I loved it!

Everyone under the age of 40 with whom I had a conversation on the topic had similar reactions: "Dragon Ball Z, I watched Dragon Ball Z, it was aired on *Club Dorothée*, that was something *Club Dorothée!*" (37-year-old male); "First [I watched] *Récré A2*, then *Club Dorothée*. (. . .) there was Goldorak, Goldorak, that I remember. (. . .) *Les Filles du Docteur March* [Ai no Wakasu Monogatari/Little Women], and *Princess Sarah*, a little later" (33-year-old female); "The *Club Dorothée* showed a lot of cartoons. There was *Candy, Remi sans Famille* . . ." (33-year-old male), "It was *Goldorak, Albator*, in other words, it was *Dorothée!* [C'était Doroteé quoi!]" (40-year-old male).

If Dorothée's programs did broadcast heavy doses of Japanese animation they also aired, however, a lot of other things—the French-produced *Boule et Bill, Bibifoc, Johan et Pirlouit*, and *Clémentine*, the American *Fantastic Four, Masters of the Universe, George of the Jungle, Thundercats*, and *Spiderman*, to name only a few. Furthermore, the immediate early success of *Goldorak* and *Candy* quickly prompted the development of numerous Franco-Japanese or Euro-Japanese co-productions that further blurred and complicated anime's cultural origins. The 1981 Franco-Japanese *Ulysse 31* loosely inspired, as its name suggests, by Homer's *Odyssey* and the 1983 Franco-Luxembourgian-Japanese series *Les Mystérieuses Cités d'Or (Taiyō no Ko Esuteban)* relating the travels of a young Spanish boy to the New World in 1532 (it aired in Japan on the educational NHK public channel) were most frequently mentioned in interviews. Both are still quite popular today, due in part to the fact that parents like to introduce their children to these highly influential texts. As one father explained, "I really liked *Ulysse 31*, and in fact, I introduced [my daughter] to it, I have the whole series, from the first to the last episode. [. . .] The *Cités d'Or* also, we know it all," to which his daughter added, "I have the theme song!" One informant even suggested that a young boy named Esteban who attended the village's school was named after the *Cités d'Or*'s main character (the show was still airing on French television in the summer of 2014).

Thus, Japanese animation entered the French media market as one element of a large repertoire of native, non-native, and co-produced texts. As *Tom Sawyer*, *Capitaine Flam*, and *La Chanson de Candy* joined such diverse titles as *Bécassine*, *C'est Guignol*, *Comme Tintin*, *Babar*, *Bravo Popeye*, *Allons Chanter avec Mickey* [Let's Go Sing with Mickey], *Snoopy*, *Mon Pinocchio*, *Les Schtroumpfs* [The Smurfs], *The Little Ewoks* (yes, the ones from *Star Wars*), and the theme songs for Disney's *Davy Crockett* or *Rox et Rouky* (*The Fox and the Hound*), in the repertoires of Dorothée and Chantal Goya, anime's hugely popular characters joined a hybrid cast of global and local icons.

When *Candy* Met *Asterix*: *Bandes Dessinées* as a Vector of Manga's Penetration

In the case of manga (which started to be distributed en masse in France in the 1990s) this process was further facilitated by the huge popularity and cultural influence of *bandes dessinées* (BD)—the much-celebrated Franco-Belgian comic books—that created a particularly favorable cultural terrain for the reception of the genre. Indeed, ever since the 1929 arrival of Tintin, the young Belgian reporter, on the Francophone popular cultural scene—followed by the Franco-Belgian *Spirou et Fantasio* in 1938, *Lucky Luke* in 1946, *Gason Lagaffe* in 1957, and the legendary Gaulois *Astérix et Obélix* in 1959 (whose magic-potion-induced resistance to Roman domination and encounters with such mythical figures as Julius Caesar and Cleopatra have made them some of the most globally famous "French" citizens despite the fact that their story takes place before France existed as a nation)—*bandes dessinées* have become an integral part of France's cultural identity. It is also a celebrated component of Francophone global cultural capital.

The fact that two of the three floors of the small community library I frequently visit when in France (located in a village of approximately 1,200 inhabitants) are dedicated to *bandes dessinées* and other graphic novels from around the globe—I found Jiro Taniguchi and Natsuo Sekikawa's excellent historical manga series *The Times of Botchan* there—provides an anecdotal illustration of the genre's importance. So does the fact that the original artwork for the cover of *Tintin en Amérique* [*Tintin in America*], the third volume of the *Adventures of Tintin* series published in 1932, recently sold for 1.3 million Euros at an auction in Paris (Lévêques and Johnny, 2012).

With comments such as "I had a neighbor friend whose father had all of [the *Tintin* and *Asterix*] [. . .] and it's thanks to her that I read them all—I didn't own all of them, but I have read them all" (40-year-old woman); "I didn't have a lot of them at home, but I got some from my cousins" (43-year-old man); "I visited people who had adolescent children and they read a lot of *Asterix* and *Obelix*, or *Gaston Lagaffe*, so it made it easy because they lent us their books" (37-year-old man); "[Our daughters] are very much into BD's right now. They started with the ones we had at home, with *Asterix*," (42-year-old mother); and "there are so many BD's, I can't even tell you which ones [I read the most]" (13-year-old girl), the French media consumers I interviewed illustrated the extent to which *bandes dessinées* were simply an unavoidable feature of growing up in France.[7]

As a result, French informants *all* remembered reading *bandes dessinées* in their youth—*Tintin, Asterix, Gaston Lagaffe, Lucky Luke, Iznogoud, Les Schtroumpfs, Yoko Tsuno, Les Tuniques Bleues*, but also more "adult" fare such as *Le Cinquième Evangile, Le Génie des Alpages*, and *Rubrique à Brac*—and, often, U.S. comics as well. As a 33-year-old man recalled, "my sister loved the Marvels. So, I ended up reading them all because she had a lot of them. So there was Spiderman and the entire Wolverine team, Captain America and all of that . . ." Many continued to read them into adulthood—as a 43-year-old man quoted above added: "I'm in the process of buying them all again."

Perhaps because *bandes dessinées* are more similar to Japanese manga than to American comics in their stylistic and thematic diversity (which ranges from science fiction and fantasy in texts such as *Yoko Tsuno, Lanfeust de Troy*, and *La Quête de l'Oiseau du Temps* to youth-oriented fare such as *The Smurfs*) and also because they are targeted to and read by adults as well as younger audiences, manga quickly resonated with French audiences. As Hermelin contends, "[manga's] popularity can no doubt be explained by the presence of a style common to these genres" (2000, p. 140; see also Garrigue, 2004, p. 110). Manga also offer a convenient, relatively cheaper alternative to the hardbound *bandes dessinées* that are released less frequently and sell for about €10 ($12 to $15) each.

As a result, manga integrated relatively easily into the French media market. In fact, France is one of the largest markets for the sale of manga outside Japan, bringing in 50 percent of all European sales (Davidson, 2012). While the distinctive aesthetic qualities of the Japanese texts are generally recognized, however, manga are not necessarily perceived in France—as is the tendency among U.S. fans (Napier, 2005, 2007)—as an entirely separate category. Manga are now exhibited at the Frankfurt international book fair and celebrated at the Angoulême festival, the "Mecca of Franco-Belgian BD" (Garrigue, 2004, p. 109). Even at the production level, manga and Franco-Belgian *bande dessinée* are becoming increasingly linked. For example, French cartoonist Frédéric Boilet's Nouvelle Manga movement "aligns like-minded creators of *bande dessinée* (BD) and *manga* under one conceptual banner" (Vollmar, 2007, p. 34) and encourages French and Japanese artists to collaborate (see also Boilet, 2006). In sharp contrast to the clearly dichotomized treatment of foreign and domestic production in the cultural policies of the French government, the consumption of manga and anime has come to represent one (important) dimension of French consumers' multidimensional engagement with global cultural production.

Anime and U.S. Academic Cultural Imperialism

Aside from challenging the stereotype of France as a culturally arrogant nation closed to outside influences, the differences between anime and manga's encounters with the French and U.S. cultural contexts point to the dangers of assuming that the Anglo-American experience of (trans)cultural negotiation matches that of the rest of the West.

On the most basic level, this assumption leads to inaccuracies in the assessment of the possible factors of influence that might have led to anime and manga's popularity in "the West." For instance, the common argument that anime's "far more open approach to sex and nudity" (Napier, 2007, p. 135)—which, according to Price is *"from a Western* perspective, certainly one of [its] most *shocking* features" (2001, p. 159, emphasis mine)—had an important impact (both negative and positive) on the genre's initial reception in "the West," does not fully apply to the fairly large portions of "the West" where sex and nudity are approached in a much more open manner (both visually and culturally) than in the United States.[8]

Similarly, the notion that anime provides an antidote to the formulaic happy endings of "Western" texts and allows "Western" audiences "to 'break the rules' of Western culture, to go beyond the Hollywood happy endings, or the need for a defined good and evil" (Napier, 2007, p. 204) may apply to parts of the U.S. audience. It does not adequately explain, however, the genre's attraction for the large portion of the "Western" audience for whom ambiguity and non-happy endings—including in texts targeted at younger audiences—are more culturally resonant. I was recently reminded, for instance, of the uncomfortably unsettling ending of Antoine de Saint-Exupéry's much celebrated *Le Petit Prince*, read by most French children as they enter third grade (and highly popular in Japan) when, incidentally, reading its graphic novel version (found in the public library described above) with my children. Remi tragically loses most of his companions in the course of his coming-of-age voyage through France in both the French novel and the Japanese animated series. Hollywood and Disney, while certainly globally influential, are not the only "Western" texts available to worldwide audiences.

This positioning of the United States as the natural representative of "the West" ignores the experiences and cultural contributions of non-U.S. (particularly non-English speaking) "Westerners" and essentializes both "the West" and Japan. As values most closely associated with U.S. culture are uncritically attributed to all of "the West"—as when Yamanaka contrasts Miyazaki's texts with the Calvinist ethic of rugged individualism, which he links to the United States but describes as "the Western model" (2008, p. 245)—"Western culture" is treated as if it were a singular homogenized entity (see, for example, Napier, 2005, 2007).

Perhaps more disturbingly, failing to compare anime and manga to a broader set of transnational cultural references results in a limited understanding of their significance as *Japanese* genres. Too close a focus on the U.S. context produces descriptions that "tend to reinforce exoticism and neonationalism" (Berndt, 2008, p. 297) by characterizing anime and manga as unique and peculiar.

Because anime consumption in the United States developed as a fan activity initially "very closely intertwined with the SF and comics fandoms from which it has grown" (Patten, 2004, p. 57; see also Cooper-Chen, 2010), U.S. consumers' engagement with the genre is generally more exclusive than in France or Japan—and, as noted above, not quite as widespread. Cultural critic Henri Jenkins' description of manga and anime's entrance into the U.S. market "through small distributors who targeted Asian immigrants" and of its spread through "fans [who] would venture into ethnic neighborhoods in search of content" or "start their own small-scale (and sometimes pirate) operations" (2011, p. 550) powerfully contrasts with *Goldorak*'s or *Candy*'s spectacular and very public (remember the *Paris Match* cover) entry onto the French popular cultural scene.

The relatively narrow focus on a more "culturally fragrant" repertoire—which typically does not include anime and manga's engagement with European or North American cultural productions (*Heidi, Tom Sawyer, Remi, Anne of Green Gables*)—further amplifies the tendency to characterize these genres as exotic and different. Price concludes, for instance, that "the way anime uses its medium of animation is so *fundamentally different* from the artistic tradition of Walt Disney, that it creates a *freshly intriguing aroma that lures foreigners* into its mist [sic]" (2001, p. 166, emphasis mine). Napier contends that "anime, at least until very recently, has been uncompromisingly true to its Japanese roots" (2007, p. 5). Celebrated manga aficionado and popular author Frederik Schodt claims that manga are "an open window onto the Japanese id, a view—not necessarily of reality itself—but of a culture's aspirations, dreams, nightmares, fantasies, and fetishes" (2008, p. vii).

This positioning of anime and manga as both highly distinctive and "representative" of Japanese culture powerfully resonates with the nationalist discourse on Japanese uniqueness promoted in Japan by conservative politicians and critics. Jacqueline Berndt, a German-born scholar who teaches at Yokohama National University, challenges such claims of "national particularity" (2008, p. 305). She warns, however, that "from a foreign perspective it is easy to repeat this position without realizing its essential conservatism" (2008, p. 305; see also Vollmar, 2007). This positioning also obscures the presence of more prosaic non-cultural factors contributing to the Japanese genres' global popularity.

Indeed, if fans' engagement with anime and manga certainly facilitated their global spread (Leonard, 2005), the facts that their exportation turned out to be highly economically viable and that the Japanese government has come to recognize them as significant tools of Japanese transnational influence—as illustrated by the Japanese Ministry of Education prize established in 1990 (Kinko, 2008)—are equally significant. In a move that he qualifies as a case of "soft nationalism," Asian and Religious studies scholar Mark MacWilliams notes, for instance, that since the Iraq war, the Japan foundation has made the broadcasting of the *Captain Tsubasa* (*Olive et Tom* in French) series—highly popular as *Captain Majed* in the Middle East since the 1990s—on Iraqi national television "one of the key priorities of its cultural diplomacy" (2008, pp. 15, 16). The Japanese coalition forces even obtained permission to put *Captain Tsubasa* stickers on their trucks. As he concludes, "In effect, Captain Tsubasa as 'Captain Majed' became an important part of the Japanese government's public relations campaign to propagandize its reconstruction efforts. . . . Here, Japanimation is used as a cipher of Japanese identity" (2008, p. 16). Political scientist Peng Er Lam similarly locates the use of manga and anime as "instruments of global outreach and appeal" within a larger effort on the part of the Japanese government to promote "a cheerful 'Japan Cool' thesis" (2007, pp. 353, 352) seeking to burnish Japan's international image (see also Condry, 2009).

Pointing to the fact that anime and manga constitute "an extraordinary successful culture industry," Berndt also reminds us that their characterization as specifically Japanese, in what she deems a form of "'economic Japaneseness,'" powerfully serves the business interests of Japanese producers (2008, p. 299). In a similar vein, Casey Brienza argues in an article in *Publishing Research Quarterly* that manga's recent popularity in the United States has more to do with a shift in publishing and distribution practices than with a sudden infatuation with Japanese culture. Critiquing current research for "relying extensively upon nebulous notions of textual exceptionalism and/or emphasizing Japan's unique talent for the creation of escapist fantasies with cross-cultural appeal," she suggests that the publishing industry's decision to migrate manga "from the comics field into the book field" (2009, p. 104) by redefining them as "graphic novels" to be sold in non-specialized stores is a better explanation for their growth in market share. While such factors are certainly not the only explanation for manga and anime's popularity, they point to the need to develop a more nuanced understanding of the articulation of different dimensions of the genre responsible for its global spread.

Unfortunately, the tendency to remain strictly focused on Japan and the United States as the two main axes on which manga and anime's status is considered results in a rather limited portrayal of global power dynamics. Japanese influence becomes an antidote to the alleged homogenizing nature of U.S.-dominated globalization: "In a world where American domination of mass culture is often taken for granted and local culture is frequently seen as either at odds with or about to be subsumed into hegemonic globalism, anime stands out as a site of implicit cultural resistance," writes Napier (2005, p. 9). Noting that "when Disney held the international monopoly on entertainment, 'globalization' was synonymous with 'Americanization,'" MacWilliams argues that "'Japanization' is now a dominant transnational economic and cultural force" (2008, p. 13). In her otherwise compelling study of Japanese characters' entry into the global imagination, cultural anthropologist Anne Allison similarly concludes: "At work here is a new kind of global imagination: new, at least, in the way it differs from an older model of Americanization" (2006, p. 275). A more translocal approach points to a more interesting phenomenon.

Anime and Manga's Multiple Resonances

Because, like hip-hop, anime and manga are globally linked to a vast array of cultural texts, considering them solely in terms of their ability to provide the world with "a window to Japan" (Poitras, 2008, p. 65)—just as considering contemporary global hip-hop solely in relationship to African American culture—does not do justice to their complexity. On a global scale, anime and manga might resonate with audiences in different cultural environments not only because they promote some sort of universal human values, as some scholars argue (see, for example, Yoshioka, 2008), but also because they resonate on different levels with a variety of elements in a given popular cultural context, including, but not limited to, "native" ones.

Indeed, the anime versions of *Heidi*, *Remi sans Famille* (*Ie Naki Ko Remi*), and *Belle et Sébastien* (*Meiken Jorii*) resonated with French audiences in part because they were based on familiar French or European children's literature—as a woman in her 50s put it, "They were from *our own books*." They also represented environments intimately familiar to French viewers. With comments such as "*Heidi*, it was—quote and quote—'our mountains'" (42-year-old woman); "*Heidi* it was for me, so faithful to our own lives, I mean for me, I lived in the Alps, in the mountains, it was so faithful to the Alps, the Alpine pasture" (32-year-old woman); or "I spent much of my childhood among the cows and the herds, and because there were [in *Remi sans Famille*] cows, fairs, people trading things and everything, you found yourself [in that universe] and you told yourself 'yes, it corresponds to the model'" (39-year-old male), informants suggested that these texts represented their *own* lives. As a result, they sometimes found it difficult to reconcile these representations with the texts' Japanese origin—as the 42-year-old woman quoted above put it, "I had trouble projecting it elsewhere."

Thus, the most interesting aspect of anime and manga is the extent to which they are able to blur cultural origin and loosen the requirements of cultural representation. As Japanese studios offer their animated versions of popular American and European literature and locate their quintessentially *shôjo* manga in foreign settings (as in *Candy* and the hugely popular *Rose of Versailles* [*Lady Oscar* in French] set in France at the time of the revolution), as Belgian artist Roger Leloup chooses to make his main character, Yoko Tsuno, Japanese in his famous 1969 science-fiction *bande dessinée*, as Japanese artists and French and Luxembourgian directors collaborate to tell the story of a young Spanish boy's 16th-century voyage to Latin America (*Les Mystérieuses Cités d'Or*/*Taiyô no Ko Esuteban*), they break down the boundaries of cultural representation.

When French viewers watch *Candy*, they, consequently, are not only engaging with foreign culture through their consumption of a text that is clearly visually marked as Japanese (and part of the larger specifically Japanese category of *shôjo* manga/anime) but also through their consumption of an exoticized (Japanese) version of America—the opening lines of the first episode state that the story takes place "on the shores of Lake Michigan." For a generation of French television viewers (of which I am part), *Tom Sawyer* is first and foremost the main (American) character of a Japanese anime text rather than the hero of a Mark Twain novel. And the aforementioned *Totally Spies!*— popular both in the United States and Japan—can draw from Japanese anime in its overall visual aesthetic, situate its main characters in a United States context (the three "spies" live in Beverly Hills), and be popularized as a French series all at the same time.

Thus, Napier is correct when she positions anime "at the forefront of creating an alternative cultural discourse that goes beyond the traditional categories of 'native' or 'international' to participate in what may well be a genuinely new form of global culture" (2005, p. 292). As she notes, this "global culture" has less to do with geography than with a broader engagement with an *imagined* global scape. When the French-language version of the Japanese *Tom Sawyer* anime series' opening song states that "Tom Sawyer, c'est l'Amérique, le symbole de la liberté [Tom Sawyer, it's America, the symbol of freedom]" it is not referring to the actual geopolitical and territorially based entity that we know as the United States, but to the global imagination of "America" as a mythical land of opportunity—an imagination to which the show powerfully contributed. It is the imagined America of the French expression "c'est l'Amérique" used to refer to great opulence or an extremely positive outcome, rather than that of Bush or even Obama. *Tom Sawyer's* or *Candy's* popularity in both France and Japan suggests that this imagination is translocally shared—in fact, the Japanese and French media consumers who participate in my research often express a very similar mix of admiration (as a producer of high-quality cultural texts) and anxiety (as a potentially cultural imperialist nation) toward the United States.

This case study demonstrates that the "global culture" to which anime and manga contribute is significantly more complicated than descriptions couched in U.S. vs. "the rest" terms—where the United States stands as the putative representative of "the West"—can account for. Japanese animation is a lot more than a window on Japanese culture or an antidote to U.S. cultural imperialism. It is one contributor to the complex process of negotiating locality and globality as mutually constitutive elements—a process that may take on different shades and nuances in different contexts, but which, overall, profoundly shapes our *collective* contemporary condition. In other words, Japanese animation is and *has long been* an important contributor to the disjunctive messiness of imagining the global.

Indeed, the "global culture" Napier describes is not as new as she suggests. Engagement with a wide range of non-domestic or "partially domestic" (co-produced) texts and characters has long been commonplace in most areas of the world. This is certainly the case in both France and Japan where Snoopy, Garfield, Winnie the Pooh, Spiderman, and the Disney Princesses easily cohabit with the (French) Barbapapas, Gaspard et Lisa, the Little Prince, and Babar; the (Belgian) Tintin; the (Italian/Japanese) Calimero; the (Finnish) Moomins; and, of course, a cast of Japanese characters too numerous to name. While the fast pace of evolution and increasingly diverse nature of glo-balized cultural forms spurred by the development of the Internet and other forms of digital communication is certainly noteworthy, what is, perhaps, most "new" and significant in the current development of "global culture" is the fact that the United States is starting to avidly consume (Kelts, 2007) rather than simply *produce* it. What is most interesting about recognizing the (often ignored) long history of Japanese animation's complex contribution to global culture is the extent to which it was *not*—despite its long-standing global spread—*previously part* of U.S. consumers' imagination of the global (at least not to the extent found in other parts of the world). In this sense, Napier (2007) is correct in identifying U.S. media consumers' engagement with non-domestic anime and manga as an important turning point. It suggests that the experience of U.S. audiences[9] is becoming more in line with that of indi-viduals across the globe.

The potential repercussions of this shift, as well as the continuing sig-nificance of the United States' historical influence, are further explored in our next chapter. Building on what we have learned so far about globalized cultural forms and drawing parallels between the three sites that constitute the focus of this book, the chapter provides a broader final exploration of the nature of individuals' imagination of the global. It considers, in particu-lar, how the different histories of transnational influence in these three sites have resulted in U.S. media consumers having a different relationship to both "global" and American texts than their Japanese and French counterparts.

// SIX //

Imagining the Global: Transnational Media and Global Audiences

So much of the way that people just operate, whatever culture they're from, is through stories. It's the way that people imagine their world and how they see things. Stories are always the backdrop. The kind of assumed things that are unspoken, find their way in the stories. And so when you see a story that comes from a different place, you . . . you run up against different assumptions. And that's always kind of exciting.
—33-year-old American male

This book has suggested that what is most distinctive about our contemporary condition is not just the extent to which different world economies and cultures are interconnected but the extent to which we are aware of this interconnection. The obvious markers of globalization surrounding us (Starbucks, sushi bars, YouTube videos in different languages) are increasingly difficult to ignore. As global media scholar Jack Lule puts it, "we feel more intensely the closeness of the world" (2012, p. 56). This sometimes creates the impression—particularly among privileged members of economically rich nations—that we live in a world in which individuals routinely communicate with *each other* across national and cultural boundaries. While this is true to a certain extent, especially for the small fraction of the world population that has access to air travel or a fast enough Internet connection, individuals' experience of "the global" remains, as we have seen, largely imagined—Lule speaks of the world as an "imagined community" (2012, p. 55). It is the product of their engagement with various transnationally distributed commodities or cultural texts rather than a sustained relationship with individuals living in different places under different conditions. In a world in which the majority of people do not have easy access to an Internet connection, "cyber-connected utopias" remain "essentially incomplete" (Shome and Hegde, 2002, p. 181).

Drawing from interviews with media consumers in France, Japan, and the United States, this chapter turns to audiences to provide a broader reflection on how this imagination of the global takes shape in individuals' daily lives and in different contexts—how, as Appadurai (1996, 2013) would put it, globalized cultural forms shape the production of locality. After a brief discussion of the mass-mediated nature of individuals' relationship to the global, it reflects on the position of the United States in the global imagination. It then considers the significance of this "imagined America" when located within the broader context of individuals' engagement with a vast array of globally distributed media. It closes with an examination of the possible consequences of the history of U.S. dominance of global cultural markets for media consumers in the United States. It concludes that this history has resulted, among U.S. media consumers, in a different kind of engagement with the hybrid globalized cultural forms described throughout this book—in a different experience of global culture, a different path, in other words, to imagining the global.

The Mass Media and the Global

Regardless of their location, the media consumers I interviewed when researching this book were highly aware of the mediated nature of their engagement with "the global." Noting that the ideal solution of "going to see for oneself" (as a 22-year-old French informant put it) is rarely available, especially when forming an informed direct impression of a place may take months or even years, they pointed to the extent to which the popular media shaped their impression of the global. Comments such as "I haven't gone to see for myself, but [I get a sense] from TV, or from the Internet" (Japanese woman in her 30s), "The only information we can get comes from the media, television, newspaper, or the Internet" (41-year-old Japanese woman), "We are necessarily tied to the media" (23-year-old French woman), "We are always more or less influenced by something, some images" (21-year-old French woman), "[We see] what transpires in the media, because, really, the only way to get information about what happens [in the world] is through the media" (21-year-old French man), "The image that is spread [in the media] is what influences us, I mean, even if we know that it isn't like this" (20-year-old French woman), frequently reoccurred in our conversations. As a 41-year-old American male concluded, "I think my interest in looking beyond my immediate [surroundings] was really through TV and film and books [. . .] I think it's interesting in the U.S. because I think media can keep you insular, but I think there is also opportunity anywhere you are to expand your horizon."

If the Internet has made access to cultural texts from a broader range of cultural perspectives a lot easier (I used to have to travel to New York City or the West Coast of the United States to find VHS copies of my favorite Japanese shows, none of which were subtitled in anything other than Chinese), sustained direct interaction between *individuals* from different parts of the world remains relatively rare—unless one considers watching a homemade 30-second YouTube video a case of sustained direct interaction. Individuals' ability to enter a global online conversation is also still often significantly restricted by technological, language, and/or cultural barriers. As the young French man quoted above explained, "my level of English does not allow me to read an American or British website or anything like that, so I have to stick with the French sites." Or as a Japanese professional woman in her 30s noted, "I have to say I try to watch BBC, CNN every day, but English is sometimes so difficult, so after 10 minutes, even 5 minutes, I give up . . ." Of course, entering the conversation is even more difficult for the millions who still lack access to the very technology that renders it possible in the first place.

Thus, despite the technical possibility of more direct means of communication and/or interaction with different cultural contexts, individuals still most frequently engage with "the global" not simply through communication technology but, more specifically, through *mass-mediated* texts. This means that the most influential global cultural producers/distributors still hold the greatest power to shape the global imagination even though people may create and distribute their own alternative cultural products. Furthermore, in a highly intertextual globalized cultural environment where cultural products frequently draw from older, previously influential texts—think, for instance, of the number of films based on earlier popular television series (*Starsky and Hutch*, *21 Jump Street*) or characters (*The Smurfs*, *Tintin*, *The Lorax*)—the historical significance of globally distributed cultural forms adds a significant dimension to their continuing influence.

Consequently, while the United States' position of complete economic domination of global cultural industries may have suffered a blow with the entry of other major players (Japanese animation companies, Bollywood, Endemol) into the competition for a piece of the worldwide mass media market, "America" still held a central position in the global imagination of the French and Japanese media I interviewed.

"America" Imagined

Whether sitting down with my daughter's 10-year-old friend to watch the *Back to the Future* trilogy (recorded for her from French television by her parents), finding myself face-to-face with the Na'vi version of Sam Worthington in every single store I entered on the day of *Avatar*'s DVD release on the French market, discussing Leonardo DiCaprio's weight gain with Japanese fans, or considering whether *Jurassic Park* is too scary for a 6-year-old to watch with a young Japanese mother, my conversations with Japanese and French media consumers and observations in both of these cultural contexts clearly pointed to the remaining global presence of U.S. texts. U.S. TV series such as *CSI* (as a young French woman explained "right now in France, you can see *CSI* on TV at least two or three times a week"), *House, M.D.*, *Desperate Housewives*, *Bones*, *Lost*, *24*, *Scrubs*, *Dexter*, or even older—and extremely "culturally fragrant"—classics such as *The West Wing*, kept on popping up in casual conversations and were discussed at length in formal interviews with both Japanese and French informants. Hollywood movies remained highly popular—an observation empirically supported by the hefty profits made globally by U.S. films (Verrier, February 23, 2011). Regardless of their age (unless they were too old to have grown up with television) or geographical location, and thanks to the low cost of reruns, people recalled growing up with *Little House on the Prairie*, *The A-Team*, and *Charlie's Angels*. Two young Japanese women who had shared their fondness for *Full House* with me when I first interviewed them as 16-year-olds in 1999 told me 10 years later that they were now watching the show with their own children.

Indeed, because cultural texts from the United States have historically been globally influential, their consumption held an element of nostalgia for many viewers, including those growing up outside the United States. Older French and Japanese informants remembered going to the movie theater, often for the first time in their lives, to see U.S. films in the immediate postwar era: "*King Kong*! I really liked that! I liked movies from the West. I loved John Wayne movies. I watched all of John Wayne's movies" (77-year-old Japanese woman); "When I was young, we went to the movie theater every week with my mother. I remember having seen *High Noon* . . . we saw a lot of American films, with Lauren Bacall" (75-year-old French woman). Those a little younger watched U.S. texts on television as well. As a 47-year-old Japanese farmer explained, "Until high school, I wasn't allowed to go to the movies, so I mainly watched movies on TV, but I liked actresses like Audrey Hepburn or Grace Kelly." A 45-year-old French woman recalled: "I watched *Tweety*, *Tom and Jerry*, the *Pink Panther* . . . the American cartoons, *Scooby-Doo*, the Road Runner . . ."

Both French and Japanese media consumers fondly recalled the Disney movies that had "cradled their [or their children's] childhood": "We never went to the movies. The only time we went to the movies was when the factory had their Christmas party [for the children of employees]. They offered us a Walt Disney" (52-year-old French woman); "There were the Disney's that we went to see at the theater when they came out and that we had on video tape. . . . *Cinderella*, I went to see with grandma, *Snow White*, *The Little Mermaid* . . . well, everything, all the classics" (28-year-old French woman); "[My daughter] loved the Disney characters like Ariel, Sleeping Beauty, and Snow White" (52-year-old Japanese woman).

Engagement in their youth with such texts as *Gone with the Wind*, *Roman Holiday*, *Casablanca*, *Planet of the Apes* (the original version), the *Star Wars* and *Indiana Jones* series, *Superman*, and *Tron* made a lasting impression on these media consumers. As a 37-year-old French man explained, "My first film [at the movie theater] was *Superman* and I also saw *Tron*. . . . *Tron*, that was phenomenal! I will be marked by *Tron* for my entire life, I never found an equivalent." Or, as the 77-year-old Japanese woman quoted above offered in a different interview: "They showed *Casablanca* on TV four or five days ago and I watched it. . . . I watched that movie when I was young and I loved it, I was very glad to be able to see it again. I loved those movies and still love them." Even younger informants felt that U.S. texts had a lasting impact on their media consumption. As a 23-year-old Japanese woman explained, "When we were little, we listened to Western music, watched *Popeye* or *Tom and Jerry*, these kinds of things. At that time, I didn't understand English, but somehow we were moved by these programs. They were so impressive that we can remember them even now."

Yet, if Japanese and French media consumers' recollections of getting up in the morning to watch *Looney Tunes* or of enjoying Disney films were often quite similar in tone to those of the U.S. consumers I interviewed (and for whom these texts were not "global" but "culturally native")—as a 40-year-old U.S. informant put it, not mentioning the Warner Brothers would be like "leaving an element off the periodic chart"—this book has demonstrated that these experiences must be interpreted with caution. Most importantly we must resist the impulse to equate the (omni)presence of U.S. texts with a kind of cultural imperialism à la Dorfman and Mattelart (1971) generating visions of non-U.S. consumers abandoning their baguettes or onigiri (Japanese rice balls) to run to the nearest McDonald after watching the latest episode of *Desperate Housewives*.

First of all, because the United States still holds a relative economic advantage in terms of its production budgets—think of the average cost of a Hollywood movie compared to a French or Japanese film[1]—these texts were frequently appreciated for the overall technical quality of their production, regardless of the value of their textual content. Both French and Japanese media consumers frequently commented on the "larger scale" and the higher production value—as one Japanese informant put it, "If you have a lot of money you can do these kinds of things"—of U.S. fare. Thus, *Avatar* was praised as a visually stunning work employing innovative production techniques (that no one outside Hollywood could ever afford to use) despite the fact that its narrative was often read as a disappointing rehashing of the too-familiar Hollywood tale of the white (North American) man saving the non-white feminized natives.

Incidentally, this perceived technical expertise and higher production capacity of the U.S. film and television industries frequently led to a rather negative comparative assessment of "native" texts. With comments such as "Growing up, I found it difficult to watch French films, I felt so much like the quality . . . it was corny, there was no action at all" (22-year-old French woman), "When they try to copy [American series] in France, it isn't worth a hoot, it's lame! I don't know, they should get a grip, it's really a catastrophe!" (42-year-old French women), "You look at *CSI* and you compare it to what they tried to do in France [rolling her eyes]" (23-year-old French woman), "I can't remember the last French series we watched that we thought wasn't too bad" (40-year-old French woman), and "We don't watch Japanese movies, we are not interested in them, on TV or at the theatre, if it's a Japanese movie, we don't watch it. If it's American, we do" (16-year-old Japanese woman), informants assertively critiqued the relatively lower production value of more "local" production.

This does not mean, however, that U.S. popular culture is uncritically consumed. As a French couple in their 40s explained:

> WIFE: There are some nights when we tell ourselves that we feel like watching something completely brainless [*une grosse daube*] and typically, brainless movies, they're American.
>
> HUSBAND: Or it could be French comedy.
>
> WIFE: Or it's bottom-line French comedy. Otherwise, the brainless movie it's something like Bruce Willis saving the world for the umpteenth time, you know . . . or the meteorite, the total catastrophe, there you go.
>
> HUSBAND: But we do get tired of these.
>
> WIFE: But sometimes, while eating sushi in front of TV, it works. Even if afterwards we go to bed telling ourselves it was really stupid!

Furthermore, appreciation for U.S.-produced texts and the recognition that "America" still maintains a privileged *symbolic* position in the global imagination does not necessarily translate into a positive assessment of the United States or into a desire to adopt values and/or practices associated with its society or culture. For instance, after commenting that "the United States, it's magical, there's a magical side. Before it was El Dorado," a French woman in her 20s nevertheless noted that she had an "extremely bad image" of the United States and "hated their politics." In a similar vein, after discussing at length their fondness for American TV series—"I watched all of *Sex and the City*, I loved it!"—or their consumption of American popular music—"lately, I've been listening to music from the old days, like the Carpenters"—a group of five Japanese women in their 30s and early 40s concluded in a 2009 interview that "America is the scariest place in the world." Or, as a French informant in her early 30s put it, "the image I have of the United States is [one of] insecurity, with lots of murders and rapes, people living in social conditions that, yes . . . with lots of violence and things like that. There is this sentiment that everyone just has to fare for themselves. It's true, I generally don't have a very positive image of the United States."

While recognizing the continuing symbolic power of "the American dream" and the frequent nostalgic association of America with freedom and opportunity—as is the case, for instance, in the Japanese animated version of *Tom Sawyer*: "With the Mississippi . . . Tom Sawyer, it makes you dream," commented a 28-year-old French woman—Japanese and French informants readily differentiated between the "America" of the global imagination (or of the French expression "c'est l'Amérique") and the United States as an actual geopolitical entity. With comments such as "I think that the image of what [the United States] actually is and the image that is given in movies or television series are completely disconnected" (40-year-old French woman), "There's a gap, a gap between the image and the reality" (23-year-old French woman), "It doesn't really correspond to what is promoted by Hollywood or TV series" (43-year-old French man), "It's the image that is promoted . . . even if we know it's not like that" (28-year-old French woman), and "What we see on TV, that's only part of America . . . The first image and the reality are a bit different" (52-year-old Japanese woman), French and Japanese media consumers alike aptly pointed to the significant disconnect between the Hollywood-influenced global image and what they could gather of the daily realities of life in the United States. Or as French rapper MC Solaar put it in his 1993 song "Nouveau western":

> While John Wayne is made up like Lucky Luke[2] [*Tandis que John Wayne est looké à la Lucky Luke*]
> Clean like an archduke. Uncle Sam dupes me [*Propre comme un archiduc. Oncle Sam me dupe*]
> Hollywood deceives us. Hollywood deceives! [*Hollywood nous berne. Hollywood berne*]

Thus, if imagined "America" might at times tint individuals' experiences of the United States as a physical space—as one French informant recalling a recent trip to Washington, DC, explained, "In fact, it's not very beautiful but you're happy to have gone because in all the American series they sit on the steps and talk and tell each other things as the sun sets. There're 50 movies in which I have seen this scene and you tell yourself, 'wow, I'm at the Lincoln

Memorial.' It's like the White House, it's super fun! We took 50 pictures in front of the White House!"—it is nevertheless generally recognized and entertained as its own separate entity. As the woman quoted above continued, "it's about the symbol." Then she added: "the image is much nicer than reality."

"America" in Context

The continuing presence of "America" as a global symbolic entity must further be carefully considered in relationship to individuals' overall consumption of globally produced and distributed media. As I hope to have demonstrated here, if people outside the United States consume impressive amounts of popular cultural fare associated with the United States, they also engage with a vast array of popular texts—music, animation, literature—produced in a number of other places, including, of course, their own "native" cultures. As a 40-year-old Japanese woman illustrated when trying to recall all the texts she enjoyed when growing up: "*Candy Candy*, I liked it. And *Sailor Moon* . . . I liked manga . . . Ghibli, like *Future Boy Conan* and *Totoro* . . . there are so many Ghibli movies and Disney too, like *Peter Pan*. When I was a child, I liked the period dramas on NHK. . . . I also liked *Rascal the Raccoon* and also *Anne of Green Gables* and *Princess Sarah*. And *Heidi*! *Tom and Jerry*, I liked that! I watched that a lot!"

Furthermore, while some texts might be more clearly associated with a specific (imagined) conceptualization of a particular place—Tom Sawyer and America as "the symbol of liberty" (as the opening song of the Japanese animated series goes), the more culturally fragrant animation and Japan as a mystical space steeped in tradition or (on the other hand of the spectrum) as a hyper-cool postmodern futuristic fantasy—others' "culture of origin" may simply not matter as much. In fact, adult informants often found it difficult to assess whether or not they knew the cultural origin of their favorite shows when they were consuming them as children—as a 22-year-old French man put it, "now it seems obvious, but I don't know if when we were kids we told ourselves 'this comes from there' when we turned the TV on," to which his friend added, "It came from the TV!" Or, as a 19-year-old recalling his early consumption of cartoons explained, "I never wondered where they came from. I watched [those shows], I enjoyed them, and it's true that Uncle Scrooge was sitting on piles of *dollar* bills, but if you asked where these came from, I wouldn't have been able to tell you they were American."

Perhaps more interestingly, while informants recalled being able to associate certain graphic features with Japanese animation or being aware that Disney was an American company, they unanimously agreed that where programs were produced ultimately did not matter to them as children: "Whether it was French or American, I didn't care" (40-year-old French woman); "I think that the first time I watched *Sleeping Beauty*, I didn't ask myself who was making the anime"[3] (28-year-old French woman); "I didn't give a damn [where the shows came from]. It absolutely didn't matter to us" (43-year-old French man).

The children I interviewed confirmed this assessment. If they were able to identify the cultural origin of some relatively culturally marked texts—such as *Pokémon* or *Spirited Away*—and knew that most of the blockbuster movies targeted at children (*Ice Age*, *Shrek*) are "made in America," they asserted not "really noticing a difference." Like their parents before them, French children consumed an assorted mix of Japanese animation (Miyazaki films, *Pokémon*, *Captain Tsubasa*, *Dragon Ball*), American fare (Disney and Pixar films, classic cartoons such as *Scooby-Doo* and *Looney Tunes* as well as newer ones, such as the currently highly popular *Ben 10*), French series (*Totally Spies!*, *Marsupilami*, *Wakfu*, *Tituf*, *Foot 2 Rue*, *Les Zinzins de l'Espace*, *Galactik Football*), and co-productions (*Les Mystérieuses Cités d'Or*, *Kirikou*). Similarly, while Japanese children certainly consumed heavy doses of Japanese fare, they mentioned enjoying a mix of "native," U.S., co-produced, and (to lesser extent) European texts—including many of those mentioned above—the origin of which they were not always able to identify. Their engagement with "non-native" media was such a routine endeavor that they simply did not give much thought to it.

Armed with impressive amounts of global cultural capital, the French and Japanese media consumers I interviewed easily navigated the highly hybrid and intertextual media environment surrounding them. They frequently employed one global text to make sense of their engagement with another. For instance, both Japanese and French manga readers traced their interest in fantasy not only to their consumption of early Japanese animation but also to the *Harry Potter* and *Lord of the Rings* series, which they saw as having sparked a resurgence in the genre. French consumers also mentioned their engagement with both classic Franco-Belgian *bandes dessinées* and American comics. Japanese readers added Chinese ghost tales to the mix.

In such a context—and because cultures represent each other as well as themselves in popular cultural texts—the global imagination of "America" is not only shaped by Hollywood's worldwide influence and by the popularity of American television series but also by the Japanese version of "America" in such globally influential texts as the *Tom Sawyer* or *Candy* animated series, the image of Beverly Hills in the French-produced *Totally Spies!*, or that of the American West in the Franco-Belgian comic *Lucky Luke*. The global imagination of Japan is likewise shaped by U.S. films such as *The Last Samurai* or *Memoirs of a Geisha* as well as Miyazaki's animation; that of Europe, by Disney classics and Japanese animation.

As suggested in chapter 5, globalized "non-native" cultural forms can even contribute to the imagination of one's own "native" environment. French consumers enjoyed Disney's renditions of European tales in part for their cultural proximity. As a 52-year-old woman noted regarding Disney's version of rural France in *Beauty and the Beast*: "I found it really really beautiful. And it really looks like Europe, Europe is represented very accurately."[4] The numerous Japanese animated series based on French or other European literature (*Remi sans Famille*, *Heidi*, *Princess Sarah*) powerfully resonated with French media consumers because they drew from texts and/or environments highly familiar to them, and which they frequently described as "theirs." These "non-native" versions of familiar texts or contexts significantly shaped their image of French culture, as well as that of other European environments. For instance, a fan of Japanese animation and manga recalled being constantly reminded of the Japanese animated series *Cathy la Petite Fermière* (*Makiba no Shôjo Katori*)[5] when visiting Finland. As another admitted, "*Remi sans Famille*, if it wasn't for the anime I wouldn't even know the story because I haven't read the Hector Malot novel!"[6]

Japanese informants, on the other hand, enjoyed these same shows in part for their exotic value—the architecture, the costumes, the scenery, even the food were frequently mentioned as pleasurable elements—but also because they capitalized on familiar themes celebrated throughout Japanese culture. Candy, Heidi, and Remi were admired, for instance, for their "*ganbare* (do your best) spirit," their ability to cheerfully endure in the face of extreme adversity. As a 33-year-old Japanese man explained: "I watched [Remi] a lot! I loved that show! The main character encounters many challenges but he faces them with courage and overcomes adversity. It's the same thing [in Heidi]. She's courageous . . . Also, the cheese, these kinds of things looked good." Or as a 40-year-old woman put it while speaking of Candy, "She's very cheerful, she had many troubles and struggles but she was always very cheerful, I thought that was good."

Thus, we must resist the temptation to draw too direct a link between a text's context of production and the meaning of its transcultural influence—anime as quintessentially Japanese, Disney as a blatant example of American or (worse) Western cultural imperialism—or its interpretation. As a 43-year-old French informant explained: "For example, the [1960s television series] *The Wild Wild West*, they speak French, but we know it takes place in the United States. [. . .] It is certainly not because it takes place in another country that that's where it's necessarily produced." As another concluded in a different interview, "it's not because [a cartoon] takes place in Japan that it's necessarily Japanese."

Global Culture and the U.S. Audience

Media consumers in different parts of the world engage with globally distributed and/or globally influenced texts in complex ways and from multiple points of entry. The differences in these points of entry became most evident in interviews with U.S. media consumers. Indeed, the historical dominance of U.S. popular cultural texts has not only resulted in consumers around the globe being familiar with Disney, Hollywood, and U.S. television series but also in a relative lack of reciprocal exposure to "non-native" culture on the part of U.S. audiences—at least when compared to the other cultural contexts considered in this book.

Aside from U.S. popular cultural production (which *everyone* seemed to be familiar with), French and Japanese informants avidly consumed numerous globally distributed texts that never made it to the mainstream in the United States. The example of Japanese animation is perhaps the most striking, but French and Japanese consumers shared a familiarity with a number of other texts. French films (which have long been easily and widely available in Japan[7]) and French *chansons* were frequently mentioned by Japanese informants as texts they remembered enjoying in their youth—older Japanese women particularly loved Alain Delon—and that they still enjoyed today. French and other European cartoon or comic book characters such as the Barbapapas, Gaspard and Lisa, Tintin, The Little Prince, Calimero, or Moomin were also familiar to them, as these have naturally joined the large cast of other *kawaii* (cute) characters omnipresent throughout the Japanese landscape.

Due in part to the historical dominance of U.S. media, particularly in the immediate postwar period when domestic production was limited by the physical destruction of their nations' infrastructure, French and Japanese consumers of all ages also more broadly shared the experience of *growing up* surrounded with global media. As a result, they expressed a relatively greater tolerance for subtitles and/or dubbing than their U.S. counterparts. I remember realizing with surprise when taking my daughters to see *Monsters Inc.* at the movie theater in Tokyo one summer that the film was in its original English-language version despite the fact that the majority of the audience in the theater seemed to be under the age of five, and consequently probably found it difficult to read the fast-moving Japanese subtitles. In contrast, the "problem" of subtitles came up frequently in interviews with U.S. consumers who felt that watching a non-English-language text required extra attention and could not be done as casually as watching a text that did not require translation. In addition, with the notable exception of animation, the dubbing of foreign-language texts is not as routinely practiced on the U.S. market as it is in France

Fig. 2. The French Barbapapas welcome customers in the tobacco shop of a small Japanese village (photo taken by the author).

or Japan where the practice is simply a natural part of watching television or going to the movie theater—as a French informant explained, "Foreign actors have French voices. If we hear them speak [their native language] it's not the same!"

Furthermore, the channels of distribution historically established though the intense importation of global media have meant that French and Japanese media consumers do not have to wait long for "foreign" texts to reach their market. For instance, Miyazaki's film *The Secret World of Arrietty* released in Japan in July 2010 reached French movie theaters in January 2011, more than a year before it was to be released in the United States. Toei Animation's *One Piece* series (based on the popular manga) was broadcast on French national television shortly after it experienced a resurgence in popularity in Japan following the release of a film version of the show in 2011 and quickly sparked a resurgence in the manga version of the text. Even films produced in the United States sometimes reach global markets before being shown domestically. The world premiere of Steven Spielberg's *The Adventures of Tintin*, for instance, took place in Brussels in October 2011, but U.S. consumers had to wait until December 21 to see it.

As a result, the media consumers I interviewed in the United States recalled engaging with relatively fewer "non-native" texts than their French or Japanese counterparts. While cultural products from outside the United States did come up in interviews—particularly British texts—they constituted a smaller portion of informants' total media consumption: "There was a little bit of it. I don't think it was a . . . mainstay of our household. But I do remember every so often going to the [independent movie theater] to watch it. I don't think we ever really . . . rented foreign films at home" (32-year-old female); "I don't think there was so much foreign stuff when I was a kid" (33-year-old female).

When specifically prompted about their consumption of global media when growing up, U.S. media consumers frequently responded that they simply "were not around." In stark contrast to Japanese and French media consumers' tales of intense and complex engagement with global culture, "foreign texts" were not among those U.S. informants considered most formative to their identity—with the possible exception of *The Smurfs*.[8] As a 35-year-old African American woman noted: "Nothing pops to mind. You know Americans always feel like that they are worldly in some way, so I have this sense that there had to be something that we saw, but I doubt it. I mean, in the house, we probably had some, like, random African stuff lying around in the household, but nothing that is really significant in my . . . nothing that I feel like 'oh yeah . . .'" Or, as a 41-year-old male recalled, "I can't think of anything that would be something [from another culture] . . . actually, when I was in my teens, I would watch *Benny Hill* with my dad."

The texts that were most frequently mentioned by U.S. consumers as highly culturally influential included *Mister Rogers' Neighborhood*—"in college I found Mr. Rogers had died, and I cried. I was like, oh my God, Mr. Rogers has died" (28-year old woman)—*Sesame Street*, *The Muppets*, *The Wizard of Oz*, the multiple *Star Wars* episodes, *The Simpsons*, Disney animation, and, as already noted, the Warner Brothers cartoons—"*Looney Tunes*. They were classic. I mean, they spanned so many different generations" (33-year-old male). As a 39-year-old woman recalled, "back in the days of thriving network TV, *The Wizard of Oz* was on, I don't know which network carried it but it was like life stopped because *The Wizard of Oz* was on and you looked forward to it every year . . . the TV was so different back then. It was like everybody in America was watching that."

The texts they identified as "stuff that was around" and that they, consequently, felt they could not avoid being exposed to included soap operas, Westerns, musicals, war and mafia films, and "classic" TV series such as *Hogan's Heroes*, *Gilligan's Island*, *The Cosby Show*, *Family Ties*, and M*A*S*H (to name only a few)—"My dad watched M*A*S*H a lot. I remember literally lying on top of my father as he was couch potatoing, watching M*A*S*H, not understanding any of the context" (31-year-old woman). As a 41-year-old man put it, watching *Happy Days* and *Laverne and Shirley* on Tuesdays and *The Cosby Show*, *Family Ties*, and *Whiz Kids* on Thursdays was the "TV experience [. . .] typical of most American kids growing up in the late 70s and 80s." With few exceptions, the texts U.S. media consumers deemed culturally important, as well as the ones they were still watching today, were similar to those frequently mentioned by French and Japanese informants in our discussions of U.S. popular culture: Disney classics, U.S. television series ranging from *Little House on the Prairie* to *Dexter*, Hollywood productions from E.T. to *Pirates of the Caribbean* and *Star Wars*.

Informants in the United States were aware that these texts were significant contributors to a global popular culture shared across national boundaries—as a 28-year-old woman recalled, "we lived in Germany for a year and a half, and I was told that I watched *Sesame Street* in German"—but they were not as familiar with other major players on the global scene. This is not to suggest that non-U.S. production is not available on the U.S. market. Certainly, texts from a broad array of cultural contexts were accessible to those who sought them out, through cable/satellite channels or VHS rentals, long before anime or Bollywood became household terms and before the Internet allowed viewers to develop a liking for Brazilian telenovelas or Korean dramas. The combination of the historical legacy of U.S. global popular cultural dominance—regardless of whether or not this dominance is waning today (Tunstall, 2007)—and of the early fragmentation of the U.S. market into niche audiences brought by the large and relatively early penetration of cable and satellite in the United States has meant, however, that the consumption of "non-native" cultural texts in the United States has been (at least until relatively recently) more of a specialized activity often linked to one's ethnic identity rather than something one simply cannot avoid doing, as Napier (2007) cogently notes.[9]

This was certainly the case among the U.S. consumers I interviewed. Nothing illustrated this fact more powerfully than our discussions about Japanese animation. While older informants did recall watching *Speed Racer* or *Kimba the White Lion*, they did not bestow on these Japanese texts the "cult" status given to the likes of *Candy Candy*, *Heidi*, and *Goldorak/Grendizer* in France or Japan, and, incidentally, throughout large areas of the world. Relatively younger informants typically pinpointed the growing influence of Japanese animation in the United States to the mid- to late 1990s—"you know, during sort of '98, '99, 2000, Japanese animation got popular" (31-year-old female)—and while some of them did fondly remember engaging with these texts, they generally located this engagement within the context of a fan or subculture activity. As a 28-year-old man interviewed in 2011 explained:

Anime I would like to think that I was one the early adopters for somebody at my age. As a kid I grew up watching *Robotech*, that was on cartoon stations in the morning, but anime, around 10 or 12, I started to become obsessed with anime. They had a small section at Blockbuster of foreign animation, and I think there was like one French, but of course it was mostly [Japanese] anime [. . .] So I think there is this element for me, part of this identity that is like I was into it before it was cool when it was still underground, something like that.

Or, as a 31-year-old woman recalled, "So I graduated high school in '97, and [got into] anime, because I was so much into the rave culture. So dressing like that, looking like one of the characters, you know from a Japananimation film, or getting into *Dragon Ball Z* . . . watching *Ninja Scroll*, watching *Ghost in the Shell* [that was part of the culture]."

Even the cultural products most frequently discussed by scholars as quintessential examples of contemporary globally influential Japanese animation were not necessarily experienced as "mainstream" cultural capital, particularly among informants who did not have children. For instance, a 28-year-old woman who had taken Japanese in high school and participated in an exchange program recalled watching Miyazaki films as part of her Japanese class: "Well, I mean in Japanese class, we used to watch, um . . . it is not manga, it's, what is it called? Anime, anime. . . . We watched *Spirited Away* and a bunch of others, and I don't remember the names. . . . And I remember watching *Spirited Away*, and we were like 'Sensei what's going on' like, this doesn't make any sense!"

In contrast to the experiences of French or Japanese media consumers who, regardless of their age, recalled growing up surrounded by "nonnative" cultural forms, U.S. media consumers' engagement with foreign texts (particularly non-English-language texts) most frequently began in (young) adulthood: "Yeah, I think I probably started watching foreign flicks in the art houses that were by the college. Like you know that college kids would go to. That's when I probably started doing that" (51-year-old female); "When I was in college I got to explore all these wonderful foreign films, I got into, you know, some French films, some German films" (41-year-old male); "[Growing up] it was like, mainstream, *The Brady Bunch*, *Nancy Drew* . . . I mean, other cultures, I didn't get that till college. I invented that for myself" (39-year-old female).[10]

Watching Miyazaki animation, Wong Kar-Wai films, and "foreign flicks in the art houses" was also more of an intellectualized and/or specialized activity—as the 39-year-old woman quoted above explained when discussing her lack of exposure to non-English-language texts when growing up: "I

was pretty white mainstream, *my parents were not arty, they weren't intellectuals.*"
Rather than being a natural and unavoidable facet of daily media consumption, their engagement with "non-native" texts stemmed from the desire to "expand [their] horizon" (41-year-old male) and learn about other cultures.[11] It came as a conscious effort, as the quote opening this chapter illustrates, to "see a story that comes from a different place" and "run up against different assumptions." As a woman in her 30s explained when asked what she enjoyed about foreign films, "We like cultural stuff. We like stuff that like . . . can . . . makes you step into something different. With, like, different languages or different . . . cultural ideals and stuff like that," or as another put it, "I like to see what life is like in other places."

Thus, the U.S. media consumers I interviewed experienced "global culture" quite differently than their French or Japanese counterparts. Of course, this is not particularly surprising considering what we know about the local negotiation of transcultural influence. What is, perhaps, more interesting is the fact that French ("Western") media consumers' engagement with global culture was more similar to that of Japanese ("non-Western") media consumers'— and vice versa—than to those born and raised in the United States ("Western"). Significant similarities between French and Japanese informants arose in their relationship to the United States as an entity whose symbolic image (the "America" of the global imagination) was avidly consumed, enjoyed, and even admired but whose status as an actual powerful geopolitical entity was seen with suspicion (the United States as a violent, scary place). On a more basic level French and Japanese media consumers shared a common history of much greater engagement with globalized popular cultural forms and familiarity with specific texts, characters, and genres that were simply never present on the U.S. cultural landscape. This fact challenges the notion that there is such a thing as an essentialized "Western" experience of cultural globalization. It also clearly establishes that the experience of media consumers in the United States cannot be taken as representative of those of individuals in other parts of "the West." As media critic Alessandra Stanley (2013) bluntly put it in a recent *New York Times* article, "American audiences today are a little like Italians in the era of Marco Polo: They have a few exotic spices and a faint sense that there may be a lot more somewhere out there."

Indeed, the history of U.S. transcultural influence has resulted in placing media consumers in the United States in a rather unique position as they negotiate global popular culture. On one hand, the historical legacy of U.S. global influence and its remaining economic edge means that U.S. popular cultural texts still frequently become instant global phenomena most people around the world are familiar with. This means that U.S. media consumers traveling to other cultural environments will necessarily encounter a certain level of familiarity with "their" culture. On the other hand, the lesser degree of ostensible penetration of non-U.S. texts into the U.S. market (the United States does not have, for instance, to establish quotas to protect its cultural industries) also means that U.S. media consumers have not, at least historically, had the same relationship with texts produced in other cultural contexts.

This, more generally, means that we must be particularly wary of theoretical arguments about the cultural dimensions of globalization based on analyses of the U.S. context. For instance, the concept of "pop cosmopolitanism" as proposed by Henri Jenkins may accurately describe the experience of privileged "younger Americans" whom he suggests "are distinguishing themselves from their parents' culture through their consumption of Japanese anime and manga, Bollywood films and bhangra, and Hong Kong action movies" (2011, pp. 546–47). It does not, however, tell us much about the process of imagining the global in other parts of the world, including in other economically powerful nations, where engagement with global culture is not something that hipsters do to "differentiate themselves from their parents," but something that has been going on for generations—not to mention the imposed transcultural influence stemming from the legacy of colonialism in less economically powerful contexts.

Such arguments also tend to place excessive emphasis on new technological developments, particularly the rise of digital communication, in their analyses of transcultural flows—"Cosmopolitans use networked communication to scan the planet in search of diversity and communicate with others of their kind around the world," writes Jenkins—and, consequently, on the experiences of the relatively privileged groups of individuals walking "a thin line between dilettantism and connoisseurship" (2011, p. 549) who enjoy easy access to it.

As I hope to have demonstrated, French and Japanese media consumers were consuming heavy doses of globalized cultural forms long before they had an Internet connection. My Japanese informants might have had to take a trip to their local *Tsutaya*—one of Japan's largest video rental chains operated by a company tellingly named the "*culture* convenience club"—when they wanted to watch a French, American, or Chinese film in the late 1990s, but they just as passionately and knowledgeably discussed global media with me then as they do today. French children may no longer have to wait for Wednesday morning to watch their favorite anime (there are now entire channels dedicated to it) or Disney films but their parents are just as likely to break into song when *Dragon Ball Z* or *Beauty and the Beast* is mentioned. While digital media may have further facilitated the sharing and spread of various cultural forms, it did not revolutionize these individuals' engagement with global culture. If anything, the Internet is allowing (middle-class) U.S. audiences to jump on a bandwagon much of the rest of the world joined half a century ago. We are yet to see the full impact of the appearance in greater numbers of Korean dramas, Japanese animated series, or French films on Netflix and cable television on U.S. consumers' imagination of the global. Future research will need to continue to explore the possible consequences of their increasingly active engagement with the inescapable hybridity of contemporary global culture described throughout this book.

SEVEN

Lessons from a Translocal Approach— or, Reflections on Contemporary Glocamalgamation

We live in a time when global technological and information systems are producing such complex cultural dynamics that the politics of colonialism, race, nation, and belonging are undergoing massive shifts. New insights and lenses are continually needed to rethink the diaspora and hybridity.
—Shome, 2006a, pp. 120–21

This book set out to examine hybridity's "finer points and meanings" (Pieterse, 2009, p. viii) through a number of case studies of globalized cultural forms and their "local" negotiation. Considering three sites in relationship to each other and in different configurations, it has explored the multiple ways in which the global/national/local are mutually constitutive elements of our contemporary era marked by an increased awareness of worldwide connectedness. The translocal mosaic sketched by its different chapters illustrates the highly hybrid nature of global culture. Moving beyond the basic recognition of hybridity's inescapability it also illustrates, however, the political nature of hybridity's formation and of its negotiation—or what Appadurai recently called the "obstacles, bumps, and potholes" (2013, p. 65) of global cultural flows. To put it differently, it answers the questions of *what* hybridity matters and *how* it contributes to the "complex, partly imagined lives" (Appadurai, 1996, p. 54) that characterize contemporary social conditions in a transcultural, deterritorialized world.

Reflecting on the lessons learned throughout the book, this chapter draws a closing assessment of what we have learned, both empirically and theoretically, from its translocal explorations. It first examines how hybridity—or what I will come to term "glocamalgamation"—normalizes the presence of "the global" in individuals' daily lives and makes its imagined dimension particularly salient as the global, national, and local are continuously (re)negotiated in relationship to each other. This chapter further reflects on the often contentious nature of this imagination of the global, particularly as it intersects with racial and gender dynamics, and explores its problematic as well as productive potential. From a more theoretical standpoint, it argues that the book's translocal approach demonstrates the need to move beyond conceptualizations of transnational cultural dynamics couched in East/West terms and/or taking the United States as the quintessential representative of "the West." It closes with a reflection on the need to decentralize the United States in our considerations of global processes while simultaneously keeping a critical eye on its continuing influence.

The Global in Everyday Life

The examples provided in this book illustrate the extent to which "the global"—as an imagined entity, a space envisioned through one's interaction with globalized cultural forms—has entered individuals' daily lives. Globalized hybridity is so much part of our contemporary condition that we rarely stop to think about it. When the "Quick" restaurants recently started to include *Totally Spies!* and *Dragon Ball Z* gifts in their boxed kids' meals, the fact that a Belgian American-style fast food chain should offer figurines from a French-produced show drawing from the visual aesthetic of Japanese animation and taking place in Beverly Hills (*Totally Spies!*) alongside characters from a seminal Japanese anime text (*Dragon Ball Z*) did not seem to faze French consumers. Hybridity is the raw material of the global imagination.

As we have seen repeatedly throughout this book, this normalization of globalized hybridity results in a situation in which the global, national, and local are constantly and simultaneously (re)negotiated in the production, distribution, and consumption of popular cultural forms. Whether in reality television, news, magazines, hip-hop, or animation, this process is more complex than can be expressed through the concepts of globalization, localization, or even glocalization. None of our current vocabulary really does justice to its multidimensional blurring of boundaries—perhaps the term "glocamalgamation" gets a little closer to describing its frustrating messiness.

Glocamalgamation signals transformations and contradictions on multiple levels. On one hand, it reminds us that corporate consolidation, conglomeration, and convergence are central trends in contemporary media industries. It reminds us that hybridity is, after all, the cultural logic of globalization—that it "is compatible with globalization *because it helps globalization rule*" (Kraidy, 2005, p. 148, emphasis mine). It reminds us that the very technologies that produce and allow us to engage with global media are often owned by large corporations operating transnationally but incorporated in the most powerful nations. It reminds us that market forces are generally behind "any fast and heavy traffic" (Appadurai, 2013, p. 69) in the global circulation of cultural forms. It points to both "the top-down push of corporate convergence" produced by increased concentration of ownership and "the bottom-up pull of grassroots convergence" (Jenkins, 2011, p. 546) characterized by increased consumer participation.

The Internet serves as a useful metaphor here. The Internet is arguably the paradigmatic example of a rhizomic, networked, decentralized arrangement (Castells, 2001). It is the stuff of social networking, flash mobs, global grassroots movements, and "Arab Spring" revolutions. Nation-states cannot seem to fully control it. On the other hand, it is the site of intensified surveillance, of invasions of privacy, of increasingly sophisticated and targeted marketing techniques (Turow, 2011), of "lateral markets that involve traffic in human organs, armaments, precious metals, and sex work" (Appadurai, 2013, p. 61). Access to much of its infrastructure and content is controlled by multibillion-dollar corporations—at least for consumers with average computer skills. It remains mostly out of the reach of the majority of the world population (Internet World Stats, 2013). Glocamalgamation reminds us of the fact that "among the most vigorous proponents of mongrelization are the world's biggest, richest, most profit-hungry corporations" (Zachary, 2000, p. xx).

But glocamalgamation is also shaping (and being shaped by) local subjectivities. Just as different elements of our daily life combine in our dreams into a phantasmagoric experience, global culture's multiple translocal references amalgamate to create "a plurality of imagined worlds" (Appadurai, 1996, p. 5) that deeply affects what Appadurai calls "the production of locality" (1996, 2003). Hybridity, like the imagination, has no limits. Actarus—Goldorak/Grendizer's pilot also known as Duke Fleed—may be the prince of the Euphor planet (Fleed in the Japanese version), but he lives on a ranch owned by an old cowboy where horses and spaceships happily cohabit. He is also, on another level, the hero of a Japanese text and a cultural icon celebrated by an entire generation of French (and Middle Eastern) viewers—all under different names. This increased role of the imagination in social life, in how we envision our place in the world, is, perhaps, one of the most defining elements of contemporary globalization.

Thus, while the words "localization" and "glocalization" still connote a sense of the merging of two or more relatively distinct entities, I propose "glocamalgamation" to suggest a more chaotic and transformative blending of multiple social, cultural, and economic dynamics that helps us address the "curious inner contradiction" (Appadurai, 2013, p. 65) of globalized cultural forms. Glocamalgamation is meant to position the global not merely as "the accidental site of the fusion or confusion of circulating global elements" but as "the site of the mutual transformation of circulating forms" (Appadurai, 2013, p. 68)—a transformation that, as Appadurai reminds us, always occurs through the work of the imagination. The term is intentionally a mouthful—a word intended to describe such a messy process should not easily roll off the tongue.

Glocamalgamation has particularly salient implications for media scholars. It means that the Japanese animated versions of classic European or American literature can be more culturally significant for French media consumers than the "original" texts on which they are based. It means that hiphop must be understood as a phenomenon drawing from multiple dimensions of individuals' imagination of the global and not just the imagination of the place(s) generally associated with its cultural roots. It means that we need to come to terms with the fact that the *Wakfu* license—composed of a televised animated series, three massive multiplayer online role-playing games, a collector card game, and a *bande dessinée*—can be graphically and textually linked to Japanese animation (the *Wakfu* is a form of energy similar to that found in *Dragon Ball* or *Naruto*, and the card game is inspired by *Pokémon* cards), make direct references to Japanese texts, use English-language titles, be reminiscent of U.S.-produced online games, and yet be claimed as an example of successful French cultural production. It means that we need to learn to better address how "different forms circulate through different trajectories, generate diverse interpretations, and yield different and uneven geographies" (Appadurai, 2013, p. 67).

While some texts retain culturally specific and/or historically conditioned elements, the vast array of globally distributed references available to both producers and consumers complicates the notion of transnational cultural influence. Thus, we must be wary of arguments positioning various texts— typically ones identified as "alternatives" to "Western" cultural production—as "representative" of the cultural environment in which they are produced, or from which they are ostensibly originating. We must also resist the related temptation to search for links between individuals' engagement with globalized culture texts and actual/physical geographies—as when Jenkins mentions that "Some anime fans do cultivate a more general knowledge of Japanese culture" and might even "travel to Japan in search of new material or to experience the fan culture there more directly" (2011, p. 550). While these links might at times exist, the examples provided in this book demonstrate that a much more significant and widespread dynamic lies in glocamalgamation's imagined dimensions. Glocamalgamation renders media scholars' job significantly more complicated. Because the global is imagined in large part through individuals' consumption of (mass-) mediated texts, genres, or formats, our job is also particularly important.

Race and Gender in the Global Imagination

As the concept of glocamalgamation suggests, the fact that hybridity has become a normalized feature of individuals' daily lives does not mean that it is devoid of political implications. Hybridity's specific character, the facets of global culture it emphasizes or represses ("what hybridity"), are contentious and contested. One of the most striking common running themes of the various cultural forms analyzed here is the centrality of race and gender dynamics in the negotiation of the global/national/local nexus. In an environment permeated with the awareness of the global, race and gender are never "simply" locally negotiated. While racial and gendered identities are certainly shaped by local conditions—instances of discrimination, legal, social, and cultural conditions—these local conditions are symbolically negotiated in relationship to the global. This book provided examples of this process in different contexts and from different angles in reality television, international news, fashion magazines, and hip-hop.

If racial and gender issues are not always ostensibly addressed and may even be assertively erased in contemporary cultural forms—as in the case of reality television in France or news of "local" dramatic events in all three cultural contexts examined—they remain an important subtext of the symbolic construction of the local/national in relationship to the global. The denying or downplaying of racial or gender prejudice in "local" texts is particularly effective when it is coupled with less generous transnational comparisons. Comparisons with other economically powerful nations are particularly compelling. Indeed, if, in all three contexts examined in this book, transnational comparisons sometimes served to locate race and gender discrimination in "less developed" nations, comparisons with other highly influential global players served to suggest that—regardless of the "local" crisis at hand—each environment was doing better than virtually *anywhere else in the world*. This process was most powerfully illustrated in the case of international news, but it is a more general dimension of individuals' engagement with the global. The global success of American gangsta rap, for instance, rests in part on the fact that it reassures transnational consumers about the comparatively less violent, racist, and sexist nature of their own "local" socio-cultural context.

In turn, the racial and gendered subtext of globalized cultural forms significantly shapes individuals' daily experiences of the local/national/global nexus as they engage in media consumption—it shapes, in other words, the production of locality. We have seen how Japanese women, for instance, find themselves in the difficult position of having to negotiate their gendered, racial, cultural, and class identities in the face of white-dominated globalized representations of upper-class fashion and feminine beauty originally heavily influenced by the United States and Europe. As illustrated in chapter 3, these different identity factors—as well as others such as age and geography—are all significant dimensions of their negotiation of a segment of global culture in which they find themselves in the position of racial minorities.

From a more theoretical point of view, chapters 5 and 6 illustrated the difficulty of adequately addressing the politics of hybridity in academic work where local identity politics and the tendency to celebrate "subaltern" speech have sometimes resulted in reductionist interpretations of global processes. Accounts positioning anime as a quintessentially Japanese alternative to Disney or global hip-hop as an imitation of an African American genre may be partially correct, but they fail to fully address glocamalgamation's multidimensional nature. Similarly, accounts celebrating the recent entry of various new actors on the global popular cultural scene must be carefully located within the global politics of hybridization. As Kraidy reminds us, "Hybridity is a risky notion, it comes without guarantees" (2005, p. vi).

Moving beyond East and West

One important boundary to blur in our theoretical engagement with contemporary hybridity is the common division of the world along East/West lines. As this book's translocal approach demonstrates, it is not a particularly useful heuristic device when it comes to understanding processes of transnational cultural influence. It results in a problematic essentializing of both sides of the axis as it "overlooks all the forms of heterogeneity that have always existed—and continue to exist—within the West" and "leaves no room for any idea that there might be a multiplicity of modernities, some of them of non-Western origin" (Morley, 2007, p. 158).

The need to resist employing such problematic shortcuts is complicated, however, by the fact that the divide is a significant subtext of the politics of hybridity. It may be strategically employed as different contexts negotiate their position in relationship to each other against the backdrop of a globalized popular cultural scene. In the case of the three sites examined here, we have seen, for instance, how news coverage in France and the United States engaged in a process of "othering" of Japan as a "non-Western" nation and how this schema intersected with the global geopolitics of race. In other words, Japan is not "Western" not only because of its different cultural and historical trajectory on its (highly successful) path to modernization, but also because it is not racially white dominated. On the other hand, opposition to "the West" is a frequent rhetorical device in Japanese nationalistic discourse that conveniently serves to veil the country's history of imperialist aggression against other Asian nations. The East/West divide further intersects with the construction of culture, race, and gender when it is employed, for example, to construct Japanese femininity in opposition to "Western" sexuality in Japanese women's magazines.

In a similar vein, critiques of "Western" transnational power paradoxically re-centralize the United States as a global cultural producer when merging U.S. cultural production with that of the rest of "the West." Positioning the United States as representative of "the West" is particularly problematic considering the fact that, as we have seen in chapter 6, U.S. media consumers' experiences of "the global" are not particularly representative of those of individuals in other parts of the world—including other parts of "the West." This book illustrated, for instance, how French and Japanese media consumers share a common history of active engagement with "non-native" U.S. popular cultural fare and with a relatively greater array of other globalized cultural forms. The U.S./West merging leads to a dismissal—or, perhaps more accurately, to a simple lack of awareness—of non-U.S. Western cultural production, especially when such production is not in the English language. It also downplays the influence of non-U.S. globally distributed cultural products in other Western contexts, as illustrated by the example of Japanese animation in France. More generally, it veils the presence of "Western" alternatives to U.S.-style capitalism and cultural policies—to, in other words, U.S.-style globalization.

The common merging of "Western" academic thought with English-language texts mostly originated in the United States and Britain similarly dismisses the possibility that alternative academic conversations may be taking place in other parts of "the West." Such conversations do take place, however, even if they are not always translated into English. French theorists,[1] for instance, differ from their colleagues across the Atlantic (and, to some extent, across the English Channel) in the amount of attention they pay to "West/West" dynamics—particularly those operating along a France/Europe/U.S. axis. While recognizing the historical impact of European imperialism on "non-Western" nations, they also locate their work within the context of power struggles waged at the national level in relationship to the United States and (not always as successfully) the rest of Europe (see, for example, Matouk, 2005; Mattelart, 2005a, 2005b; Warnier, 2004).

This different positioning has resulted in a characterization of globalization subtly different than that found in the works of Anglo/U.S. scholars. The common use of the term of Latin origin "mondialisation" over the more direct English translation "globalization" reflects this different angle of vision. While "globalisation" is also used, "mondialisation" serves to describe the more complex sum of cultural, linguistic, political, and economic processes that characterize the formation of global modernities and their local manifestations (Matouk, 2005). More than a simple reaction against another "Anglicisme" (even though certainly partly that), mondialisation provides a "Western" alternative to the Anglo/U.S. concept of globalization. It linguistically and conceptually separates Francophone scholars from their Anglophone counterparts—and potentially links them to Latin American intellectuals who have similarly opted for the term "*mundialización*" in their translation of the English term into Spanish (Stald and Turfe, 2002). The twin concepts of mondialisation/mundializacion characterized by Stald and Turfe as "the process where a process of world modernity is developing, but articulated and differentiated according to the particular historical circumstances of each country" (2002, p. 4) serve as acts of resistance against Anglo/American power to define the terms through which transnational influence is understood and discussed in intellectual discourse. They at least help diversify the debate by providing a potentially alternative vision (Matouk, 2005).[2]

These different philosophical positions—Yúdice speaks of "a kind of transcultural and translational parallax" (2001, p. xviii) in his introduction to the English-language edition of García Canclini's *Consumers and Citizens*—further point to differences in the nature of identity politics on either side of the Atlantic (particularly between the United States and non-English-speaking Europe) and between the United States and other parts of America. As García Canclini notes, "If the Anglo-American and Latin American worlds experience globalization differently it is because of the different ways in which they conceptualize their multicultural character" (2001, pp. 9–10). These differences were empirically illustrated in this book in the contrasting ways in which French and U.S. popular cultural texts—reality television, news, hip-hop—dealt with the ethnically and racially diverse nature of their respective sociocultural contexts. They are further reflected in the different theoretical positions on race historically held by French and U.S. scholars (for an excellent detailed description of these dynamics see Stam and Shohat, 2012). Working translocally exposes the political nature of these various boundaries placed on identity—East vs. West, color blindness vs. multiculturalism, global vs. local—both in popular cultural texts and in academic discourse. It forces us to conceptualize identities in their "unavoidable relation to hybridity" (García Canclini, 2011, p. 11).

The United States in the Global Imagination

Such a conceptualization also requires us to challenge the position of the United States as the natural representative of "the West"—and, by extension, of global capitalism—in our examinations of processes of globalization. Recognizing the political nature of this positioning and the presence of alternative perspectives and modes of cultural production decentralizes the role of the United States as the source of "Western" transnational cultural influence and, more generally, as an unavoidable and totalizing model of modernity. This does not mean, however, that we should ignore the historical legacy of its global cultural influence or its continuing transnational power. The role of the United States must be differently centralized to focus on its complex engagement with globalized hybridity—or, to put it differently, on its historical, economic, and symbolic contribution to glocamalgamation.

This book demonstrated that even as new players are becoming increasingly globally influential, we cannot ignore the historical impact of U.S. transnational cultural power. As discussed in chapter 6, transnational media consumers' imagination of the global and of their own locality are significantly shaped by the experience of growing up surrounded by Hollywood, Disney, and U.S. television series. While these are certainly not the only globalized cultural forms French or Japanese media consumers were exposed to with in their youth—chapter 6 demonstrated, for instance, the equally significant presence of Japanese animation in the French context—these texts continue to hold a special, and often nostalgic, position in individuals' imagination. If this engagement with "imagined America" must be carefully differentiated from individuals' attitudes toward the United States as a geopolitical entity, the symbolic status of "America" remains an influential subtext of the process of imagining the global (including, ironically, in texts produced in other parts of the world). Media scholars must contend with this subtext not as a blatant example of U.S. cultural imperialism but as one ingredient of globalized hybridity—one important dimension of contemporary glocamalgamation.

Interestingly, the nostalgia surrounding "classic" globalized cultural products can easily be cultivated today as digital technology facilitates the re-release of older texts for newer generations. Indeed, if digital technology facilitates the development and spread of new globalized cultural forms, it also permits us to (re)engage with old ones. A large portion of contemporary popular culture is simply recycled stuff—periodic DVD re-releases of classic Disney animation, film remixes of popular Marvel comics, the return to the theater of the Star Wars prequel (itself drawing on a entire generation's nostalgic engagement with the earlier trilogy) this time in 3D. Parents who participated in my research frequently turned to the Internet to share with their children the texts that had shaped their own childhood—hence young informants' ability to sing the Candy theme song. Searching for a specific text might, in turn, lead to the (re)discovery of another in the vast pool of shared memories and fan favorites making up much of YouTube. This nostalgic dimension of global culture means that historically influential texts may remain significant well beyond the generations that first experienced them. In this context, the historical legacy of U.S. global cultural power, the fact that it has provided much of the "original" raw materials of globalized hybridity—even if these were subsequently remixed, re-interpreted, and/or re-appropriated—remains significant even as new actors are assertively entering the scene of global cultural production.

The United States' relative economic power and its historical influence also mean that its cultural industries retain much power to borrow, remix, and redistribute globalized cultural forms. Texts such as *Slumdog Millionaire* (Bollywood), *Speed Racer* (classic Japanese animation), *The Smurfs, The Adventures of Tintin* (Franco-Belgian *bandes dessinées*), and *Ugly Betty* (telenovela) are relatively recent examples. Hollywood studios and U.S. television producers are not the only media companies engaged in this process—as we have seen, Japanese animation studios have long been selling European culture back to Europe (and to much of the rest of the world)—but they remain influential. We must keep a critical eye on their ability to serve as a filter through which cultural forms from relatively less economically powerful cultural producers must pass if they are to reach a truly global status—we need to remain attuned, in other words, to the "blockages, bumps, and interference" (Appadurai, 2013, p. 69) that line the circuits of culture. After all, the *Smurfs* come home to their destroyed village only to rebuild it in New York City's image at the end of the 2011 Columbia Pictures film.

On the other hand, these texts actively draw on contemporary media consumers' large pool of global cultural capital. Viewers are expected to "get" the references to the "original" text or genre—as when Tintin finds a picture of himself (as he is drawn in the Franco-Belgian *bande dessinée*) in the market in the Steven Spielberg movie. In a globalized media market, these "American" texts may even be mainly targeted at a non-U.S. audience—as noted, *Tintin* was first released in Belgium and France, then in Quebec, before it opened in the United States and English-speaking Canada. Furthermore, the need to carefully locate U.S. influence within the broader context of media consumers' engagement with a wide array of globalized cultural forms has been well established throughout this book. I will not return to it here. These examples suggest that we need to continue to explore how cultural forms produced in the United States contribute to glocamalgamation's intense blurring of boundaries and to the imagination of the global in different localities.

More interesting, and less frequently recognized, side effects of the legacy of U.S. transnational cultural power discussed in chapter 6 are its consequences for U.S. media consumers who do not share the history of naturalized engagement with "non-native" media found in other environments. Thus, the most important dimension of the increased hybridity of globalized cultural forms may not be its ability to mitigate U.S. global cultural influence, even though that is certainly important, but its power to bring U.S. media consumers' imagination of the global a step closer to that of individuals in other parts of the world. As texts produced and originally distributed in other cultural contexts are increasingly becoming readily available on the U.S. market—*The Mysterious Cities of Gold* (the classic animated series so frequently mentioned by French and Japanese consumers) can now be viewed instantly on Netflix—and as Hollywood increasingly ostensibly draws its raw materials from globalized cultural forms, U.S. media consumers are given new points of entry into various elements of global culture. They are encouraged to more fully engage with the globalized hybridity that characterizes our contemporary era. The door may still only be cracked open (Stanley, 2013), but they are given more of a glimpse at the glocamalgamation surrounding them. This, in turn, might help them develop a more nuanced understanding of the fact that the notion of "the United States as the repository of good in the world" (Shor, 2010, p. 32) is but one mythical element of the global imagination.

Thinking in terms of glocamalgamation helps us understand *how* hybridity matters. It matters because it normalizes the presence of the global in our daily lives and blurs the boundaries of cultural representation. It matters because it is a contentious subtext of the negotiation of racial, gendered, class, and cultural identities under conditions of globalization. It matters because it decentralizes the role of the United States as a geopolitical entity while exposing its continuing symbolic power. It matters because it has the potential to challenge the "fetishism of boundaries" (Pieterse, 2003/2009, p. 98), to deconstruct *all sorts* of identities. It matters because it points to the bumps, roadblocks, and traffic jams in the flows of global culture that shape the imagination of the global.

Perhaps most importantly, thinking in terms of glocamalgamation can help us better understand how local subjectivities are constructed through "temporary negotiations between various globally circulating forms" (Appadurai, 2013, p. 69). It can help us wrap our heads around the fact that these subjectivities "are not subordinate instances of the global, but in fact the main evidence of its reality" (2013, p. 69). The case studies discussed in this book have started to sketch the contours of some of these temporary negotiations. We must continue to work to empirically identify and theoretically explore glocamalgamation's productive potential. Doing so will require us to further expand our horizon to include other contexts, other points of entry, other ways to experience the world in our academic texts. It will require a more translocal perspective.

Conclusion: Getting over
Our "Illusion d'optique"

Last, and most daunting, is the prospect that we shall have to find ways
to connect theories of intertextuality to theories of intercontextuality. . . .
Yet a framework for relating the global, the national, and the local has
yet to emerge.
—Appadurai, 1996, pp. 187–88

In his seminal work on the hybrid nature of contemporary cultures, Argentinian Mexican cultural critic Néstor García Canclini describes the anthropologist as entering the city by foot, the sociologist "by car and via the main highway," and "the communications scholar by plane" (1995, p. 4). The empirically informed theory of translocalism developed in this book aims at bringing communication scholars a little closer to the ground while keeping in mind the "bigger picture" of globalization. Heeding Kraidy and Murphy's suggestion that "it is through the comparative study of local life in various locations that a living, breathing sense of global communication flows, processes, and outcomes can be comprehensively grasped" (2008, p. 339), a multisited comparative analysis approaches the local/national/global as mutually constitutive elements of our contemporary condition. Considering the concrete conditions under which various local/national environments relate to each other in a globalized world and putting the emphasis on the multi-faceted relations, connections, and dynamics between local sites, it "[refocuses] on the local . . . without disengaging from issues involving global forces" (Kraidy and Murphy, 2008, p. 339). The three-way comparison encourages us to move beyond dichotomized conceptualizations. It forces us to develop thicker descriptions of both "local" processes and "global" interactions. It helps complicate our understanding of the local/national/global nexus. It gets us a step closer to developing "a practice of representation that illuminates the power of large-scale, imagined life possibilities over specific life trajectories" (Appadurai, 1996, p. 55).

A translocal approach is always necessarily partial. This book's focus on three powerful cultural producers aimed at deconstructing the common division of the world along East/West lines by pointing to significant differences within "the West" and drawing connections between contexts rarely considered in relationship to each other. By pointing to the continuing significance of racial and gendered dynamics in these three sites' negotiation of local/national/cultural identities it also challenged the notion that these economically powerful nations (including those classified as "Western") are comfortably installed in the "posts"—postracial struggle, postfeminism, postmodernity. It suggested that the intersection of race, ethnicity, and gender with definitions of national/cultural identity remains highly contentious in all three contexts, even if it is not as ostensibly recognized as it might be in environments—such as the Middle East (Echchaibi, 2011; Kraidy, 2009) and India (Hegde, 2011b; Parameswaran, 2011)—positioned as currently negotiating their entry into (post)modernity.

Translocal comparisons focusing on other contexts would be equally, if differently, productive. Other scholars have already engaged in them from different angles, even if the focus has thus far mostly remained on theoretical debates and intellectual positions (for examples, see McMillin, 2007; Stam and Shohat, 2012). I hope this book will inspire further work in this direction. Particularly needed is the kind of "more situated and empirically driven research" moving "beyond abstract and acontextual theorizations" (Shome, 2006b, p. 257) that scholars have identified as a crucial building block to our understanding of "how globalizing forces are working, or not working, in culture" (Morris, 2004, p. 181). Work, in other words, employing empirical evidence as a vital starting point to theorizing.

Scholarship at its best is a collective endeavor, a conversation based on mutual engagement, a "multidirectional polylogue" (Stam and Shohat, 2012, p. xix). While no individual scholar can provide a fully developed picture of processes of globalization spanning the entire globe—at least not when one is trying to develop the kind of "thick descriptions" advocated in this book—each contributes one building block of a larger intellectual edifice. Each strand of this conversation is necessarily affected by the context in which a scholar operates. Even "transnational interdisciplinarity is very much tied to, although not fixed by, the politics of the geography from within which we perform it" (Shome, 2006c, p. 21).

While this is, to some extent, unavoidable, developing a theory of translocalism requires us to develop a greater awareness of our own location(s). Exposing hybridity's normality and "exploring its genealogies" (Pieterse, 2003/2009, p. 91) require us to recognize both the productive potential and the possible blind spots of our own identities. It requires us, in other words, to tease out the politics of our own hybridity. Because "powerful interests are invested in boundaries and borders" (Pieterse, 2003/2009, p. 145), this is not always an easy task—including within an academic context where "boundary fetishism" often remains. Scholars' work is, for instance, frequently interpreted in light of their perceived membership in rigidly defined groups—"Western," "non-Western," "White," "minority," "woman"—with little consideration to the specific intricacies of their multiple selves (Shome, 2006c). Those who do not neatly "fit" in these categories are encouraged to "pick a camp." Under such conditions, as Stam and Shohat explain, the challenge is to engage in "a synergistic coalition rather than a competitive cockfight in which hyphenated Americans fight for the leftovers from the master's table" (2012, pp. 79–80).

Thus, one central task of the translocal project is to develop a critical awareness of the boundaries placed upon us by the culture of academia. This book has discussed some of the blind spots specific to the U.S. academic context and their possible influence on our conceptualizations of processes of globalization and transnational influence. More generally, because academic culture, wherever it might be, "takes its capital from the scholarly tradition, from the machineries of literacy and education, which are affordable only to a privileged few" (Chow, 1993, p. 114), it fosters (upper-) class biases. We must be careful not to assume that the experiences of cosmopolitan, middle-class, educated individuals (the kinds of people academics are most frequently in direct contact with) can be taken as the norm when considering individuals' engagement with the global.

Particularly problematic, as far as studies of global media are concerned, are the assumptions regarding the use of technology that permeate English-speaking academic culture. We may know that the majority of the world population does not have the kind of access to technology that academics typically enjoy, but moving beyond a purely intellectual recognition of this fact to imagine its ramifications is not an easy task. Furthermore, even in highly economically powerful nations where technology is widely available, rural, relatively lower-class (the two are frequently related) individuals may have quite a different relationship to it than upper-class and/or urban folks. For instance, the rural informants who participated in my research (both in France and Japan) frequently differentiated themselves from urbanites by pointing to what they characterized as the latter's obsession with technology. Privileging personal interaction over virtual engagement they often chose to use email or cell phones sparingly—I had to learn to resist my instinct to try to set up interviews through email as my messages were left unanswered for weeks at a time. Their Internet use tended to be hyperlocal—listings of the films to be shown at the community center, local flea-market summer schedule—and pragmatic. They distanced themselves from the YouTube obsessed, Facebook fixated Twittering crowd of the city. In other words, when engaging with digital technology, they negotiated their local/rural identities in relationship to the urban and national, as well as the global.

Other scholars have pointed to the urgent need to move beyond the study of metropolitan and urban practices in a number of other environments (for examples, see Shome, 2009; Spivak, 2004). While the Internet and other digital technologies are certainly shaping the way people engage with the global—as well as the national, local, and, more generally, each other—our understanding of these relatively new developments must be nuanced by an active commitment to placing them within their proper context.

As García Canclini reminds us, "It is not enough to study only from the metropolis, or from the context of peripheral or postcolonial nations, or even from one isolated discipline, or even a totalizing knowledge. An effective study of culture focuses on the intersections" (2001, p. 12). By forcing us to move beyond dualism(s) and binary thinking, an empirically driven and multisited translocal approach pushes us to recognize "the in-between the interstices" (Pieterse, 2003/2009, p. 120, emphasis in the text), the "cracks and crevices, and silences and sutures of the global" (Shome, 2006c, p. 3). It raises our awareness of the "fateful optical illusion" (Warnier, 2004, p. 91) created by the politics of the geography from which we perform research and, more generally, by the socio-cultural context in which we evolve—an illusion that necessarily shapes contemporary discourses about globalization.

In his recent sequel to *Modernity at Large*, Appadurai proposes that we start thinking about research as a human right. Calling for a reconceptualization of research as "the capacity to systematically increase the horizons of one's current knowledge," he proposes that we work to make this capacity "more widely available to all human beings" (2013, pp. 282, 283). Because it encourages us to destabilize the boundaries of all identities (including our own), a critical translocal perspective moves us a step closer to this more fluid and deparochialized definition of research as part of everyday life, wherever in the world we might be. A translocal perspective expands and complicates our imagination of the global.

Notes

Introduction

1. It is important to note, however, that while France's policies are frequently portrayed as idiosyncratic by the U.S. media and U.S. scholars alike, the policies of other non-English-speaking European nations (including other larger nations such as Spain, Italy, and Germany) are generally much closer to those of France than to those of the United States or Britain (McPhail, 2010).

2. The historical and institutional origins of the East/West dynamic are numerous and complex, but the most obvious ones include: (1) the disciplinary division into area studies that scholars must "fit into" if they are to receive funding and the complex identity politics arising from this division; (2) the historical influence of postcolonial theory on studies of globalization (Kraidy, 2005); and (3) the influence of the 1970s debates regarding the New World Information and Communication Order, which led to an additional focus on North/South dynamics (Mowlana, 1986/1997). Today, these two dividing lines are often used interchangeably. For instance, in *Grassroots Globalization and the Research Imagination*, Appadurai speaks in the same paragraph of the "cultural wars of the Western academic world" and the "theory mill of the North" (2001, p. 5).

3. Shome also frequently uses the terms "North Atlantic," "America," "U.S.," "Anglo," "West," and "Western" interchangeably in her work (see, for example, 2006c, p. 8; 2009, p. 700). While she carefully acknowledges that when she uses such terms as "Western students," "students in the West," or the "western academy," she is "thinking of the U.S. or U.K. primarily" (2009, p. 696) one wonders why these more general terms have to be used at all.

4. I am not mentioning these slippages here to dismiss these influential scholars' otherwise enlightening work (the extent to which they are cited throughout this book demonstrates the significance of their contribution), but to point to the persisting nature of these biases in English-language work coming out of a U.S. academic context. To use Shome's own words, "Recognizing such issues is less to point fingers and more to understand the (geo)politics informing the travel and recognition of politically committed interdisciplinary scholarship" (2006c, p. 7).

5. Condry emphasizes the performative aspects of the *genba* in his work and would, consequently, probably not apply the term to some of the texts examined here. I contend, however, that the concept of *genba* as sites offering a contextualized space through which to examine the simultaneous negotiation of global, national, and local identity under specific circumstances can be extended to other aspects of cultural production. After all, even "big media," while financed by large corporations often portrayed as faceless monolithic entities by globalization scholars, are produced and con-

sumed by individuals who, at least to some extent, express and negotiate their identity in the process.

Chapter 1

1. TF1 was the first French channel to be privatized by then prime minister Jacques Chirac in 1987. Today, the French television system consists of six analog channels (known as the "chaînes Hertziennes"), including two free private channels (TF1 and M6), one pay private channel (Canal +), and three free public channels (France 2, formerly Antenne 2; France 3, formerly France Régions; and France 5/Arte, which share a channel with France 5 broadcasting during the day and the Franco-German Arte in prime time). Since 2005, 18 free additional channels and 10 pay digital channels known as the TNT system (*télévision numérique terrestre*/digital terrestrial television), also available with a decoder, and several Internet providers also offer additional digital channels for free with an Internet subscription.

2. A product of the European Broadcasting Union, which also produces the Eurovision Contest, *Jeux sans Frontières* owes its original concept to former French president Charles de Gaulle who wanted to provide a forum through which German and French youth could meet in order to heal the wounds of World War II. Eurovision television, the programming branch of the European Broadcasting Union, proposed to resurrect the show in 2007, but ultimately cancelled production due to financial difficulties (European Broadcasting Union, n.d.).

3. The celebration of holidays and customs of religious (typically Catholic) origin on the part of non-practicing Christians (and, often, non-Christians) is not uncommon in France where the Catholic religion is generally perceived as one element of the country's cultural and historical fabric rather than as a personal lifestyle choice. Thus, viewers would be more likely to interpret *Star Academy*'s nod to Candlemas as pointing to a cultural tradition rather than to a religious practice. The different approach to religion in the United States and France is further illustrated, for instance, by the fact that individuals of all faiths (or no faith at all) send their children to Catholic schools, including a large section of France's Muslim population attracted by these private schools' greater tolerance for the display of religious symbols—including the veil— prohibited in public schools.

4. The show aired continuously from 2001 to 2008 with 2008 featuring two seasons.

5. Cyril was the first black candidate to win *Star Academy* in the show's 6th season (2006–7).

6. The constitution of the 5th French Republic states that "France is a Republic . . . that guarantees the equality of all citizens in the eyes of the law, regardless of origin, race or religion."

7. The French republic is divided into 27 administrative regions—22 in metropolitan France and 5 overseas. Martinique is one of France's 5 overseas regions.

8. A Franco-Congolese rapper, originally part of the group Ministère AMER, to be further discussed in chapter 4.

9. For example, Jenifer, the show's first winner in 2002, has released four albums since and has won an MTV Europe music award. In 2007, her effigy was included in the Grévin wax museum in Paris.

10. Such as the award of the 2008 Nobel Prize in literature to French writer Jean-Marie Gustave Le Clézio, which Prime Minister François Fillon claimed "blatantly refutes the theory of a so-called decline of French culture" (Lyall, October 9, 2008).

11. The shows may actually be recorded but are shown as if they happened in real time.

Chapter 2

1. Speaking of a "transatlantic short circuit" in the ways French and U.S. intellectuals approach race relations and multiculturalism, Stam and Shohat highlight the historical significance of race relations in the competitive relationship between France and the United States. They argue, for instance, that France's postwar embrace of African American artists and intellectuals (fueled in part by the influx of African American soldiers on French soil) "while undoubtedly sincere . . . also afforded a narcissistic payoff for French whites, who could simultaneously demonstrate their relative lack of racism while also using blacks as a vehicle for expressing resentment against U.S. power in Europe" (2012, p. 47).

2. One editorial was titled "Nation Must Pool Wisdom to Prepare for Unforeseeable," but actually consisted of a call for local governments to pool their resources together and for stronger safety checks on nuclear reactors (April 10, 2011). Another warned in its headline that "Excessive Self-Restraint May Hinder Recovery" (April 8, 2011), but focused on the possible economic consequences of failing to return to normal levels of consumption.

Chapter 3

1. Pseudonyms are used throughout the book to identify all informants. In the case of Japanese informants, the use of first name ("Takako") or last name followed by the title "san" ("Horie-san") is employed to indicate the nature of my relationship with different informants—first name only for those informants with whom I conducted extensive participant observation and with whom I have a relatively close relationship, and the more commonly used last name followed by "san" for those informants with whom my relationship was more formal.

2. The East/West division is alive and well in Japanese popular discourse. The term "Western" is generally used in Japan to refer to a hybrid mix of Euro-American cultural influences.

3. Many Caucasian models in Japanese magazines are actually from Eastern Europe.

4. Of course, my informants' professed admiration for Caucasian features may have had something to do with my presence in the interviews. Because of our close relationship, the women I interviewed were probably careful not to hurt my feelings by criticizing the physical appearance of members of my race. While this may have been at least partially the case, a number of factors suggest that this was not the only possible explanation. For one thing, my informants typically did not hesitate to criticize Western women on numerous other levels—deeming them, among other things, selfish, lazy, and sexually promiscuous. Furthermore, strangers stopped me in the streets of the village to comment on how white, beautiful, and tall I was. A woman once com-

mented to me at the public bath that "all *gaijin* have such good bodies"—a statement clearly not empirically supported by the presence of my then pregnant, and starting to show, naked body.

5. Note the association of "America" with "whiteness."

6. It should also be noted that hip-hop has not reached the kind of popularity in the Japanese countryside that it enjoys in Tokyo where, as will be discussed in chapter 4, hip-hop clubs allow fans to directly engage with DJs and the broader hip-hop culture.

7. A highly popular pop artist in the late 1990s, Namie has since successfully redefined herself as an R&B star. She is partly responsible for making identification with African American styles more appealing to young women in Japan.

8. I am aware that other identity factors—such as sexual orientation and ability—also enter into the equation here. These factors, however, were not ones I had enough of a chance to explore with my informants to knowledgeably discuss in this chapter.

Chapter 4

1. Scholars have noted that it is through rapping that hip-hop most powerfully inscribes itself in different socio-cultural and linguistic contexts (Pecqueux, 2007). Consequently, while the terms "hip-hop" and "rap" will both be used in this chapter, greater focus will be placed on rapping than on other constitutive elements of hip-hop such as dance or graffiti. Furthermore, the globally distributed cultural production of French artists in the hip-hop genre is generally known as "French rap."

2. Scholars have described a similar process in places as diverse as Puerto Rico (Baez, 2006), Slovakia (Barrer, 2009), Newfoundland (Clarke and Hiscock, 2009), Algeria (Davies and Bentahila, 2006), Malawi (Gilman and Fenn, 2006), Montreal (Low, Sarkar, and Winer, 2009), Colombia, Cuba, and Mexico (Tickner, 2008) to name only a few of the most recent examples.

3. While the roots of hip-hop are complex and debated, scholars generally agree to pinpoint the origins of the global phenomenon that we know today as hip-hop to the East Coast of the United States in the 1970s (Dyson, 2007; Mitchell, 2001; Rose, 2008).

4. All artists in the tradition of socially engaged singer-songwriters.

5. Metropolitan France is often referred to as "the hexagon" because of its somewhat hexagonal shape.

6. One of the world's best-known francophone singers, Renaud (his full name is Renaud Séchan) is a politically engaged singer-songwriter with leftist, environmentalist, and, at times, anarchist leanings whose songs are often highly critical of French culture and politics.

7. A former member of the group NTM—which, as discussed, can either stand for "le Nord Transmet le Message" or "Nique Ta Mère" (fuck your mother)—along with Kool Shen. Formed in 1989, NTM was a highly influential force in the development of French rap, particularly in its more openly violent form.

8. French rappers also frequently engage in the long tradition of "letters to the President"—songs written as open letters to France's leader—that Pecqueux (2007) identifies as a significant element of France's cultural heritage. Written and first interpreted by Boris Vian in 1954 (who was himself inspired by a longer 19th-century tradition of calling draftees to desert in songs), the "original" letter titled

"Le Deserteur"—in which Vian declared his refusal to fight in the Algerian war— was later interpreted by, among others, Marcel Mouloudji, Maxime Le Forestier, and Johnny Hallyday, before Michel Sardou offered his own version in 1979 ("Monsieur le Président de France") followed by Renaud in 1983 ("Déserteur"). The tradition was then taken up by rappers such as Lionel D. in 1990 ("Monsieur le Président") and Fabe in 1997 ("Lettre au Président"). Salif's 2001 song "Notre Vie S'Résume en une Seule Phrase" also refers to the practice, even though he refuses to engage in it: "Pour parler au président pas b'soin de faire de letters / Si j'puis me permettre qu'il aille se faire mettre" [To talk to the president no need to write a letter / If I may say so, he can go do himself].

9. French schools have historically been closed on Wednesdays.

10. In one of the most famous songs of the French version of the musical, the character of Gavroche sings "Je suis tombé par terre / c'est la faute à Voltaire" [I fell on the ground / it's Voltaire's fault].

11. I am consciously choosing to use the term "black" American rather than "African" American because if the term "African American" refers to a racial (black) as well as cultural characteristic in the U.S. context, this is not necessarily the case in other parts of the world. Algerian rappers, for instance, are (North) African but (typically) not racially black, and the politics of race they discuss significantly differ from those faced by American rappers.

12. A variation on the American "N" word sometimes used in the Japanese hip-hop scene.

13. The reasons why I am choosing to define Solaar as a French rapper rather than as Senegalese will, I hope, become obvious later in the chapter.

14. The so-called Carignon Law (named after then minister of communication Alain Carignon) passed in 1994 and modified in 2000 (Conseil Superieur de L'Audiovisuel, n.d.).

15. He has indeed been one of most globally influential French artists since the mid-1990s. In addition to multiple tours throughout Europe, Africa, and the United States, he has appeared in several Bollywood films. One of his songs was used as the soundtrack for the final episode of the U.S. television series *Sex and the City*.

16. He even was one of the first celebrities to be caricatured as a puppet, along with the likes of Johnny Hallyday, Vanessa Paradis, Josiane Balasko, and Gérard Depardieu (to name a few), in *Les Minikeums*—a youth program parodying various aspects of French (and global) popular culture in short skits.

17. Second-generation immigrants, generally of Arab descent.

18. Incest, homosexuality, pedophilia, and eroticism were constant themes in his songs and films.

19. The ban is discussed in some of Brassens' letters displayed at the Espace George Brassens in Sete, France.

20. *Burakumin* are descendents of members of Japanese society historically outcast because of their professional activity—butchers, tanners, executioners, gravediggers. They still face severe discrimination today in employment and marriage. *Nikkeijin* are second- and third-generation descendents of Japanese emigrants who settled in South America (especially Brazil) starting in the late 19th century. Often of mixed racial heritage, *nikkeijin* and their spouses are allowed to work as migrant workers in Japan (Roth, 2003; Sellek, 1997).

21. While, from a Western point of view, Korean and Japanese might appear to share an "Asian" racial identity, Yoshino Kosaku (1997) describes a tendency among Japanese to think of themselves as a distinct racial group (see also Kondo, 1990).

22. Couscous is a popular dish in France that is generally associated with the cuisine of North African immigrants.

Chapter 5

1. Blyton's books and characters are still highly popular in France today, as her original series such as *Noddy* (*Oui-Oui* in French), *The Famous Five* (*Le Club des Cinq*), and *The Secret Seven* (*Le Clan des Sept*) have been reprinted for a new generation of young readers to enjoy. *Noddy* was also turned into a television series.

2. Goldorak appeared under the title *Grandizer*—with an "a" as opposed to *Grendizer*, the more commonly romanization of the Japanese グランダイザ found in other parts of the world—in Jim Terry's *Force Five* series produced in response to the popularity of the Shogun Warrior's toys. The series was not shown nationally, however, only briefly appearing in a handful of local markets.

3. One of the first and most globally successful anime series, *Candy* enjoyed great popularity throughout Europe, Southeast Asia, Africa, and Latin America. In a recent personal email exchange regarding the global influence of Japanese animation, a Mexican journalist had this comment: "*Candy Candy* and some other Japanese cartoons were part of my childhood too, even nowadays my friends and I talk about them, they became 'a cult' television show . . . they had successful re-runs until a few years ago . . . and they even became one of best seller DVDs in the black market in Mexico! But it's funny to hear how my friends still talk about falling in love the very first time with Anthony or Terry [Candy's two consecutive love interests]. Those stories have created a great impact and identification among people from different countries."

4. In an anecdotal illustration of this process, my younger daughter recently called on her sister to "come watch the Japanese show" when watching *Olive et Tom* (*Captain Tsubasa*) on French television. When I asked her how she knew this show featuring a relatively culturally odorless soccer team was Japanese, she answered "the faces."

5. The generation following the "generation *Goldorak*" is frequently referred to in France as "the Club Dorothée generation."

6. He is referring to the original *Dragon Ball* Toei Animation series (not the later *Dragon Ball Z*) broadcast in Japan from 1986 to 1989 and in France starting in 1988.

7. These comments were reminiscent of those of Japanese informants who all remembered growing up with manga. They contrasted, however, with those of U.S. consumers who often noted that comics were not really something they engaged with while growing up: "Comic books did not grab me, they were not around. Nobody that I knew was reading comic books," (35-year-old female); "I didn't have any friends that did the comic book thing" (32-year-old female); "Comic books was like . . . I don't know, the direction of the books confuses us. Like I don't know where to read what, do you know what I mean?" (28-year-old female); "I just never read comic books. I just was never interested in them" (33-year-old male); "My parents wouldn't allow [comic books] in the house" (55-year-old female). While some (mostly male) U.S. media consumers did remember enjoying comic books, the level of penetration of the genre in the United States does not match that found in France or Japan. Comic book charac-

ters, however, such as Spiderman, Batman, and Flash Gordon were certainly familiar to U.S. (and, incidentally, global) consumers: "[The original *Batman* series] was the only thing we could watch at night. And *Flash Gordon*. If we ate . . . if we ate all our food and helped with clean up, we could watch *Flash*" (55-year-old female).

8. A 2005 survey of advertising in women's magazines in seven countries (Brazil, China, France, India, South Korea, Thailand, and the United States) found that French (and Thai) advertisements "showed the highest levels of sexuality" (Nelson and Paek, 2005, p. 380). The United States was somewhere in the middle.

9. I am aware that, considering the wide diversity of the U.S. population, the suggestion that there is such a thing as "the U.S. audience" is essentializing. I hope the reader will excuse this temporary oversimplification, as the nature of U.S. consumers' experiences of global culture will be further elaborated in chapter 7.

Chapter 6

1. The average cost of a film produced in France was $7.3 million in 2010, up 13.5 percent from $6.8 million in 2009 (Leffler, January 13, 2011). Compare that to the United States where the average cost of a major studio movie was about $65 million when the MPAA stopped tracking the number in 2006 (Glossary of Movie Business Terms, 2014). *Avatar* cost about $280 million, the third *Pirates of the Caribbean* $300 million—not counting marketing costs (Keegan, December 22, 2009).

2. The cowboy hero of the Franco-Belgian *bande dessinée* of the same name.

3. The fact that she used the term "anime" to refer to the Disney film illustrates how blurry the cultural distinction between different texts can be.

4. The consumption of Disney fare was further complicated for both Japanese and French informants (particularly relatively younger ones) by the fact that Disney has been physically reterritorialized into their own national geographies in the form of theme parks in their respective capitals (Tokyo Disneyland and Disney Paris): as a 15-year-old French woman exclaimed, "Disney, it's in Paris!" For rural informants living hundreds of miles away from these parks—most frequently visited within the context of a (school) trip to the capital—Disney symbolized the urban/national as well as the global.

5. The series takes place in Finland under Russian occupation and relates the adventures of a young girl forced to work on a farm after her mother's departure for Germany.

6. Note here that while she may not have read it, she is familiar with the novel and can identify its author.

7. When I first moved to Japan in the mid-1990s, I was happy to find out that French films and even television series were much more widely and rapidly available there than in the United States. I was able to catch up on much French popular culture I had missed while living in the United States.

8. The *Smurfs* animated series was indeed frequently mentioned in interviews, possibly due to the fact that interviews with U.S. informants took place relatively shortly after the release of the Hollywood movie of the same name. While the animated television series was produced in the United States, the fact that the characters themselves are classic Franco-Belgian *bandes dessinées* characters complicates their identity.

9. The U.S. media consumers I interviewed frequently linked their *overall* media

consumption to their racial or ethnic identity: "the *Cosby Show* was huge thing for me as a teenager, because I lived in a black family with two professional parents, and I felt like, hey it is us, we exist on TV. I felt that was a positive representation of black people that was closer to my reality" (35-year-old African American woman); "We saw *Kung Fu Theater* a lot growing up. Because it was about Asians and we never saw Asians on TV" (38-year-old Asian American woman). A 31-year-old Italian American fondly recalled, "the *Golden Girls*, it is like a huge part of my relationship with my grandma . . . she loved them, and my family is very identifiable Italian Americans. The grandma Sophia Petrolo was Sicilian, although to my grandma she does not make that distinction, so that was a huge shared experience."

10. Of course, like their French or Japanese counterparts U.S. informants may have consumed non-U.S. fare (in particular British texts) without being aware of their cultural origin while growing up. The fact that, as adults, they could not recall engaging with global culture at the time significantly differs, however, from the experiences described by French and Japanese media consumers.

11. As noted in the introduction, the media consumers I interviewed in the United States were relatively more urban and more highly educated than my informants in France and Japan. Thus, their tendency to actively engage with foreign texts as an intellectualized activity might in part stem from this different status.

Chapter 7

1. By "French theorists" I mean intellectuals operating within the French cultural environment and academic system. Thus, Mattelart, while born in Belgium, would fit this category as a professor at Paris VIII and researcher at MSH-Paris-Nord. It should be noted, however, that theorists outside the French environment, while facing different global circumstances, might share some of the elements of these individuals' approach to globalization. Canada's situation vis-à-vis the United States, or Quebec's complex relationship to both the United States and France, for instance, cannot be adequately understood in conceptualizations of globalization focusing solely on East/West or North/South power dynamics.

2. The term "alter-mondialisme," used to refer in French to what in English is generally characterized as "anti-globalization," further illustrates the key philosophical differences between globalization and mondialisation. Rather than negatively defining the movement as an *oppositional* position, it (literally) recognizes it as a valid *alternative*.

Bibliography

Abelson, Reed, and Alan Feuer. "10,000 Patients and Staff Members Await Evacuation from Barely Functional Hospitals." *New York Times*, September 1, 2005.

"Aeon Store Reopens in Disaster-Hit City." *Yomiuri Shimbun/Daily Yomiuri*, April 1, 2011.

Allison, Anne. *Millennial Monsters: Japanese Toys and the Global Imagination*. Berkeley: University of California Press, 2006.

Andrejevic, Mark. *Reality TV: The Work of Being Watched*. Lanham, MD: Rowman & Littlefield Publishers, 2003.

Ang, Ien. *Watching Dallas: Soap Opera and the Melodramatic Imagination*. London: Methuen, 1985.

Appadurai, Arjun. "Disjuncture and Difference in the Global Cultural Economy." *Theory, Culture and Society*, no. 7 (1990): 295–310.

Appadurai, Arjun. *Fear of Small Numbers*. London: Duke University Press, 2006.

Appadurai, Arjun. *The Future as Cultural Fact: Essays on the Global Condition*. New York: Verso, 2013.

Appadurai, Arjun. "Grassroots Globalization and the Research Imagination." In *Globalization*, edited by Arjun Appadurai, 1–21. Durham, NC: Duke University Press, 2001.

Appadurai, Arjun. *Modernity at Large: Cultural Dimensions of Globalization*. Minneapolis: University of Minnesota Press, 1996.

Armstead, Ronni. "Las Krudas, Spatial Practice, and the Performance of Diaspora." *Meridians: Feminism, Race, Transnationalism* 8, no. 1 (2008): 130–43.

Arupsu no shôjo Haiji no kitte [Heidi girl from the Alps stamp]. 2013. http://www.post.japanpost.jp/kitte_hagaki/stamp/tokusyu/2012/h250123_t.html.

Báez, Jillian M. "'En Mi Imperio': Competing Discourses of Agency in Ivy Queen's Reggaetón." *Centro Journal* 18, no. 11 (2006): 63–81.

Barrer, Peter. "'My White, Blue, and Red Heart': Constructing a Slovak Identity in Rap Music." *Popular Music & Society* 32, no. 1 (2009): 59–75.

Basu, Dipannita, and Pnina Werbner. "Bootstrap Capitalism and the Culture Industries: A Critique of Invidious Comparisons in the Study of Ethnic Entrepreneurship." *Ethnic and Racial Studies* 24, no. 2 (2001): 236–62.

Bazin, Hugues. "Préface." In *Rap, Expression des Lascars: Significations et Enjeux du Rap dans la Société Française* [Rap, the expression of rascals: Rap's significance and stakes in French society], by Manuel Boucher, 10–16. Paris: L'Harmattan, 1998.

Beau, Marie-Agnès. "Hip Hop and Rap in Europe. The Culture of the Urban Ghetto's." In *Music, Culture and Society in Europe*, edited by Paul Rutten, 129–34. Brussels: European Music Office, 1996.

Belson, Ken. "As Routines Falter, So Does National Confidence." *New York Times*, March 16, 2011.

Belson, Ken, and Norimitsu Onishi. "In Deference to Crisis, a New Obsession Sweeps Japan: Self-Restraint." *New York Times*, March 28, 2011.

Belson, Ken, Hiroko Tabuchi, and Keith Bradsher. "Japan Races to Restart Reactors' Cooling System." *New York Times*, March 19, 2011.

Bennett, Andy. "Hip-Hop am Main, Rappin' on the Tyne: Hip-Hop Culture as a Local Construct in Two European Cities." In *That's the Joint! The Hip-Hop Studies Reader*, edited by Murray Forman and Mark A. Neal, 177–200. New York: Routledge, 2004.

Bernard, Philippe. "Banlieues: La Provocation Coloniale [Suburbs: The colonial provocation]." *Le Monde*, November 19, 2005.

Berndt, Jaqueline. "Considering Manga Discourse: Location, Ambiguity, Historicity." In *Japanese Visual Culture: Explorations in the World of Manga and Anime*, edited by Mark W. MacWilliams, 295–310. New York: M. E. Sharpe, 2008.

Bernstein, Richard. "Despite Minor Incidents, Chance of Large-Scale Riots Elsewhere in Europe Is Seen as Small." *New York Times*, November 8, 2005.

Bernstein, Richard. "The View from Abroad." *New York Times*, September 4, 2005.

Bird, S. Elizabeth. *For Enquiring Minds: A Cultural Study of Supermarket Tabloids*. Knoxville: University of Tennessee Press, 1992.

Blum, Françoise. "Ils Sont Entrés en Politique [They entered politics]." *Le Monde*, November 11, 2005.

Bocquet, Jean-Louis, and Philippe Pierre-Adolphe. *Rap Ta France—Les Rappeurs Français Prennent La Parole* [Rap your France: Rappers speak up]. Paris: J'ai Lu, 1999.

Bordenave, Yves, and Mustapha Kessous. "Une Nuit avec des 'Émeutiers' qui ont 'la Rage' [A night with angry rioters]." *Le Monde*, November 8, 2005.

Boucher, Manuel. *Rap, Expression des Lascars: Significations et Enjeux du Rap dans la Société Française* [Rap, the expression of rascals: Significance and stakes of rap in French society]. Paris: L'Harmattan, 1998.

Bouthier, Antoine. "Japon: Le Gouvernement Appelé à plus de Transparence [Japan: Government calls for more transparence]." *Le Monde*, March 14, 2001.

Bouthier, Antoine. "Nucléaire: La Presse Japonaise Critiquée [Nuclear: The Japanese press criticized]." *Le Monde*, March 21, 2001.

Boyle, John Hunter. *Modern Japan: The American Nexus*. Fort Worth, TX: Harcourt Brace College, 1993.

Bradsher, Keith, and Hiroko Tabuchi. "Workers Brave Radiation Risk at Failing Japan Reactors." *New York Times*, March 16, 2011.

Brassens, Georges. "Le Gorille." *La Mauvaise Reputation*. LP. Paris: Polydor, 1952.

Brassens, Georges. "Le Nombril des Femmes d'Agents." *Chanson Pour L'Auvergnat*. CD. Paris: Intsm, 1995.

Brienza, Casey E. "Books, Not Comics: Publishing Fields, Globalization, and Japanese Manga in the United States." *Publishing Research Quarterly* 25, no. 2 (2009): 101–17.

Bronner, Luc, and Mustapha Kessous. "Des Cités à la Cité [From the cities to the housing project]." *Le Monde*, March 23, 2006.

Bronner, Luc, and Catherine Simon. "Clichy-sous-Bois Cristallise les Tensions Politiques et Sociales [Clichy-sous-Bois Crystallizes Political and Social Tensions]." *Le Monde*, November 2, 2005.

Brooks, David. "Katrina's Silver Lining." *New York Times*, September 8, 2005.

Bynoe, Yvonne. "Getting Real about Global Hip Hop." *Georgetown Journal of International Affairs* 3, no. 1 (2002): 77–84.

Byrka, Delphine. "Les Sacrifiés de Fukushima [Sacrificed at Fukushima]." *Paris Match*, April 8, 2011.

Calhoun, Lindsay. "Will the Real Slim Shady Please Stand Up?": Masking Whiteness, Encoding Hegemonic Masculinity in Eminem's *Marshall Mathers' LP*." *Howard Journal of Communication*, 16, no. 4 (2005): 276–94.

Cannon, Steve. "Paname City Rapping: B-Boys in the Banlieues and Beyond." In *Postcolonial Cultures in France*, edited by Alec Hargreaves and Mark McKinney, 150–66. London: Routledge, 1994.

Caramel, Laurence. "Venir en Aide à la Troisième Puissance Mondiale, une Situation Inédite pour les Organisations Humanitaires [Coming to the aid of the third most powerful power, a new situation for humanitarian organizations]." *Le Monde*, March 20, 2011.

Castells, Manuel. *The Internet Galaxy: Reflections on the Internet, Business and Society.* Oxford: Oxford University Press, 2001.

Castells, Manuel. *The Power of Identity: The Information Age: Economy, Society and Culture.* Oxford: Blackwell, 2003.

Castells, Manuel. *The Rise of the Network Society: The Information Age: Economy, Society and Culture.* Oxford: Blackwell, 2000.

Ceaux, Pascal. "Les Policiers Dénoncent Désormais l'Action de 'Bandes Organisées' [The police now denounce the action of organized gangs]." *Le Monde*, November 4, 2005.

Chaillou, Philippe. "Ces Brimades qui Empoisonnent l'Atmosphère des Banlieues [Those vexations that poison the suburbs' atmosphere]." *Le Monde*, January 17, 2006.

"Chaos en Louisiane Après les Ravages de Katrina [Chaos in Louisiana after Katrina's devastation]." *Le Monde*, September 3, 2005.

Chemin, Anne. "Pour sa Famille, the Jeune Fouad 'Est Devenu un Symbole' [For his family, the young Fouad 'became a symbol']." *Le Monde*, November 16, 2005.

Choo, Kukhee. "Girls Return Home: Portrayal of Femininity in Popular Japanese Girls' Manga and Anime Texts During the 1990s in *Hana yori Dango* and *Fruits Basket*." *Women: A Cultural Review* 19, no. 3 (2008): 275–96.

Chow, Rey. *Writing Diaspora: Tactics of Intervention in Contemporary Cultural Studies.* Bloomington: Indiana University Press, 1993.

Clarey, Christopher. "Athletes Come Out in Support of Japan." *New York Times*, March 20, 2011.

Clarke, Sandra, and Philip Hiscock. "Hip-hop in a Post-insular Community: Hybridity, Local Language, and Authenticity in an Online Newfoundland Rap Group." *Journal of English Linguistics* 37, no. 3 (2009): 241–61.

Coles, Les. "Japan Rallies for Victims of Hurricane Katrina." *Yomiuri Shimbun/Daily Yomiuri*, September 29, 2005.

Condry, Ian. "Anime Creativity: Characters and Premises in the Quest for Cool Japan." *Theory, Culture & Society* 26, no. 2–3 (2009): 139–63.

Condry, Ian. *Hip-Hop Japan: Rap and the Paths of Cultural Globalization.* Durham, NC: Duke University Press Books, 2006.

Condry, Ian. "Japanese Hip-Hop and the Globalization of Popular Culture." In *Urban Life: Readings in the Anthropology of the City*, edited by George Gmelch and Walter P. Zenner, 357–87. Prospect Heights, IL: Waveland Press, 2001.

Condry, Ian. "The Social Production of Difference: Imitation and Authenticity in Japanese Rap Music." In *Transactions, Transgressions, Transformations: American Culture in Western Europe and Japan*, edited by Uta G. Poiger and Heide Fehrenbach, 166–84. New York: Berghahn Books, 2000.

Conrad, Kate, Travis L. Dixon, and Yuanyuan Zhang. "Controversial Rap Themes, Gender Portrayals and Skin Tone Distortion: A Content Analysis of Rap Music Videos." *Journal of Broadcasting & Electronic Media* 53, no. 1 (2009): 134–56.

Conseil Superieur de L'Audiovisual. n.d. "Les Obligations de Diffusion d'Oeuvres Audiovisuelles [Obligations of diffusion of audiovisual works]." http://www.csa.fr/Television/Le-suivi-des-programmes/La-diffusion-des-oeuvres/Les-obligations-de-diffusion-d-aeuvres-audiovisuelles.

Cooper-Chen, Anne M. *Cartoon Cultures: The Globalization of Japanese Popular Media*. New York: Peter Lang Publishing, 2010.

Cornyetz, Nina. "Fetishized Blackness: Hip Hop and Racial Desire in Contemporary Japan." *Social Text* no. 41 (1994): 113–39.

"Cosmopolitan." n.d. http://www.cosmomediakit.com/r5/home.asp.

Cowell, Alan. "What Britain Can Tell France about Rioters." *New York Times*, November 20, 2005.

Creighton, Millie R. "Imaging the Other in Japanese Advertising Campaigns." In *Occidentalism: Images of the West*, edited by James G. Carrier, 135–260. New York: Oxford University Press, 1995.

Cross, Gary. "Foreword." In *Millennial Monsters: Japanese Toys and the Global Imagination*, by Anne Allison, xv–xviii. Berkeley: University of California Press, 2006.

Dao, James. "The Misery Is Spread Equally." *New York Times*, August 31, 2005.

Darling-Wolf, Fabienne. "From Airbrushing to Liposuction: The Technological Reconstruction of the Female Body." In *Women's Bodies, Women's Lives: Health, Well-Being and Body Image*, edited by Miedema Baukje, Janet M. Stoppard, and Vivienne Anderson, 277–93. Toronto: Second Story Press, 2000b.

Darling-Wolf, Fabienne. "Gender, Beauty, and Western Influence: Negotiated Femininity in Japanese Women's Magazines." In *The Gender Challenge to Media: Diverse Voices from the Field*, edited by Elizabeth L. Toth and Linda Aldoory, 267–415. Cresskill, NJ: Hampton Press, 2000a.

Darling-Wolf, Fabienne. "Getting over Our 'Illusion d'Optique': From Globalization to Mondialisation (Through French Rap)." *Communication Theory* 18, no. 2 (2008): 187–209.

Darling-Wolf, Fabienne. "The Men and Women of *non-no*: Gender, Race, and Hybridity in Two Japanese Magazines." *Critical Studies in Media Communication* 23, no. 3 (2006): 181–99.

Darling-Wolf, Fabienne. "SMAP, Sex, and Masculinity: Constructing the Perfect Female Fantasy in Japanese Popular Music." *Popular Music and Society* 27, no. 3 (2004): 357–70.

Davet, Gérard, and Fabrice Lhomme. "La Version Policière des Évènements of Clichy-sous-Bois [The police's version of the Clichy-sous-Bois events]." *Le Monde*, November 11, 2005.

Davidson, Danica. "Manga Grows in the Heart of Europe." CNN, January 26, 2012.

Davies, Eirlys E., and Abdelali Bentahila. "Code Switching and the Globalisation of Popular Music: The Case of North African Rai and Rap." *Multilingua—Journal of Cross-Cultural and Interlanguage Communication* 25 (2006): 367–92.

Dawson, Michael C. "Dis Beat Disrupts: Ideology and the Politics of Race." In *The Cultural Territories of Race: Black and White Boundaries*, edited by Michele Lamont, 318–42. Chicago: University of Chicago Press, 1999.

De Beer, Arnold S., and John C. Merrill. *Global Journalism: Topical Issues and Media Systems*. Boston: Allyn & Bacon, 2008.

Dee Nasty. *Paname City Rappin'*. CD. Maison Alfort, France: Cabana Music, 1984.

Delberghe, Michel. "Fuite des Classes Moyennes [The flight of the middle classes]." *Le Monde*, November 6, 2005.

Demers, David. *Global Media: Menace or Messiah?* Cresskill, NJ: Hampton Press, 1999.

Dennis, Christopher. "Afro-Colombian Hip-Hop: Globalization, Popular Music and Ethnic Identities." *Studies in Latin American Popular Culture* 25 (2006): 271–95.

Dewan, Shaila, and Janet Roberts. "Louisiana's Deadly Storm Took Strong as Well as the Helpless." *New York Times*, December 18, 2005.

"Disasters Top This Year's News." *Yomiuri Shimbun/Daily Yomiuri*, December 30, 2005.

"Dog Rescued from Debris Floating off Miyagi Pref." *Yomiuri Shimbun/Daily Yomiuri*, April 3, 2011.

Dollase, Hiromi Tsuchiya. "Early Twentieth Century Japanese Girls' Magazine Stories: Examining Shôjo Voice in Hanamonogatari (Flower Tales)." *Journal of Popular Culture* 36, no. 4 (2003): 724–55.

Dollase, Hiromi Tsuchiya. "Girls on the Home Front: An Examination of Shôjo no tomo Magazine 1937–1945." *Asian Studies Review* 32, no. 3 (2008): 323–39.

Dorfman, Ariel, and Armand Mattelart. *How to Read Donald Duck: Imperialist Ideology in the Disney Comic*. New York: International General, 1971.

Dov, Shinar. "'Re-membering' and 'Dis-membering' Europe: A Cultural Strategy of Studying the Role of Communication in the Transformation of Collective Identities." In *Globalization, Communication and Transnational Civil Society*, edited by Sandra Braman and Annabelle Sreberny-Hohammadi, 89–103. Cresskill, NJ: Hampton Press, 1996.

Dower, John W. "Peace and Democracy in Two Systems: External Policy and Internal Conflict." In *Postwar Japan as History*, edited by Andrew Gordon, 3–33. Berkeley: University of California Press, 1993.

Drazen, Patrick. *Anime Explosion! The What? Why? & Wow! of Japanese Animation*. Berkeley: Stone Bridge Press, 2003.

Du Gay, Paul. "Introduction to the First Edition." In *Doing Cultural Studies: The Story of the Sony Walkman*, second edition, edited by Paul Du Gay, Stuart Hall, Linda Janes, Anders Hoed Madsen, Hugh MacKay, and Keith Negus, xxviii–xxxii. Thousand Oaks, CA: Sage, 2013.

Durham, Meenakshi Gigi. "Displaced Persons: Symbols of South Asian Femininity and the Returned Gaze in U.S. Media Culture." *Communication Theory* 11, no. 2 (2001): 201–17.

Duus, Peter. *Modern Japan*. Boston: Houghton Mifflin, 1998.

Dwyer, Jim, and Christopher Drew. "Fear Exceeded Crime's Reality in New Orleans." *New York Times*, September 29, 2005.

Dyson, Michael Eric. *Know What I Mean? Reflections on Hip-Hop*. New York: Basic Civitas Books, 2007.

Echchaibi, Nabil. "Gendered Blueprints: Transnational Masculinities in Muslim Televangelist Cultures." In *Circuits of Visibility: Gender and Transnational Media Cultures*, edited by Radha Hegde, 89–102. New York: New York University Press, 2011.

"Elle: About Us." n.d. http://www.ellemediakit.com/r5/showkiosk.asp?listingid=4172450.

Enloe, Cynthia. *The Curious Feminist: Searching for Women in an Age of Empire*. Berkeley: University of California Press, 2004.

Eudes, Yves. "Après l'Évacuation de la Nouvelle Orléans, Toute l'Amérique S'Interroge [After New Orleans evacuation, all of America wonders]." *Le Monde*, September 6, 2005.

Eudes, Yves. "Les Blancs Ont Réussi à Partir: Ils Savent Comment Voyager et Ils Ont de l'Argent [Whites managed to leave: They know how to travel and they have money]." *Le Monde*, September 4, 2005.

Eudes, Yves. "Katrina: Cinq Jours de Cauchemar au Charity Hospital [Katrina: Five days of nightmare at charity hospital]." *Le Monde*, September 18, 2005.

"Excessive Self-Restraint May Hinder Recovery." *Yomiuri Shimbun/Daily Yomiuri*, April 8, 2011.

Fackler, Martin. "Misery and Uncertainty Fill up Shelters." *New York Times*, March 17, 2011.

Fackler, Martin. "Quietly, U.S. Troops Help Reopen Japanese Airport." *New York Times*, April 14, 2011.

Fackler, Martin. "Severed from the World, Villagers Survive on Tight Bonds and To-Do Lists." *New York Times*, March 24, 2011.

Fackler, Martin, and Makiko Inoue. "Misery and Uncertainty Fill up Shelters." *New York Times*, March 19, 2011.

Fackler, Martin, and Mark McDonald. "Anxiety and Need Overwhelm a Nation." *New York Times*, March 15, 2011.

Fackler, Martin, and Mark McDonald. "As Death Toll Rises, a Frantic Effort to Rescue Survivors." *New York Times*, March 13, 2011.

Fackler, Martin, and Hiroko Tabuchi. "In Visit to Japan, Biden Seeks to Inspire Recovery." *New York Times*, August 24, 2011.

Faiola, Anthony. "Japan's Empire of Cool." *Washington Post*, December 27, 2003.

Feigenbaum, Harvey B. "Hegemony or Diversity in Film and Television? The United States, Europe and Japan." *Pacific Review* 20, no. 3 (2007): 371–96.

Fernandes, Sujatha. "Island Paradise, Revolutionary Utopia or Hustler's Heaven? Consumerism and Socialism in Contemporary Cuban Rap." *Journal of Latin American Studies* 12, no. 3 (2003): 359–75.

"Final Miyakejima Evacuees Return Home." *Yomiuri Shimbun/Daily Yomiuri*, April 2, 2011.

Flores, Juan. "Puerto Rocks: Rap, Roots, and Amnesia." In *That's the Joint! The Hip-Hop Studies Reader*, edited by Murray Forman and Mark A. Neal, 69–86. New York: Routledge, 2004.

Forman, Murray. "Introduction." In *That's the Joint! The Hip-Hop Studies Reader*, edited by Murray Forman and Mark A. Neal, 1–12. New York: Routledge, 2004.

Gainsbourg, Serge. *Sensuelle Et Sans Suite*. LP. Vu De L'Exterieur. Paris: Philips, 1973.

García Canclini, Néstor. *Consumers and Citizens: Globalization and Multicultural Conflicts*. Minneapolis: University of Minnesota Press, 2001.

García Canclini, Néstor. *Hybrid Cultures: Strategies for Entering and Leaving Modernity*. Minneapolis: University of Minnesota Press, 1995.

Garrigue, Anne. *L'Asie en nous* [The Asia in us]. Arles, France: Editions Philippe Picquier, 2004.

Gates, Kelly. "Introduction: Media Studies Futures: Past and Present." In *The International Encyclopedia of Media Studies*, edited by Angharad. N. Valdivia, Vol. VI, *Media Studies Future*, edited by Gates, 1–28. Oxford: Wiley-Blackwell, 2013.

Geertz, Clifford. *Local Knowledge: Further Essays in Interpretive Anthropology*. New York: Basic Books, 1983.

Giddens, Anthony. *The Consequences of Modernity*. Cambridge: Polity, 1990.

Giddens, Anthony. *Runaway World: How Globalization Is Reshaping Our Lives*. London: Profile Books, 1999.

Gilens, Martin. "Race and Poverty in America: Public Misperceptions and the American News Media." *Public Opinion Quarterly*, no. 60 (1996): 515–41.

Gilman, Lisa, and John Fenn. "Dance, Gender, and Popular Music in Malawi: The Case of Rap and Ragga." *Popular Music* 25, no. 3 (2006): 369–81.

Gilroy, Paul. "It's a Family Affair." In *That's the Joint! The Hip-Hop Studies Reader*, edited by Murray Forman and Mark A. Neal, 87–94. New York: Routledge, 2004.

Gilroy, Paul. *Small Acts: Thoughts on the Politics of Black Cultures*. New York: Serpent's Tail, 1993.

Glanz, James, and Norimitsu Onishi. "Japan's Strict Codes and Drills Are Seen as Lifesavers." *New York Times*, March 12, 2011.

Glossary of Movie Business Terms. *The Numbers*. 2014. http://www.the-numbers.com/glossary.php.

Gonzalez, David. "From Margins of Society to Center of the Tragedy." *New York Times*, September 2, 2005.

Gluck, Carol. "The Past in the Present." In *Postwar Japan as History*, edited by Andrew Gordon, 64–95. Berkeley: University of California Press, 1993.

Gordon, Andrew, ed. *Postwar Japan as History*. Berkeley: University of California Press, 1993.

Gordinier, Jeff. "Restaurateur's 'Japantown' Helps Victims." *New York Times*, March 30, 2011.

Goué, Emmanuel. "Il existe un Énorme Mouvement de Solidarité [There is an enormous movement of solidarity]." *Le Monde*, March 20, 2011.

"Government to Send Researchers to Louisiana." *Yomiuri Shimbun/Daily Yomiuri*, September 6, 2005.

Grewal, Inderpal, and Caren Kaplan. "Warrior Marks: Global Womanism's Neo-Colonial Discourse in a Multicultural Context." In *Multiculturalism, Postcoloniality, and Transnational Media*, edited by Ella Shohat and Robert Stam, 256–78. New Brunswick, NJ: Rutgers University Press, 2003.

Grimes, William. "Forget the Freedom Fries: All is Forgiven, Chérie." *New York Times*, February 3, 2006.

Grossberg, Lawrence. "Bringin' It All Back Home—Pedagogy and Cultural Studies." In *Between Borders: Pedagogy and the Politics of Cultural Studies*, edited by Henry A. Giroux and Peter McLaren, 1–28. New York: Routledge, 1993.

Grossberg, Lawrence. "On Postmodernism and Articulation: An Interview with Stuart Hall." In *Stuart Hall: Critical Dialogues in Cultural Studies*, edited by David Morley and Kuan-Hsing Chen, 131–50. New York: Routledge, 1996.

Haberman, Clyde. "Japan Learning to Accept Help in Disaster's Wake." *New York Times*, March 15, 2011.

Hachten, William A. *Troubles of Journalism: A Critical Look at What's Right and Wrong with the Press*. Mahwah, NJ: Lawrence Erlbaum Associates, 2005.

Hafstrand, Helene. "Consumer Magazines in Transition: A Study of Approaches to Internationalization." *Journal of Media Economics* 8, no. 1 (1995): 1–12.

Hall, Stuart. "The Whites of Their Eyes." In *Gender, Race, and Class in Media: A Critical Reader*, edited by Gail Dines and Jean M. Humez, 81–84. Thousand Oaks, CA: Sage, 2011.

Harvey, David. *The Conditions of Postmodernity*. Malden, MA: Blackwell, 1989.

Haugen, Jason D. "'Unladylike Divas': Language, Gender, and Female Gangsta Rappers." *Popular Music and Society* 26, no. 4 (2003): 429–44.

Hegde, Radha. "Introduction." In *Circuits of Visibility: Gender and Transnational Media Cultures*, edited by Radha Hegde, 1–17. New York: New York University Press, 2011a.

Hegde, Radha. "Spaces of Exception: Violence, Technology, and the Transgressive Gendered Body in India's Global Call Centers." In *Circuits of Visibility: Gender and Transnational Media Cultures*, edited by Radha Hegde, 178–95. New York: New York University Press, 2011b.

Hennion, Antoine. "Musiques, Présentez-Vous ! Une Comparaison entre le Rap et la Techno [Music, introduce yourself: A comparison between rap and techno]." *French Cultural Studies* 16, no. 2 (2005): 121–34.

Herbert, Bob. "No Strangers to the Blues." *New York Times*, September 8, 2005.

Hermelin, François. "La 'Dangereuse' (?) Explosion des Mangas et des Jeux Video [The 'dangerous' (?) explosion of mangas and video games]." In *Japon, Chine, Corée . . . Cette Asie qui Dérange* [Japan, China, Korea . . . The Asia that bothers us], edited by Henry Lelievre, 133–46. Paris: Editions Complexe, 2000.

Holmes-Smith, Christopher. "Method in the Madness: Exploring the Boundaries of Identity in Hip-Hop Performativity." *Social Identities* 3, no. 3 (1997): 345–74.

Horioka, Charles Yuji. "Consuming and Saving." In *Postwar Japan as History*, edited by Andrew Gordon, 259–92. Berkeley: University of California Press, 1993.

IAM. "Achevez-Les." *Ombre Est Lumière*. CD. Paris: Virgin France, 2007.

IAM. "Do the Raï Thing." *De la Planète Mars*. CD. Paris: EMI France, 2003.

IAM. "Mars Contre Attaque." *Ombre Est Lumière*. CD. Paris: Virgin France, 2007.

IAM. "Noble Art." *Revoir Un Printemps*. CD. Paris: Virgin France, 2003.

Inoshita, Hiroshi. "Mother Smiles Again after Being Reunited with Son." *Yomiuri Shimbun/Daily Yomiuri*, April 16, 2011.

Inoue, Miyako. "Things That Speak: Peirce, Benjamin, and the Kinesthetics of Commodity Advertisement in Japanese Women's Magazines, 1900 to the 1930s." *Positions* 15, no. 3 (2007): 511–52.

"In Paris, Tough Talk Isn't Enough." *New York Times*, November 4, 2005.

"Internet World Stats: Usage and Population Statistics." 2013. Retrieved from http://www.internetworldstats.com/stats.htm.

Iriye, Akira. *Across the Pacific: An Inner History of American-East Asian Relations*. New York: Harcourt Brace Jovanovich, 1967.

Ivy, Marilyn. *Discourses of the Vanishing*. Chicago: University of Chicago Press, 1995.

Iwabuchi, Koichi. "Introduction: Cultural Globalization and Asian Media Connections." In *Feeling Asian Modernities: Transnational Consumption of Japanese TV Dramas*, edited by Koichi Iwabuchi, 1–22. Hong Kong: Hong Kong University Press, 2004.

Iwabuchi, Koichi. "Japanese Popular Culture and Postcolonial Desire for 'Asia'." In *Popular Culture, Globalization and Japan*, edited by Matthew Allen and Rumi Sakamoto, 15–35. New York: Routledge, 2006.

Iwabuchi, Koichi. *Recentering Globalization: Popular Culture and Japanese Transnationalism.* Durham, NC: Duke University Press Books, 2002.

"Japan Government, Firms Join Relief Effort to Hurricane Victims." *Kyodo News International,* September 2, 2005.

"Japan NGO Members to Visit Houston to Help Hurricane Victims." *Kyodo News International,* September 12, 2005.

"Japan Ready to Double Hurricane Aid to $1 Million." *Kyodo News International,* September 7, 2005.

"Japan's Multiple Calamities." *New York Times,* March 15, 2011.

Jenkins, Henri. "Pop Cosmopolitanism: Mapping Cultural Flows in an Age of Media Convergence." In *Gender, Race, and Class in Media: A Critical Reader,* edited by Gail Dines and Jean M. Humez, 545–51. Thousand Oaks, CA: Sage, 2011.

Jones, Andrew. *Globalization: Key Thinkers.* Malden, MA: Polity, 2010.

Jost, François. *Le Culte du Banal: De Duchamp à la Télé-Réalité* [The cult of banality: From Duchamp to reality TV]. Paris: CNRS Editions, 2007.

Jost, François. *L'Empire du Loft (La Suite)* [The big brother empire (follow up)]. Paris: La Dispute, 2002/2007.

"Katrina's Grim Reminder." *Japan Times,* September 7, 2007.

Keegan, Rebecca. "How Much Did *Avatar* Really Cost?" *Vanity Fair,* December 22, 2009.

Kelts, Roland. *Japanamerica: How Japanese Pop Culture Has Invaded the U.S.* New York: Palgrave Macmillan, 2007.

Kessous, Mustapha. "Le Collectif Devoir de Mémoires Demande un Débat Public sur les Violences Policières [The collective duty to remember requires a debate on police violence]." *Le Monde,* November 20, 2005.

Kessous, Mustapha. "L'Imam a Raison, Il Faut Respecter Ce Pays [The imam is right, we must respect this country]." *Le Monde,* November 6, 2005.

Kilborn, Richard. *Staging the Real: Factual TV Programming in the Age of Big Brother.* Manchester, UK: Manchester University Press, 2003.

Kinko, Ito. "Manga in Japanese History." In *Japanese Visual Culture: Explorations in the World of Manga and Anime,* edited by Mark W. MacWilliams, 26–47. New York: M. E. Sharpe, 2008.

Kitch, Carolyn L. *The Girl on the Magazine Cover: The Origins of Visual Stereotypes in American Mass Media.* Chapel Hill: University of North Carolina Press, 2000.

Kondo, Dorinne K. *About Face: Performing Race in Fashion and Theater.* New York: Routledge, 1997.

Kondo, Dorinne K. *Crafting Selves: Power, Gender, and Discourses of Identity in a Japanese Workplace.* Chicago: University of Chicago Press, 1990.

Kosaku, Yoshino. "The Discourse of Blood and Racial Identity in Contemporary Japan." In *The Construction of Racial Identities in China and Japan,* edited by Frank Dikötter, 199–211. Honolulu: University of Hawaii Press, 1997.

Kossity, Lord. "Gladiator." *Everlord.* CD. Paris: Naïve, 2001.

Kraidy, Marwan M. *Hybridity: Or the Cultural Logic of Globalization.* Philadelphia: Temple University Press, 2005.

Kraidy, Marwan M. "My (Global) Media Studies." *Television and New Media* 10, no. 1 (2009b): 88–90.

Kraidy, Marwan M. *Reality Television and Arab Politics: Contention in Public Life.* Cambridge, MA: Cambridge University Press, 2009a.

Kraidy, Marwan M., and Patrick D. Murphy. "Shifting Geertz: Toward a Theory of Translocalism in Global Communication Studies." *Communication Theory* 18, no. 3 (2008): 335–55.

Kraszewski, Jon. "Country Hicks and Urban Cliques: Mediating Race, Reality, and Liberalism on MTV's The Real World." In *Reality TV: Remaking Television Culture*, edited by Susan Murray and Laurie Ouellette, 179–96. New York: New York University Press, 2004.

Krims, Adam. *Rap Music and the Poetics of Identity*. New York: Cambridge University Press, 2000.

Kristof, Nicholas D. "The Japanese Could Teach Us a Thing or Two." *New York Times*, March 20, 2011.

Kristof, Nicholas D. "The Larger Shame." *New York Times*, September 6, 2005.

Lachaud, François. "Ces Japonais à l'Héroïsme Poignant [The poignant heroism of the Japanese]." *Le Monde*, March 17, 2011.

Lam, Peng Er. "Japan's Quest for 'Soft Power': Attraction and Limitation." *East Asia* 24 (2007): 349–63.

Lapassade, George, and Philippe Rousselot. *Le Rap ou la Fureur de Dire* [Rap or the furor to say]. Paris: Loris Talmart, 1990.

La Rumeur. "Là Où Poussent Mes Racines." *Du Coeur à l'Outrage*. CD. Paris: Da Buzz, 2007.

Leffler, Rebecca. "French Film Production up 13.5% in 2010." *Hollywood Reporter*. January 13, 2011.

Le Guay, Damien. *L'Empire de la Télé-Réalité: Ou Comment Accroître le Temps de Cerveau Disponible* [Reality TV's empire: Or how to increase one's available brain space]. Paris: Presses de la Renaissance, 2005.

Le Hir, Pierre, and Hervé Morin. "A Fukushima, un Combat Acharné pour Tenter de Stabiliser la Situation [At Fukushima, a desperate struggle to attempt to stabilize the situation]." *Le Monde*, March 19, 2011.

Leonard, Sean. "Progress Against the Law: Anime and Fandom, with the Key to the Globalization of Culture." *International Journal of Cultural Studies* 8, no. 3 (2005): 281–305.

Leser, Eric. "Les Forces de l'Ordre Ont Repris le Contrôle du Centre de la Nouvelle Orléans [Police forces regain control of New Orleans' center]." *Le Monde*, September 4, 2005.

Leser, Eric. "Les Médias Américains Sans Complaisance [No indulgence from American media]." *Le Monde*, November 15, 2005.

Leslie, D. A. "Global Scan: The Globalization of Advertising Agencies, Concepts, and Campaigns." *Economic Geography* 71, no. 4 (1995): 402–26.

Lesnes, Corine. "Les Américains Consternés par la Fragilité de Leur Puissance [Americans appalled by the fragility of their power]." *Le Monde*, September 3, 2005.

Lesnes, Corine. "Après Katrina, le Monde Tend la Main à une Amérique Humiliée [After Katrina, the world holds its hand out to a humiliated America]." *Le Monde*, September 4, 2005.

Lesnes, Corine. "La Jeunesse Américaine Redécouvre la Lutte Contre l'Inégalité Raciale [American youth rediscovers the struggle against racial inequality]." *Le Monde*, January 18, 2006a.

Lesnes, Corine. "SOS pour la Nouvelle Orléans [SOS for New Orleans]." *Le Monde*, January 18, 2006b.

Lévêques, Thierry, and Johnny Cotton. "La Couverture de 'Tintin en Amérique' Vendue 1,3 Million d'Euros ['Tintin in America' cover sold for 1.3 million Euros]." *Reuters*, June 3, 2012.

Liebes, Tamar, and Elihu Katz. *The Export of Meaning: Cross-Cultural Readings of Dallas.* Cambridge, MA: Oxford University Press, 1990.

Liu, Catherine. "French Rap / M.C. Solaar." *Journal of Twentieth-Century/Contemporary French Studies* 1, no. 1 (1997): 327–43.

Livingstone, Sonia. "The Challenge of Communication or, What Is the Audience Researcher to Do in the Age of the Internet?" *European Journal of Communication* 19, no. 1 (2004): 75–86.

"Locals Musicians Support 'Big Easy'." *Yomiuri Shimbun/Daily Yomiuri*, November 21, 2005.

Loupias, Bernard. "Le Rap? Il Parle la France. [Rap? It speaks of France]." *Le Nouvel Observateur*, March 21–27, 1996.

Low, Bronwen, Mela Sarkar, and Lise Winer. "'Ch'us Mon Proper Bescherelle': Challenges from the Hip-Hop Nation to the Quebec Nation." *Journal of Sociolinguistics* 13, no. 1 (2009): 59–82.

Lule, Jack. *Globalization and Media: Global Village of Babel.* Lanham, MD: Rowman & Littlefield, 2012.

Lyall, Sarah. "French Writer Wins Nobel Prize." *New York Times*, October 9, 2008.

Machin, David, and Theo Van Leeuwen. "Language Style and Lifestyle: The Case of a Global Magazine." *Media, Culture & Society* 27, no. 4 (2005): 577–600.

MacWilliams, Mark W. "Introduction." In *Japanese Visual Culture: Explorations in the World of Manga and Anime*, edited by Mark W. MacWilliams, 3–25. New York: M. E. Sharpe, 2008.

Mark, Cristoph. "The Kids (and Parents) Will Be All Right." *Yomiuri Shimbun/Daily Yomiuri*, March 27, 2011.

Marti, Pierre-Antoine. *Rap 2 France: Les Mots d'une Rupture Identitaire* [Rap of France: The words of an identity rupture]. Paris: L'Harmattan, 2005.

Matouk, Jean. *Mondialisation Altermondialisation* [Globalization alterglobalization]. Toulouse, France: Les Essentiels Milan, 2005.

Mattelart, Armand. *Diversité Culturelle et Mondialisation* [Cultural diversity and globalization]. Paris: La Découverte, 2005b.

Mattelart, Armand. *La Mondialisation de la Communication* [The globalization of communication]. Paris: Presses Universitaires de France, 2005a.

McGray, Douglas. "Japan's Gross National Cool." *Foreign Policy* 130 (2002): 44–54.

McMillin, Divya. *International Media Studies.* Malden, MA: Blackwell, 2007.

McPhail, Thomas. *Global Communication: Theories, Stakeholders, and Trends.* 3rd ed. London: Wiley-Blackwell, 2010.

McVeigh, Brian J. *Nationalisms of Japan: Managing and Mystifying Identity.* Lanham, MD: Rowman & Littlefield Publishers, 2004.

McVeigh, Brian J. *Wearing Ideology: State, Schooling and Self-Presentation in Japan.* New York: Berg Publishers, 2000.

Mesmer, Philippe. "Au Japon, les ONG Antinucléaires Ont du Mal à se Faire Entendre [In Japan, anti-nuclear NGOs find it difficult to be heard]." *Le Monde*, March 26, 2011.

Mesmer, Philippe. "La Puissance du Lobby Pronucléaire Japonais Annihile Toute Velléité de Débat [The power of the Japanese pronuclear lobby eliminates all possibility of debate]." *Le Monde*, March 19, 2011.

Mesmer, Philippe. "Tepco, une Entreprise Trop Sûre d'Elle-Même [Tepco, an overconfident company]." *Le Monde*, March 16, 2011.

Meyers, Marian. "African American Women and Violence: Gender, Race, and Class in the News." *Critical Studies in Media Communication* 21, no. 2 (2004): 95–118.

Ministère AMER. "Brigitte (Femme de Flic)." *Pourquoi Tant de Haine?* CD. Paris: Hostile, 1992.

"Miracle Rescue, 9 Days Later / Octogenarian, Teenage Grand." *Yomiuri Shimbun/Daily Yomiuri*, March 22, 2011.

Mitchell, Tony. "Doin' Damage in My Native Language: Resistance Vernaculars in Hip Hop in France, Italy and Aotearoa / New Zealand." *Popular Music* 24, no. 3 (2000): 41–55.

Mitchell, Tony. "Introduction: Another Root—Hip-Hop Outside the USA." In *Global Noise: Rap and Hip-Hop Outside the USA*, edited by Tony Mitchell, 1–38. Middletown, CT: Wesleyan University Press, 2001.

Mizuno, Shota. "Tsunami-Hit Soy Sauce Company Comes Back in Iwate Prefecture." *Yomiuri Shimbun/Daily Yomiuri*, April 3, 2011.

Moeran, Brian. "The Portrayal of Beauty in Women's Fashion Magazines." *Fashion Theory* 14, no. 4 (2010): 491–510.

Monhanty, Chandra Talpade. *Feminism without Borders: Decolonizing Theory, Practicing Solidarity.* Durham, NC: Duke University Press, 2003.

Mohanty, Chandra Talpade. "Under Western Eyes: Feminist Scholarship and Colonial Discourses." In *Third World Women and the Politics of Feminism*, edited by Chandra Talpade Mohanty, Ann Russo, and Lourdes Torres, 33–60. Bloomington: Indiana University Press, 1991.

Molinero, Stéphanie. *Les Publics du Rap: Enquête Sociologique* [Rap's publics: A sociological inquiry]. Paris: L'Harmattan, 2009.

Montaigne, Véronique. "Joey Starr dans l'Arène Civique [Joey Starr in the civic arena]." *Le Monde*, October 2006.

"More Japanese Firms Join Hurricane Relief Efforts." *Kyodo News International*, September 5, 2005.

Morgan, Joan. "Hip-Hop Feminism." In *That's the Joint! The Hip-Hop Studies Reader*, edited by Murray Forman and Mark A. Neal, 277–81. New York: Routledge, 2004.

Morimoto, Mariko, and Susan Chang. "Western and Asian Models in Japanese Fashion Magazine Ads: The Relationship with Brand Origins and International Versus Domestic Magazines." *Journal of International Consumer Marketing* 21, no. 3 (2009): 173–87.

Morley, David. *Media, Modernity and Technology: The Geography of the New.* New York: Routledge, 2007.

Morley, David. "Unanswered Questions in Audience Research." *Communication Review* 9, no. 2 (2006): 101–21.

Morris, Meagan. "Transnational Imagination in Action Cinema: Hong Kong and the Making of a Global Popular Culture." *Inter-Asia Cultural Studies* 5, no. (2004): 181–99.

Mowlana, Hamid. *Global Information and World Communication: New Frontiers in International Relations.* Thousand Oaks, CA: Sage Publications, 1986/1997.

Murphy, Patrick D., and Marwan M. Kraidy. "Towards an Ethnographic Approach to Media Studies." In *Global Media Studies: Ethnographic Perspective*, edited by Patrick D. Murphy and Marwan M. Kraidy, 3–19. New York: Routledge, 2003.

"'My Grandma Is Inside!' / Teen Escapes Rubble after 9 Days." *Yomiuri Shimbun/Daily Yomiuri,* March 22, 2011.

Napier, Susan J. *Anime from Akira to Howl's Moving Castle: Experiencing Contemporary Japanese Animation.* New York: Palgrave Macmillan, 2005.

Napier, Susan J. *From Impressionism to Anime: Japan as Fantasy and Fan Cult in the Mind of the West.* New York: Palgrave Macmillan, 2007.

"Nation Must Pool Wisdom to Prepare for Unforeseeable." *Yomiuri Shimbun/Daily Yomiuri,* April 10, 2011.

Neate, Patrick. *Where You're At: Notes from the Frontline of a Hip-Hop Planet.* New York: Riverhead, 2004.

Nelson, Michelle, R., and Hye-Jin Paek. "Cross-Cultural Differences in Sexual Advertising Content in a Transnational Women's Magazine." *Sex Roles* 53, no. 5/6 (2005): 371–83.

Niezen, Ronald. *A World beyond Difference: Cultural Identity in the Age of Globalization.* Malden, MA: Blackwell, 2004.

Nossiter, Adam. "Dispute over Historic Hospital for the Poor Pits Doctors against the State." *New York Times,* December 17, 2005.

Nossiter, Adam. "New Orleans Crime Swept Away, with Most of the People." *New York Times,* November 10, 2005.

Nossiter, Adam. "New Orleans Landlords Are Pitted against Tenants in Court." *New York Times,* November 4, 2005.

Onishi, Norimitsu. "At Age 84, a City's Last Geisha Defies Time and a 4th Tsunami." *New York Times,* April 5, 2011.

Onishi, Norimitsu. "'Safety Myth' Left Japan Ripe for Nuclear Crisis." *New York Times,* June 25, 2011.

Onishi, Norimitsu, and Ken Belson. "Culture of Complicity Tied to Stricken Nuclear Plant." *New York Times,* April 27, 2011.

Onishi, Norimitsu, and Martin Fackler. "In Nuclear Crisis, Crippling Mistrust." *New York Times,* June 13, 2011.

Onishi, Norimitsu, and Martin Fackler. "Japan Held Nuclear Data, Leaving Evacuees in Peril." *New York Times,* August 9, 2011.

Orlando, Valérie. "From Rap to Raï in the Mixing Bowl: Beur Hip-Hop Culture and Banlieue Cinema in Urban France." *Journal of Popular Culture* 36, no. 3 (2003): 395–415.

Ossman, Susan. "Seeing Princess Salma: Transparency and Transnational Intimacies." In *Circuits of Visibility: Gender and Transnational Media Cultures,* edited by Radha Hegde, 21–34. New York: New York University Press, 2011.

Osumare, Halifu. "Beat Streets in the Global Hood: Connective Marginalities of the Hip Hop Globe." *Journal of American & Comparative Cultures* 24, no. 1/2 (2001): 171–81.

Ouellette, Laurie, and Susan Murray. "Introduction." In *Reality TV: Remaking Television Culture,* edited by Susan Murray and Laurie Ouellette, 1–15. New York: New York University Press, 2004.

Oware, Matthew. "A 'Man's Woman'? Contradictory Messages in the Songs of Female Rappers, 1992–2000." *Journal of Black Studies* 39, no. 5 (2009): 786–802.

Parameswaran, Radhika. "E-racing Color: Gender and Transnational Visual Economies of Beauty in India." In *Circuits of Visibility: Gender and Transnational Media Cultures,* edited by Radha Hegde, 68–86. New York: New York University Press, 2011.

Parameswaran, Radhika. "Facing Barack Hussein Obama: Race, Globalization, and Transnational America." *Journal of Communication Inquiry* 33, no. 3 (2009): 195–205.

Parameswaran, Radhika. "Global Media Events in India: Contests over Beauty, Gender and Nation." *Journalism & Communication Monographs* 3, no. 2 (2001): 52–105.

Parameswaran, Radhika. "Global Queens, National Celebrities: Tales of Feminine Triumph in Post-Liberalization India." *Critical Studies in Media Communication* 21, no. 4 (2004a): 346–70.

Parameswaran, Radhika. "Spectacles of Gender and Globalization: Mapping Miss World's Media Event Space in the News." *Communication Review* 7, no. 4 (2004b): 371–406.

Parameswaran, Radhika. "Western Romance Fiction as English-Language Media in Postcolonial India." *Journal of Communication* 49, no. 3 (1999): 84–105.

Parameswaran, Radhika, and Kavitha Cardoza. "Melanin on the Margins: Advertising and the Cultural Politics of Fair/Light/White Beauty in India," *Journalism and Communication Monographs*, 11, no. 3 (2009): 213–74.

Passi. "Dieu Créa." *Genèse*. CD. Paris: Sony, 2000.

Patten, Fred. *Watching Anime, Reading Manga: 25 Years of Essays and Reviews*. Berkeley: Stone Bridge Press, 2004.

Pecqueux, Anthony. *Voix du Rap: Essai de Sociologie de l'Action Musicale* [The voice of rap: Essays on the sociology of musical action]. Paris: L'Harmattan, 2007.

Peterson, Theodore. *Magazines in the Twentieth Century*. Urbana: University of Illinois Press, 1964.

Peterson, Shani H., Gina M. Wingood, Ralph J. DiClemente, Kathy Harrington, and Susan Davies. "Images of Sexual Stereotypes in Rap Videos and the Health of African American Female Adolescents." *Journal of Women's Health* 16, no. 8 (2007): 1157–64.

Pieterse, Jan Nederveen. *Globalization and Culture: Global Mélange*. 2nd ed. Lanham, MD: Rowman & Littlefield Publishers, 2003/2009.

Poitras, Gilles. "Contemporary Anime in Japanese Pop Culture." In *Japanese Visual Culture: Explorations in the World of Manga and Anime*, edited by Mark W. MacWilliams, 48–67. New York: M. E. Sharpe, 2008.

Pons, Philippe. "L'Étonnante Maîtrise de Soi des Japonais [The striking self-control of the Japanese]." *Le Monde*, March 15, 2011.

Pons, Philippe. "Une Politique Sans Boussole [Politics without a compass]." *Le Monde*, March 17, 2011.

Pough, Gwendolyn D., Elaine Richardson, Aisha Durham, and Rachel Raimist. *Home Girls Make Some Noise: Hip Hop Feminism Anthology*. Mira Loma, CA: Parker.

Prévos, André J. M. "Hip-Hop, Rap, and Repression in France and the United States." *Popular Music and Society* 22, no. 2 (1998): 67–95.

Price, Shinobu. "Cartoons from Another Planet: Japanese Animation as Cross-Cultural Communication." *Journal of American & Comparative Cultures* 24, no. 1/2 (2001): 153–69.

Purdum, Todd S. "Across U.S., Outrage at Response." *New York Times*, September 3, 2005.

Purnick, Joyce. "In the Capitol, Nervous Evacuees Fear Biting a Hand That Might Help." *New York Times*, September 14, 2005.

Rantanen, Terhi. *The Media and Globalization*. Thousand Oaks, CA: Sage.

Reid-Brinkley, Shanara R. "The Essence of Res(ex)pectability: Black Women's Negotiation of Black Femininity in Rap Music and Music Video." *Meridians: Feminism, Race, Transnationalism* 8, no. 1 (2008): 236–60.

Renaud. "Déserteur." *Morgane De Toi*. LP. Paris: Polydor, 1983.

Renaud. "Hexagone." *Amoureux de Paname*. LP. Paris: Polydor, 1975.

Renaud. "Je Suis un Voyou." *L'Absolument Meilleur de Renaud*. CD. Paris: EMI Import, 1996.

"Rescued Dog Reunites with Owner." *Yomiuri Shimbun/Daily Yomiuri*, April 6, 2011.

Rhoden, William C. "Pity the Poorest While America Waves the Flag." *New York Times*, September 10, 2005.

Roque, Eva. "Comment Star Ac' Attire les Stars [How Star Ac' attracts stars]." *Télé 7 Jours*, December 15, 2007.

Rose, Tricia. *Black Noise: Rap Music and Black Culture in Contemporary America*. Middletown, CT: Wesleyan University Press, 1994.

Rose, Tricia. *The Hip Hop Wars: What We Talk About When We Talk About Hip Hop—and Why It Matters*. New York: Basic Civitas Books, 2008.

Roth, Joshua Hotaka. *Brokered Homeland: Japanese Brazilian Migrants in Japan*. Ithaca, NY: Cornell University Press, 2003.

Sabbagh, Daniel. *L'Égalité par le Droit: Les Paradoxes de la Discrimination Positive aux États Unis* [Equality by right: The paradoxes of positive discrimination in the United States]. Paris: Broché, 2003.

Sakamoto, Kazue. "Reading Japanese Women's Magazines: The Construction of New Identities in the 1970s and 1980s." *Media, Culture & Society* 21, no. 2 (1999): 173–93.

Salles, Alain. "Après Katrina, l'Amérique S'Interroge sur les Failles de son Modèle [After Katrina, America wonders about the failures of its model]." *Le Monde*, September 8, 2005.

Samuel, David. "The Rap on Rap: The 'Black Music' That Isn't Either." In *That's the Joint! The Hip-Hop Studies Reader*, edited by Murray Forman and Mark A. Neal, 147–53. New York: Routledge, 2004.

Sanger, David E., and William J. Broad. "Data Show Radiation's Spread; Frantic Repairs Go On." *New York Times*, March 18, 2011.

Sanger, David E., and Matt Wald. "Japan Reels as Toll Rises and Nuclear Risks Loom." *New York Times*, March 14, 2011.

Schodt, Frederik L. *The Astro Boy Essays: Osamu Tezuka, Mighty Atom, and the Manga/Anime Revolution*. Berkeley: Stone Bridge Press, 2007.

Schodt, Frederik L. *Dreamland Japan: Writings on Modern Manga*. Berkeley: Stone Bridge Press, 1996.

Schodt, Frederik L. "Foreword." In *Japanese Visual Culture: Explorations in the World of Manga and Anime*, edited by Mark W. MacWilliams, vii–ix. New York: M. E. Sharpe, 2008.

Schodt, Frederik L. *Manga! Manga! The World of Japanese Comics*. New York: Kodansha USA, 1983.

Sciolino, Elaine. "Chirac, Lover of Spotlight, Avoids Glare of France's Fires." *New York Times*, November 10, 2005.

Sciolino, Elaine. "Immigrants' Dreams Mix with Fury Near Paris." *New York Times*, December 12, 2005.

Sellek, Yoko. "Nikkeijin: The Phenomenon of Return Migration." In *Japan's Minorities: The Illusion of Homogeneity*, edited by Michael Weiner, 187–92. New York: Routledge, 1997.

"Shocking Scenes of Rioting." *Asahi Shimbun*, November 11, 2005.

Shohat, Ella. "Area Studies, Gender Studies, and the Cartographies of Knowledge." *Social Text* 20, no. 3 (2002): 67–78.

Shohat, Ella, and Robert Stam. "Introduction." In *Multiculturalism, Postcoloniality, and Transnational Media*, edited by Ella Shohat and Robert Stam, 1–17. New Brunswick, NJ: Rutgers University Press, 2003.

Shohat, Ella, and Robert Stam. "Outing Whiteness." *Critical Studies in Media Communication* 17, no. 3 (2000): 366–71.

Shome, Raka. "Interdisciplinary Research and Globalization." *Communication Review* 9, no. 1 (2006c): 1–36.

Shome, Raka. "Post Colonial Reflections on the 'Internationalization' of Cultural Studies." *Cultural Studies* 23, no. 5–6 (2009): 694–719.

Shome, Raka. "Thinking through the Diaspora: Call Centers, India and a New Politics of Hybridity." *International Journal of Cultural Studies* 9, no. 1 (2006a): 105–24.

Shome, Raka. "Transnational Feminism and Communication Studies." *Communication Review* 9, no. 4 (2006b): 255–67.

Shome, Raka, and Radha S. Hegde. "Culture, Communication and the Challenge of Globalization." *Critical Studies in Media Communication* 19, no. 2 (2002): 172–89.

Shor, Francis. *Dying Empire: US Imperialism and Global Resistance*. New York: Routledge, 2010.

Shpigel, Ben, and Richard Sandomir. "After Tsunami, Igawa Leaves Yankees' Camp." *New York Times*, March 12, 2011.

Skeggs, Beverley. "Two Minute Brother: Contestation through Gender, Race and Sexuality." *Innovation in Social Sciences Research* 6, no. 3 (1993): 299–322.

Slack, Jennifer Daryl. "The Theory and Method of Articulation in Cultural Studies." In *Stuart Hall: Critical Dialogues in Cultural Studies*, edited by David Morley and Kuan-Hsing Chen, 113–30. New York: Routledge, 1996.

Smith, Craig S. "Angry Immigrants Embroil France in Wider Riots." *New York Times*, November 5, 2005.

Smith, Craig S. "Chirac Appeals for Calm as Violent Protests Shake Paris's Suburbs." *New York Times*, November 3, 2005.

Smolar, Piotr. "Violences dans les Banlieues [Violence in the suburbs]." *Le Monde*, November 11, 2005.

Sniper. "Arabia." *À Toute Épreuve*. CD. Paris: Belive, 2011.

Sniper. "Bollywood Style." *Puissance Rap 2012*. CD. Paris: SmI, 2012.

Sniper. "La France." *Du Rire aux Larmes*. CD. Paris: East West France, 2001.

Sniper. "Retour aux Racines." *Trait pour Trait*. CD. Paris: Up Music, 2006.

Solaar, MC. "Nouveau Western." *Le Tour de la Question*. CD. Paris: Polygram, 1993.

Solaar, MC. "La Vie N'est Qu'un Moment." *MC Solaar*. CD. Paris: Polygram, 1998.

Solomon, Thomas. "'Living Underground Is Tough': Authenticity and Locality in the Hip-Hop Community in Istanbul, Turkey." *Popular Music* 24, no. 1 (2005): 1–20.

Sommers, Samuel R., Evan P. Apfelbaum, Kristin N. Dukes, Negin Toosi, and Elsie J. Wang. "Race and Media Coverage of Hurricane Katrina: Analysis, Implications, and Future Research Questions." *Analyses of Social Issues and Public Policy* 6, no. 1 (2006): 39–55.

Sontag, Deborah. "With New Orleans's Future in Flux, Anxiety about a Life without Roots." *New York Times*, November 5, 2005.

Sorge, Arndt. *The Global and the Local: Understanding the Dialectics of Business Systems*. New York: Oxford University Press, 2005.

Souyri, Pierre-François. "Le Tsunami Oblige le Japon à Repenser Sa Politique [The tsunami forces Japan to rethink its policies]." *Le Monde*, March 15, 2011.

Spivak, Gayatri Chakravorty. "Can the Subaltern Speak?" In *Marxism and the Interpretation of Culture*, edited by Cary Nelson and Lawrence Grossberg, 271–313. Urbana: University of Illinois Press, 1988.

Spivak, Gayatri Chakravorty. "Righting Wrongs." *South Atlantic Quarterly* 24, no. 2/3 (2004): 523–81.

Stald, Gitte, and Thomas Tufte. "Introduction." In *Global Encounters: Media and Cultural Transformation*, edited by Gitte Stald and Thomas Tufte, 1–8. Luton, UK: University of Luton Press, 2002.

Stam, Robert, and Ella Shohat. *Race in Translation: Culture Wars around the Postcolonial Atlantic*. New York: New York University Press, 2012.

Stam, Robert, and Ella Shohat. "Transnationalizing Comparison: The Uses and Abuses of Cross-Cultural Analogy." *New Literary History* 40, no. 3 (2009): 473–99.

Stanley, Alessandra. "The Elusive Pleasures of French TV." *New York Times*, August 29, 2013.

Stapleton, Craig Roberts. "Du 11 Septembre à Katrina [From September 11 to Katrina]." *Le Monde*, September 11, 2005.

Starr, Joey. "Gare au Jaguarr." *Gare au Jaguarr*. CD. Jive/epic, 2006.

Steger, Manfred. *Globalization: A Very Short Introduction*. Oxford: Oxford University Press, 2009.

Stephens, Vincent. "Pop Goes the Rapper: A Close Reading of Eminem's Genderphobia." *Popular Music* 24, no. 1 (2005): 21–36.

Sterne, Jonathan. "Out with the Trash: On the Future of New Media." In *Residual Media*, edited by Charles R. Acland, 6–31. Minneapolis: University of Minnesota Press, 2007.

Straubhaar, Joseph D. *World Television: From Global to Local*. Thousand Oaks, CA: Sage Publications, 2007.

Swedenburg, Ted. "Islamic Hip-Hop vs. Islamophobia: Aki Nawaz, Natasha Atlas, Akhenaton." In *Global Noise: Rap and Hip-Hop Outside the USA*, edited by Tony Mitchell, 57–85. Middletown, CT: Wesleyan University Press, 2001.

Tabuchi, Hiroko, Ken Belson, and Norimitsu Onishi. "Dearth of Candor from Japan's Leadership." *New York Times*, March 17, 2011.

Tabuchi, Hiroko, and Matthew L. Wald. "Japan Scrambles to Avert Nuclear Meltdowns." *New York Times*, March 13, 2011.

Tabuchi, Hiroko, and Matthew L. Wald. "Second Explosion at Reactor as Technicians Try to Contain Damage." *New York Times*, March 14, 2011.

Tagliabue, John. "French Lesson: Taunts on Race Can Boomerang." *New York Times*, September 21, 2005.

Takakura, Masaki, and Yu Hinatani. "Hospital Emerges as Center of Hope." *Yomiuri Shimbun/Daily Yomiuri*, March 28, 2011.

Talbot, Margaret. "The Year in Ideas: Pokémon Hegemon." *New York Times*, December 15, 2002.

Tay, Jinna. "'Pigeon-Eyed Readers': The Adaptation and Formation of a Global Asian Fashion Magazine." *Continuum: Journal of Media & Cultural Studies* 23, no. 2 (2009): 245–56.

Tickner, Arlene B. "Aquí en el Ghetto: Hip Hop in Colombia, Cuba and Mexico." *Latin American Politics and Society* 50, no. 3 (2008): 121–46.

Tomlinson, John. *Globalization and Culture*. Chicago: University of Chicago Press, 1999.

Treaster, Joseph B., and John Desantis. "With Some Now at Breaking Point, City's Officers Tell of Pain and Pressure." *New York Times*, September 6, 2005.

Tunstall, Jeremy. *Media Are American*. New York: Columbia University Press, 1979.

Tunstall, Jeremy. *The Media Were American: U.S. Mass Media in Decline*. New York: Oxford University Press, 2008.

Turow, Joseph. *The Daily You: How the New Advertising Industry Is Defining Your Identity and Your Worth*. New Haven, CT: Yale University Press, 2011.

Uesugi, Hiroshi, Masanori Yamashita, Hironori Kanashima, Yosuke Honbu, and Kenichiro Tashiro. "Survivors Fete Miraculous Return to Life." *Yomiuri Shimbun/ Daily Yomiuri*, March 30, 2011.

"U.S. Envoy Schieffer Thanks Japan for Hurricane Aid." *Kyodo News International*, September 9, 2005.

Valdivia, Angharad. "The Gendered Face of Latinidad: Global Circulation of Hybridity." In *Circuits of Visibility: Gender and Transnational Media Cultures*, edited by Radha Hegde, 53–67. New York: New York University Press, 2011.

Van Dijk, Teun Adrianus. *Racism and the Press*. London: Routledge, 1991.

Van Ginneken, Jaap. *Understanding Global News: A Critical Introduction*. Thousand Oaks, CA: Sage Publications, 1998.

Vernet, Daniel. "Katrina Bouscule la Diplomatie Américaine [Katrina unsettles American diplomacy]." *Le Monde*, September 9, 2005.

Verrier, Richard. "Industry Report: International Box-Office Revenue Soars in 2010." *The Los Angeles Times*, February 23, 2011.

Vigoureux, Elsa. "Enfants du Hip-Hop et de Derrida: Les Intellos du Rap [Children of hip-hop and Derrida: The intellectuals of Rap]." *Le Novel Observateur*, May 18, 2006.

Volčič, Zala, and Karmen Erjavec. "Constructing Transnational Divas: Gendered Productions of Balkan Turbo-Folk Music." In *Circuits of Visibility: Gender and Transnational Media Cultures*, edited by Radha Hegde, 35–52. New York: New York University Press, 2011.

Vollmar, Rob. "Frédéric Boilet and the Nouvelle Manga Revolution [Frédéric Boilet and the new manga revolution]." *World Literature Today* 81, no. 2 (2007): 34–41.

Warnier, Jean-Pierre. *La Mondialisation de la Culture* [The globalization of culture]. Paris: La Découverte, 2004.

"While Paris Burns." *New York Times*, November 8, 2005.

Wilgoren, Jodi. "After 14 Weeks, Evacuees Settle into 14th Home." *New York Times*, December 13, 2005.

Wines, Michael. "In Japan's Chaos, Order and Civility at Shelters." *New York Times*, March 26, 2011.

Wollan, Malia. "After the Japan Quake, Sister Cities Rally for Relief." *New York Times*, March 20, 2011.

"Worldwide Plastic Surgery Statistics Available for the First Time." *Medical News Today*, August 10, 2010. http://www.medicalnewstoday.com/releases/197293.php.

Yako, Nao. "Giving Kids Something to Smile About." *Yomiuri Shimbun/Daily Yomiuri*, April 9, 2011.

Yamada, Tetsuro. "NYT: Reactor Core Probably Leaked." *Yomiuri Shimbun/Daily Yomiuri*, March 28, 2011.

Yamanaka, Hiroshi. "The Utopian 'Power to Live': The Significance of the Miyazaki Phenomenon." In *Japanese Visual Culture: Explorations in the World of Manga and Anime*, edited by Mark W. MacWilliams, 237–55. New York: M. E. Sharpe, 2008.

"A Year of Natural Violence." *Yomiuri Shimbun/Daily Yomiuri*, December 29, 2005.

Yegenoglu, Meyda. *Colonial Fantasies: Towards a Feminist Reading of Orientalism.* Cambridge, MA: Cambridge University Press, 1998.

Yoshioka, Shiro. "Heart of Japaneseness: History and Nostalgia in Hayao Miyazaki's *Spirited Away.*" In *Japanese Visual Culture: Explorations in the World of Manga and Anime,* edited by Mark W. MacWilliams, 256–73. New York: M. E. Sharpe, 2008.

Yúdice, George. "From Hybridity to Policy: For a Purposeful Cultural Studies" (translator's introduction). In *Consumers and Citizens: Globalization and Multicultural Conflicts,* by Néstor García Canclini, ix–xxxviii. Minneapolis: University of Minnesota Press, 2001.

Zachary, Pascal. *The Global Me: New Cosmopolitans and the Competitive Edge: Picking Globalism's Winners and Losers.* New York: Public Affairs, 2000.

Zeller, Tom, Jr. "Experts Had Long Criticized Potential Weakness in Design of Stricken Reactor." *New York Times,* March 16, 2011.

Index